SHAKESPEARE IN THE PARKING LOT

three plays for the inner child

Peter Fenton

This work is published by Ornithology Media, an imprint of
www.byPeterFenton.com

Copyright © 2021 by Peter Fenton

All rights reserved. No part of this publication may be reproduced, stored or transmitted in any form or by any means, electronic, mechanical, photocopying, recording, scanning, or otherwise without written permission from the publisher. It is illegal to copy this book, post it to a website, or distribute it by any other means without permission.

Professionals and amateurs are hereby warned that this material, being fully protected under the Copyright Laws of the United States of America and all other countries of the Berne and Universal Copyright Conventions, is subject to a royalty. All rights including, but not limited to, professional, amateur, recording, motion picture, recitation, lecturing, public reading, radio and television broadcasting, and the rights of translation into foreign languages are expressly reserved.

Reading editions of Peter Fenton's plays, *Knights of the Square Table* (under the title *Good Knight and Goodbye*) and *The Thousand-Year Rose*, are included as part of this anthology for the benefit of the reader and are not authorized for performance use. To obtain performance rights and cast scripts for either play, contact Heuer Publishing LLC.

A reading edition of Peter Fenton's play *See Amid the Winter Snow* is included as part of this anthology for the benefit of the reader and is not authorized for performance use. To obtain performance rights and cast scripts for this play, visit www.byPeterFenton.com

First edition

ISBN: 978-1-7376182-8-7

Edited by Ciera McElroy

Contents

Introduction   v

I   Good Knight and Goodbye

Author's Preface to Good Knight and Goodbye	3
A Personal Message	8
For King and Country	16
An Honest Question	29
Questionable Life Choices	36
Bored On a Boat	44
Exactly Two Radishes	53
Prolonged Sounds of Warning	61
Rescue at Sea	71
The Trial of Torte	78
Quiet Evening in the Forest	88
Kill the Beast	99
Backward Kingdom	108

II   The Thousand-Year Rose

Author's Preface to The Thousand-Year Rose	125
Planter's Warts	129
Dank Mythology	137
The Pure of Heart	146
Forsaking Duty and Jet Lag	157
Stage Fright	166

To Begin a Witch Hunt	178
The Good Kind of Betrayal	183
White Lies	193
Reading the Map	199
Six Minutes	207
Platform Peril	214
Lo, How a Rose E'er Blooming	224

III See Amid the Winter Snow

Author's Preface to See Amid the Winter Snow	239
The Sundae Bet	243
In the Name of Christmas Magic	249
Maureen Gaines Claus	259
The Elephant in the Steakhouse	269
Chinese Take-Out	276
Yuletide Pandemonium	284
Dancing in the Eye of the Storm	299
It's Cold Outside	316
The Hood, the Wolf, the Granny, and the Axe	323
Over the River and Through the Woods	329
To Grandmother's House We Go	336

Acknowledgments	348
About the Author	350
Your Next Read	351

Introduction

At the beginning of each of my fall semesters in undergrad, the Wheaton College theatre department would host a Shakespeare in the Park event. "Shakespeare in the Park" is exactly what it sounds like: Arena Theatre, which was the troupe of "serious theatre" folks, would put on a genuinely impressive Shakespeare show or two or three on a stage in the park just off-campus. It was always a great time gathering a group of friends together to see those shows, we would carry in our own foldable lawn chairs to the little patch of grass and made sure to find a spot that no trees or telephone poles would obstruct anyone's view. While none of my friends and I had quite the literary palate to truly appreciate all the playful nuance of Elizabethan English scattered throughout *All's Well that Ends Well* or *The Taming of the Shrew*, once each performance began, it was mystifying to see the beautiful, intricate costume design and to see just how professional the lighting and the acting and all of the other elements of production design completely pulled you into the world. You would never know the stage and production infrastructure had been loaded in just hours earlier and didn't live in this park permanently. It was without a doubt some of the most immersive theatre magic I've ever experienced . . . it truly was Shakespeare, in the Park.

As a communication major who concentrated in interpersonal studies, I was not part of Arena Theatre—no, no. I was involved with—and later, in senior year, was the President of—Wheaton College's other student performing arts troupe, Jukebox Theater. To date in my life, and especially in undergrad, I've never been much for the straightforward, "classically trained" professionalism offered by conservatories or MFA writing circles. I have pretty much always gravitated toward the weird, unconventional opportunities when seeking to express my creative side. When it came to my brief stint in campus journalism, for example, I chose not to join the team on the official campus newspaper, *The Wheaton Record*, but instead, I wrote for the *Onion*-style Wheaton satire paper, *Off the Record*. In 2014, when *The Somewhat True Tale of Robin Hood*—a tongue-in-cheek retelling of the classic tale—was revealed to be Jukebox Theater's fall play, the title alone spoke to me. I went ahead and auditioned for that production, booked a role, and went on to play a delightfully psychotic Prince John that October. The best way I have found of comparing the two performing arts groups at Wheaton is to use a sports analogy, of all things: if Arena Theatre was a varsity program, then Jukebox Theater was our intramurals. You might have also noticed that we spelled Jukebox "Theater" with an "er" at the end rather than an "re" . . . that should maybe tell you everything you need to know.

My point is, Jukebox Theater often had to get creative with how we brought shows to life. We often had to do a whole lot more with a whole lot less. While Arena Theatre had the resources to pull off that annual Shakespeare in the Park event—as seen from the makeup and costuming alone, let alone perfect lighting to match the mood of each moving performance from student artists taking themselves seriously for the sake of Art (with a capital A!)—if Jukebox had been put in charge of organizing an event like that, knowing Jukebox Theater, we would absolutely have the same level of heart and energy poured into the production as the main Shakespeare in the Park event, but the overall aesthetic would be a little more . . . let's go with "homespun." Putting on a show is serious business whether you have a feast of funds or have to get by with scraps; whether you produce light-hearted comedy or heart-wrenching drama.

If Jukebox were to mount an outdoor play extravaganza, we would be armed with not much more than a silly script selected by that year's President and cabinet, and we would probably end up doing the very pragmatic thing of having the company perform under the lampposts in the parking lot outside Buswell Library so that nobody would have to rent or rig up a lighting system . . . come Hell or high water, we would have made this hypothetical event work. We would have called it Shakespeare in the Parking Lot.

Perhaps our efforts would draw a crowd, perhaps we would just be performing for our roommates. Audience reception—or whether there was an audience to receive the work at all—would really be a roll of the dice no matter what we did, but none of that would matter. Shakespeare in the Parking Lot would be all about the thrill of telling a story by bringing it to life, no matter how quirky the end product would be.

This book is a bit like Jukebox Theatre. Welcome to *Shakespeare in the Parking Lot*. This literary event is meant to be a fun night of three adventure comedies performed back-to-back-to-back:

- *Good Knight and Goodbye:* A legendary knight is sent on a quest for the princess's hand in marriage but finds himself falling in love with the king's humble messenger while an evil threat lurks beneath his nose.
- *The Thousand-Year Rose:* Three bickering witches conspire to find a lost treasure, which will only appear for a pure heart. They decide to kidnap the sassy college intern who is also hunting for the treasure.
- *See Amid the Winter Snow:* The simple love story of the Claus family publicist and a village schoolteacher is threatened when a blackmail scandal breaks in Santa's Workshop during Mrs. Claus's campaign for Mayor of the North Pole.

Each of these plays were developed during my time at Wheaton. While I wrote the first draft and staged the world premiere of *Good Knight and Goodbye* when I was in high school and I finally got around to writing the first draft and world premiere of *See Amid the Winter Snow* after graduating, whenever I had a spare moment in undergrad, I put significant work on each of these three scripts. I adopted a distinct tone and style to these three plays that I like to say is written for the "inner child" rather than for children in general. The wacky worldbuilding, bright colors, and optimistic endings were born out of a love for my boyhood worlds of Disney and Nintendo, but the cutting wit and humor was inspired by my early college love affair with *Arrested Development*.

I would certainly call myself a verbal processor, which is something you can pretty safely assume about most writers of creative non-fiction. As much as putting pen to paper and telling stories has become my life's work (supplemented by my day job of the week—which, at the time of publication, is working as a bartender at a gastropub in a classy Philadelphia suburb), writing these stories was vital journaling work. I processed my own world and personal development through creating fantastical stories. We all go through high-stress periods of time in our lives, and it's important to find healthy ways of processing them. I do this work with words.

On the face of it, this book is an anthology comprised of the three plays I developed during my Wheaton years, and it certainly is . . . but I don't think that's the end of it. There has to be a reason this collection exists, otherwise, I would have split these three works into separate volumes. I think I've landed on what the reason may be.

As I reread each of my plays and got them ready for the average reader to pick up and comprehend, I realized every one of us is a storyteller in some fashion. The stories we choose to share and the details we choose to highlight or downplay reflect what is important to us at the time we tell them, and as we grow and change, our stories evolve with us even if we are telling the story of the same event.

I present the collection of plays before you as evidence that something similar goes on when fiction writers create works of any genre—these stories don't come from a vacuum, they are told from a place of hurt or joy or curiosity informed by the author's lived experience. They are snapshots of who the author was and what they valued at the time they put pen to paper, and laying stories by the same author in chronological order one after the other can inform the reader how that author grew in their priorities and personhood from work to work.

In rereading each of *Good Knight and Goodbye*, *The Thousand-Year Rose*, and *See Amid the Winter Snow* in order as I prepared to publish them, I followed the story of one boy who found his place in the world and sense of identity through writing, lost his way when it consumed him, and found it again when he grew more secure in his personhood.

I pray, for my own journey, that this collection is a fitting closure for each individual work, to almost place them together as a museum exhibit. In as much as I hope you get any enjoyment out of the funny stories and the clever jokes in this book, I hope you can appreciate my journey. If nothing else, the human in me wants to show the human in you how I got started as a writer.

Any way you slice this book, it's a labor of love, and it's ultimately not that serious . . . it's Shakespeare in the Parking Lot.

Shakespeare in the Parking Lot is a compilation of the three works I developed through undergrad and is, fittingly enough, dedicated to my three roommates from Wheaton College who remain my best friends on planet Earth: Jake Steggerda, Jake Stauber, and Brendan Jones.

Jake Steggerda, for reading every word I've ever written—each of these scripts, my senior thesis, my blogs, my social media posts—and for listening to every word I've ever spoken. Through your friendship, I always feel heard.

Jake Stauber, for never holding anything back—in casual conversation, deep philosophical argument, or *Mario Kart*, I know exactly your hopes, dreams, and goals and you challenge me to express my own. Through your friendship, I always feel seen.

And Brendan Jones, for being by my side since the day we met as overwhelmed eighteen-year-olds in the Traber 6 bathroom during freshman orientation—through the ups and downs of writing *Knight* and helping me produce it when we were sophomores, to staying up and eating ramen with me at two a.m. when I was figuring out how to cast *Rose* during senior year. Through your friendship, I always feel understood.

Good Knight and Goodbye

est. 2009, revised in 2014

Peter Fenton

I dedicate this play to the very first woman to direct my work: my eighth-grade English teacher and lifelong supporter, Suzanne Fisher. May no one ever forget the first one to believe in them.

Author's Preface to Good Knight and Goodbye

I hope to God I'm done working on *Good Knight and Goodbye* forever. Seriously, someone personally come and stop me if Future Peter Fenton announces he's releasing a "brand new, definitive edition" of the tale of Sir Galahad, Lady Heron, Princess Jacqueline, and everyone else in the Kingdom of Slekochovakia in any medium ever again. And of course, you and I both know exactly what's going to happen someday since I've immortalized those words in print in the year of our Lord 2021 . . . if you once loved something, time has a funny way of bringing it back to the forefront of your mind whether you asked for it or not.

I'll give you the lowdown on my relationship with this play as quickly as I can. Over the years, I have developed such a love-hate relationship with *Good Knight and Goodbye* to the point where I could (and probably will) someday write an entire memoir just about how formative this text has been, for better and for worse, as a writer and as a human being. I can trace this complicated history to the moment the germ of this story (and quite a bit of the dialogue existing within) was born in Mrs. Fisher's English classroom in 2009.

I wrote *Good Knight and Goodbye* when I was in eighth grade in my hometown of Lancaster, Pennsylvania. As a cast member in the generic adventure comedy play Conestoga Valley Middle School staged that spring, I remember fourteen-year-old Peter rather arrogantly declaring, with his nose buried in the script, "This is garbage. I can write better than this crap."

Mrs. Fisher turned to me with an encouraging smirk and replied, "Then write me a better play."

So naturally, I went home and wrote a play. By July, I had finished the first draft and I gave it to Mrs. Fisher to have a look. *She loved it.* She made a call to my parents' landline phone and asked me for a meeting where we agreed she would direct the world premiere of *Good Knight and Goodbye* performed by the seventh and eighth graders in the following school year, and buzz was built in south-central Pennsylvania. I became the gentleman of the hour with my picture and an article by Jane Holahan on the front page of the Lancaster New Era—above the fold—and Anne Shannon later interviewed me during the week of the world premiere on our local NBC affiliate. Lancaster County's U.S. Representative in Congress at the time added me as a friend on Facebook. Once the performances came, the audiences were crazy—each performance was to a packed house with standing room only. I was signing autographs on people's playbills at intermission and outtake, and people older than me were gushing about what an inspiration I was—how I was "gonna be someone" someday. However real any of this attention was, it certainly gave me the impression practically everyone in the county—my teachers, fellow students, and friends of my grandparents—were all brimming with the question, 'What did that boy wonder Peter Fenton do?'

The thing about your fifteen minutes of fame is that surely enough, the sixteenth minute will come. The clock will strike midnight and your Ferrari will turn back into a Honda Civic. I was able to leverage my experience as a teenage playwright to stand out when it came time to apply for colleges and that certainly helped me get into a nice one, but otherwise, I was an ordinary student at Conestoga Valley High School. This experience writing *Good Knight and Goodbye* became the picture of success to my impressionable teenage heart. I tried, I really tried, to resurrect that success and recapture the feeling of wowing the masses by writing a new draft of the play once I got to college—staying up to ungodly hours in my freshman dorm room—in hopes of impressing my friends. While my friends at the time didn't end up caring about my play nearly as much as I did, this rewrite actually was a great exercise for me as a budding writer and ended up being a net gain for script and story. I stand by that decision.

The decision I no longer stand by is when I made the choice to take that rewritten script and mount a deeply troubled production the following year. This was my shot, I thought, at mainstream popularity at Wheaton College. The assignment? Direct a very much stripped-down "film adaptation" of *Good Knight and Goodbye* as the sophomore class's offering at the Wheaton College Class Film Festival in 2015. I'm sure this could have been a fine production had I been in the right headspace, had I not hinged an incredibly unhealthy amount of my sense of worth on the production's success. My quiet longing in freshman year to be seen once again by my peers as "that boy wonder Peter Fenton" had turned to ugly desperation by sophomore year. I'd gotten in my head that if this iteration of *Good Knight and Goodbye* fascinated my classmates in college the way it fascinated their high school counterparts, then I would be worth something . . . I might "be someone" someday. It does truly sound silly when I spell it out like that, but the struggle was so real and this battle was taking place so much at the core of my humanity. Needless to say, this life-or-death environment I built for myself and my crew on set was not one conducive for growth, or happy thoughts, or joy, or peace, or any other fruits of the spirit.

For what it's worth, with the cinematic eye of my talented co-director and an epic score written by a classmate studying music composition, the cast and I put together a well-intentioned final product for the festival. Some people in the audience really did end up liking what we had created with that production, but the people I specifically wanted to impress didn't seem to care for it. Of the four films screened at the Wheaton College Class Film Festival in 2015, three of them won awards. Guess which one didn't.

I was bawling. I darted out the side door of the building out to the street, not wanting to see another soul that night. My heart had really split in two when it was revealed I lost Best Screenplay to the Junior Class Film, and it was only salt in the wound when we still had not won a single award by the final one (Best Supporting Actress) and even then, they hadn't thrown Alexa Dava a bone for her portrayal of Princess Jacqueline. It was April in Chicagoland, so I could still see my breath as the tears kept falling. I had left in such a hurry my jacket was still on the chair inside, so I was out there shivering and alone with just the fog of my breath rising from my lips. The moment was fitting enough.

The whole experience with the class film festival left me feeling gutted to the point where I was unsure if I was going to pick up a pen (or, you know, open Microsoft Word) ever again. I wanted to quit writing altogether before my career had even begun.

But you know what's funny? Here I am, writing this preface and getting vulnerable with you to share some of the history that has led to these tangled up attachments and complicated feelings I get when I think about that story that I wrote eons ago, and yet—you hold this script in your hands right now, and chances are, if you don't know me personally or if you've met me within the past couple of years, you might not know it existed. You are a clean slate, you have none of that experience tied to the work. You have the chance to separate the art from the artist. You'll read the play, you'll like it or not as you will, and then you get to move on with your life.

Honestly? There is a part of me that envies you because I do believe *Good Knight and Goodbye* is a very fun play at its core. As I went back through the entire manuscript and rewrote the stage directions for the benefit of a general reader, the silly characters and not-particularly-serious storyline made me smile all over again.

It's a first play. It's not the first draft—not even close—I counted them out, and I believe with the publication of this reader's edition in *Shakespeare in the Parking Lot*, there have been seventeen drafts of *Good Knight and Goodbye/Knights of the Square Table/Late Knight Request* (yes, this same story has been told under three titles!).

I hope something in the pages that follow through Sir Galahad's journey makes you smile, too. As I've created more and more work in my lifetime from *Rose* to *Abandon All Hope* and everything that will come beyond, my craft has gotten more refined. The characters have been better-developed and the plots have been better thought-out, because as the author, more experience means I've gained more command of the medium of the stage, screen, or page—but I will always have *Good Knight and Goodbye* to point to

and say, "This is truly where it all began."
All of this being said—have a little fun in Slekochovakia for me.

A Personal Message

Act One, Scene 1

O nce upon a time, the world was filled with very silly kingdoms ruled by very silly kings. Just north of Prance and east of Gortupal (and a ways south from Just Okay Britain) was the silliest kingdom of them all—Slekochovakia.

The morning begins as it always does in the courtyard of Rumplegoose Castle. King Carlton IV's soldiers converse jovially right outside the castle as they await their commander. SIR KRAUSE, LADY SOBERICK and SIR HUMMEL huddle in one corner as the legendary SIR GALAHAD rushes into the room a bit disheveled after oversleeping. Sir Galahad scans the crowd and sees Sir Traber motion to him. Sir Galahad crosses to his friend as Sir Traber smirks.

SIR TRABER. Late again, Sir Galahad? That's three days in a row now, you better watch yourself!

SIR GALAHAD. Hey man, cut me some slack! I was gone for five years. Coming back, it takes some getting used to! Lord Diehm knows that.

SIR TRABER. Yeah, yeah, I guess so, but you're still late! One more and you'll have to cower before the king. Some legendary knight you are—

SIR GALAHAD. Pssshaw. I can handle the king with one hand tied behind my back.

A PERSONAL MESSAGE

SIR TRABER. Listen to yourself . . . *(Playfully mocking.)* "I'm Sir Galahad—I lived in Gortupal for five years—I'm too good for this place now."

SIR GALAHAD. Maybe. Look, the king and queen are lovely people. They're just . . . dull.

SIR TRABER. Delightfully dull. *(Grinning.)* But hey, they must've done something right if Jacqueline came from 'em.

SIR GALAHAD. *(Flatly.)* "The headstrong beauty of Slekochovakia."

SIR TRABER. Come on, it's Princess Jacqueline! Man, is something wrong with you or something?

SIR GALAHAD. I've never really bothered with women.

SIR TRABER. With all of your legendary quests, or whatever, I expected you to be much more of a romantic—or at least a little more into that princess. Maybe you should tie one hand behind your back and look again!

SIR GALAHAD. I don't write the legends, Jeff, I live 'em.

Sir Galahad and Sir Traber continue their conversation. The focus shifts to Sir Krause and Lady Soberick. Sir Hummel crosses to join them.

SIR HUMMEL. Sir Krause! What's new with you, my friend?

SIR KRAUSE. That's a stupid question. Nothing ever changes in this kingdom.

LADY SOBERICK. Things change from time to time. Sir Galahad came back last week.

SIR KRAUSE. Galahad? Pfft. They say that man's such a legend—that he struck down an entire army with a donkey's jawbone—that everything he touches turns to gold.

SIR HUMMEL. Wasn't that Sir Midas?

SIR KRAUSE. I didn't ask you.

LADY SOBERICK. I heard he did a lot of good for Gortupal these past five years. I'm sure he knows how to command an army . . .

SIR HUMMEL. Do you think King Carlton wants Galahad to take over for Diehm?

LADY SOBERICK. Lord Diehm is leaving?

SIR HUMMEL. Yeah, yeah! I overheard him say the other day he's leaving for the peace treaty conference in Gentlemandia.

LADY SOBERICK. It's an interesting thought. I think Galahad would be a fantastic commander. He's—

SIR KRAUSE. *(Interrupting.)* Look, Galahad's been here a week and I haven't seen a thing that tells me that he's such a big shot. King Carlton's a bonehead, begging the king of Gortupal to give him back. Waste of breath—the guy shows up late every day.

LADY SOBERICK. I don't know if you're in a position to criticize the king and queen . . . You think you'd make a better king?

SIR KRAUSE. Now that's a stupid question. Of course I'd be a better king. For one, Princess Jacqueline would be mine, there'd be no meetings, and people could have a second or two to breathe without the royal messenger

A PERSONAL MESSAGE

showing up—

Right on cue, the uptight commander of the forces, LORD DIEHM, enters with the royal family's chief communicator, LADY HERON.

LORD DIEHM. Ladies, gentlemen, I present the royal messenger, Lady Heron.

All bow.

LORD DIEHM. Lady Heron.

Lady Heron pulls out a scroll and clears her throat.

LADY HERON. Hear ye, hear ye: I bring you a message from the royal eminence himself, King Carlton.

SIR KRAUSE. What's the breaking news? Has the king blown his nose again?

LADY HERON. I bring you the message: *(Mindlessly reading scroll.)* "Bananas, chocolate, onions, pasta, carr—" This is my grocery list.

Lady Heron switches scrolls.

LADY HERON. *This* is the royal message: "The King has called a meeting with the Knights of the Square Table regarding the recent territorial acquisition following your morning duties. Please be prompt."

LORD DIEHM. Thank you, Lady Heron. You are dismissed.

Lady Heron starts to exit, but drags her feet—there's something else on her mind.

LORD DIEHM. Get to your morning duties. Chop, chop.

Knights exit in all directions as Sir Galahad crosses to a large basket and picks it up. Lord Diehm heads toward the castle with purpose, but not about to do hard labor. Lady Heron spots this as her opportunity to approach Sir Galahad—she moves to him as she crosses the crowd, trying to get his attention.

LADY HERON. Sir Galahad! Caleb! Sir Caleb—Galahad!

Sir Galahad turns around, holding the basket in his hands.

SIR GALAHAD. Yes, those are my names.

LADY HERON. Yeah. Hey, sorry. Didn't want to make a big scene back there, but you have a message of your own—it's more of a—personal message.

SIR GALAHAD. *(With slight worry.)* Oh, really? To whom do I owe the pleasure?

LADY HERON. This one's from . . . me. I have a message for you.

Sir Galahad turns to leave.

SIR GALAHAD. Hate to be rude, but this doesn't sound pressing. If you'll excuse me—

LADY HERON. Well, uh . . . It really depends on how you . . . prioritize—

Lady Heron grabs the basket from Sir Galahad's hand.

SIR GALAHAD. . . . What?

LADY HERON. Okay—

Lady Heron looks down at the basket in her hand.

LADY HERON. *This* is yours.

Lady Heron gives Sir Galahad the basket back.

LADY HERON. Mmm . . .there's not really an easy way to pivot into this . . .

A beat. They hang in comfortable—though slightly awkward—silence.

LADY HERON. So . . .are you seeing anyone right now?

SIR GALAHAD. No.

LADY HERON. Wonderful! *(Pulls out scroll.)* So, here's your message: "Bananas, chocolate, onions, pasta, carr–..." (Smiles.) That's my grocery list again. Well—

Lady Heron looks around on her person to find the scroll, realizes she has none.

LADY HERON. so I didn't actually write anything down, so just bear with me, okay?

SIR GALAHAD. Lady Heron, I—

LADY HERON. Please, call me Andrea.

SIR GALAHAD. Okay, uh . . .listen, Andrea—could we maybe do this later?

LADY HERON. No.

This "No" pierces Sir Galahad. He refocuses his attention to Lady Heron.

LADY HERON. I'll only be a second, I swear. Just let me get through this.

SIR GALAHAD. *(Nodding.)* Fine.

LADY HERON. I've heard a lot about what you've done over the years. I've only been in the castle for two years now, but I've heard all the legends. You are so brave, so handsome—

SIR GALAHAD. Uhh, yeah, ummm—Lady Her—*(Corrects himself.)* Andrea... I think you've got the wrong... impression.

LADY HERON. If I'm wrong—*(Smiles.)* then I want the right impression. Would you like to have dinner tonight?

SIR GALAHAD. Well, uh, this is a first.

LADY HERON. It's the tenth century, Sir Galahad, there's a first time for everything.

SIR GALAHAD. Listen, Andrea—you seem really cool. And brave. Really brave. I like what you're doing here...in theory. But the fact of the matter is, I just got here. Four days ago. Right now, I need to dedicate myself to the kingdom. So it's a thank you, but not now. Would you like me to introduce you to, uh—Sir Lancelot? He's a—wonderful man.

LADY HERON. He's a cad.

Lady Heron turns to walk away.

SIR GALAHAD. Andrea—

Lady Heron stops.

SIR GALAHAD. I didn't say... never.

LADY HERON. Oh—that's all right. I'll just go eat some pudding or something...

Lady Heron exits, silently asking herself, "Why on earth did I just say that?" Sir Galahad looks at the basket for a moment, picks it up, and exits in the opposite direction.

For King and Country

Act One, Scene 2

The Hall of the Square Table in Rumplegoose Castle, later that day. Sir Galahad, Sir Traber, Lady Soberick, Sir Hummel, and Sir Krause are seated at the Square Table. A trumpet blares as Lord Diehm enters. All rise in respect of their commander.

LORD DIEHM. Knights of the Square Table: your king and queen.

KING CARLTON and QUEEN VICTORIA enter with a couple of stoic HANDSERVANTS following them. The king and queen are seated at their throne-like chairs at the Square Table, after which all take their seats. The handservants stand in line along the wall behind the Square Table.

All hang in awkward silence as an idea visibly pops into King Carlton's head.

KING CARLTON. Lord Diehm.

LORD DIEHM. Your highness.

KING CARLTON. Please do that thing where you say these people's names.

LORD DIEHM. . . . Call roll, your highness?

KING CARLTON. Yes. Do that.

LORD DIEHM. Right away.

King Carlton very clearly spends this time organizing notes and obnoxiously rehearsing what he needs to say.

LORD DIEHM. Lady Soberick?

LADY SOBERICK. Here.

LORD DIEHM. Sir Galahad?

SIR GALAHAD. Here.

LORD DIEHM. Sir Hummel?

SIR HUMMEL. Present.

A handservant tosses an ornately wrapped box to Sir Hummel, who nonchalantly catches it and stores it under the table.

LORD DIEHM. Sir Krause?

SIR KRAUSE. Here.

LORD DIEHM. Sir Lancelot?

A beat.

LORD DIEHM. Sir Lancelot?

A beat. Knights look back and forth at each other. Sir Hummel speaks up.

SIR HUMMEL. Haven't seen him in days—

SIR TRABER. Weeks.

SIR HUMMEL. Haven't seen Gwen, either, now that you mention it—

SIR TRABER. Do you think she and Sir Lancelot...?

SIR HUMMEL. Oh *baby*, Sir Lancelot!

LADY SOBERICK. He's a cad.

LORD DIEHM. *(Sharply.)* Enough. Your highness, Sir Lancelot is not accounted for.

King Carlton has heard none of this exchange, as he continues to practice his speech. Lord Diehm clears his throat.

LORD DIEHM. Your highness—

The king pays him no attention.

QUEEN VICTORIA. Carlton!

KING CARLTON. Yes, dear?

Queen Victoria motions to Lord Diehm.

LORD DIEHM. Sir Lancelot is not accounted for.

KING CARLTON. Who?

LORD DIEHM. Sir Lancelot.

King Carlton is genuinely confused.

KING CARLTON. And . . . why would I care?

QUEEN VICTORIA. The roll call, dear. You requested it.

KING CARLTON. Right. Thank you, Lord Diehm.

LORD DIEHM. Sir Traber?

SIR TRABER. Here.

KING CARLTON. *(Simultaneously, to Lord Diehm.)* Well now what are you doing?

LORD DIEHM. Calling roll as you requested, your highness.

KING CARLTON. Come now, there's no need for that. I am ready now. Have a seat.

A bewildered Lord Diehm sinks down into his chair.

KING CARLTON. Now, to the important business at hand: my business. The kingdom of Slekochovakia has been an empire to be reckoned with since the reign of Sylvester the Third when the Slek Republic and the kingdom of Chovakia were unified into one virtuous empire, but we have grown so far past that mere accomplishment under my reign. I managed to acquire the vital seaport of Cape Emerald after a bidding war down at the moat of Farris—in Prance, of course. A little manly charm from such a wonderful king as myself sealed the deal. My bold act of heroism is cause for celebration . . . *(To Handservant.)* A bottle of my finest champagne, and a fresh cake.

Handservant exits.

QUEEN VICTORIA. *(To herself.)* I say let 'em eat cake.

KING CARLTON. Of course, the issue at hand is that Cape Emerald is so far away from our landlocked dominion that our regular army will not be able to protect the port. And naturally, in addition to the regular threats of vandals, thieves, wildfire, plague, bears, and global warming we are right up on the coast, which means there's now the threat of pirates. We don't want to deal with pirates. They're scary. Anyway, to make a long story short . . .

A beat. The king has lost his train of thought.

KING CARLTON. Oh, dearest me. What was I talking about?

SIR HUMMEL. Scary pirates...

The assembled grow increasingly agitated with King Carlton's trailing monologue. Handservant enters, carrying champagne and cake.

KING CARLTON. Right! Pirates! Now there is no pirate so valiant as I, but the presence of these seafaring warriors will be a formidable match for most of the kingdom. Now, these swashbuckling folk are sometimes employed by the crown to ravage other nations' seaports—when that happens, they're called privateers. As Slekochovakia has been landlocked for the duration of its history, we have employed no privateers. Though maybe we should.

King Carlton turns to the handservant.

KING CARLTON. And, while I'm thinking about it, send for six hundred topiary artists from across the countryside.

Handservant nods and exits.

KING CARLTON. We need a few more of them around the castle. You see, the topiary artist is much like a privateer in that they are a people employed by the king to do the will of the king—

ALL KNIGHTS. Get on with it!!!

KING CARLTON. Dreadfully sorry. I am forever distracted by topiary artists.

King Carlton clears his throat.

KING CARLTON. My kingly duties prevent me from overseeing the acquisition of Cape Emerald, so I would like one of you to lead an exploration to the new seaport. Provided you bring me back some little tiny topiaries, I shall consider naming you governor, serving as a trusted advisor under me, of course.

SIR HUMMEL. But who will be sent for the job?

KING CARLTON. Lord Diehm—

Lord Diehm rises.

LORD DIEHM. Your highness.

KING CARLTON. What were you doing earlier when you were saying the names of uh, those people?

LORD DIEHM. Calling roll, your highness.

KING CARLTON. Yes. Who was the last name you called?

LORD DIEHM. Sir Traber.

KING CARLTON. *(With a grand gesture.)* Masterful! Sir Truscott—

LORD DIEHM. Traber.

KING CARLTON. Traber—of the Square Table shall lead the inaugural expedition to Cape Emerald.

A beat. King Carlton looks around the table as he is not entirely sure which one is Sir Traber.

KING CARLTON. Would Sir Traber please rise?

Sir Traber rises. King Carlton is a little surprised, but nonetheless, he rises and walks over to Sir Traber to personally shake his hand.

KING CARLTON. I believe in you, Sir . . .

SIR TRABER. Traber.

KING CARLTON. Traber. I trust you will be great because I chose you. Lady Heron!

Lady Heron enters.

LADY HERON. Yes, your majesty?

KING CARLTON. Send word to—someone—that this brave knight Sir Chumbert will lead an expedition to Cape Emerald.

LADY HERON. I could send word to the stables to prepare a horse for him.

KING CARLTON. Yes. Do that.

Lady Heron exits.

KING CARLTON. And now, the meeting is adjourned.

A beat. A devilish smile spreads across King Carlton's face.

KING CARLTON. Go on, now, say the thing.

All knights rise.

ALL KNIGHTS. *(Reciting together.)* "I am a Knight of the Square Table of Slekochovakia. I swear to protect the walls of Rumplegoose Castle and obey King Carlton the Fourth, who was chosen by God and therefore he is an incredible genius and very handsome—"

The headstrong, beautiful PRINCESS JACQUELINE abruptly bursts into the room, mercifully interrupting the knights' oath.

PRINCESS JACQUELINE. Wait!

Knights are unsure whether they should remain standing or return to their seats.

PRINCESS JACQUELINE. I have an important announcement to make!

QUEEN VICTORIA. The princess has the floor. Be seated.

Knights return to their seats.

PRINCESS JACQUELINE. As you know, my courtship with Prince Charming ended abruptly—something about a glass slipper. Whatever. I didn't care to listen. Anyway, I'm offering my hand in marriage to any brave knight who wants to go on a quest. It's not a bad deal really, you just go on an epic adventure and then you get to marry me. So, any takers?

Nobody moves. Princess Jacqueline nods.

PRINCESS JACQUELINE. Well then. You can just, uh, you can just have some time to think about it. It's better this way. Mother!

QUEEN VICTORIA. Yes, dear?

PRINCESS JACQUELINE. Have a plate of brownies sent to my chambers. That is all.

Princess Jacqueline exits, wiping away a single tear.

KING CARLTON. Meeting adjourned.

LORD DIEHM. Report to the feasting room at once. I hear Chef Torte has prepared the finest ribs today.

Most of the knights exit. King Carlton places his hand on Sir Galahad's shoulder.

KING CARLTON. Sir Galahad. A word?

SIR GALAHAD. Yes, your highness.

Out of the corner of his eye, Sir Krause notices Sir Galahad stay behind. As the rest of the knights mill out of the room, Sir Krause nonchalantly crouches behind a plant to eavesdrop as Sir Galahad returns to the Square Table to face King Carlton and Queen Victoria.

KING CARLTON. So you have been here four days. I have heard—

Sir Galahad assumes he is in trouble.

SIR GALAHAD. Oh—your highness—it's a new schedule . . . I think I'm in a different time zone, but I—I'll get there. I'll figure it out soon—

The King and Queen have no idea what Sir Galahad is talking about.

KING CARLTON. Erm—ah—

Sir Galahad cocks his head.

SIR GALAHAD. Your highness?

QUEEN VICTORIA. We wished to speak with you about our daughter.

SIR GALAHAD. Oh—yeah, what about her?

QUEEN VICTORIA. Sir Galahad, you are a good knight, the greatest on the continent. There was a reason we bargained so deeply with Gortupal for your return. We wanted you not simply for your service as a Knight of the Square Table, but we . . . *(Heavily.)* we have something important to request of you.

SIR GALAHAD. Sure.

Queen Victoria attempts to continue, but bursts into tears. Feeling a little awkward, Sir Galahad comforts Queen Victoria with a couple of taps on the shoulder. King Carlton speaks up.

KING CARLTON. I am dying, Sir Galahad.

Queen Victoria composes herself.

QUEEN VICTORIA. Our finest physicians have told us he will die within the year.

Lady Heron enters.

LADY HERON. The horses are ready whenever Sir Traber is, your highness.

KING CARLTON. Lady Heron, we will speak on this later. If you would leave us be, please.

Lady Heron backs out of view to eavesdrop.

KING CARLTON. I want to give my daughter away at her own wedding.

QUEEN VICTORIA. And we would like Princess Jacqueline to marry you.

KING CARLTON. You see, I never bore a son of my own—

SIR GALAHAD. Well—I don't think that's . . . anatomically . . . possible? For you? I could be wrong . . . ?

King Carlton does not hear Sir Galahad.

KING CARLTON. —and I want you to take up Princess Jacqueline's quest. I want you to marry her and ascend to the throne when I pass. I have full faith in you. I want her to be married when I pass from this world into the next, and if there is no man so formidable as I to rule this kingdom in the coming days, I would like it to be you.

SIR GALAHAD. Uh . . . Wow. Yes. Anything for you, your highness. I'll—take the quest. Sure. It would be an honor to marry Princess Jacqueline.

Lady Heron exits slowly. She's a little confused, given the conversation she had with Sir Galahad earlier that day, but on some level understands.

KING CARLTON. Wonderful! Your quest begins right now! You are to complete three tasks to prove your worthiness to marry Princess Jacqueline. Go to the monastery at once. Friar Wesley has a special task for you there.

Sir Galahad nods.

KING CARLTON. You will be a mighty king, Sir Galahad. Do not take this lightly.

Sir Galahad exits. Sir Krause stumbles out from his hiding place behind the plant, which falls to the floor. King Carlton and Queen Victoria are a bit alarmed.

SIR KRAUSE. Your majesty—the name's Krause. Sir Krause.

KING CARLTON. Ah yes, I . . . know you?

SIR KRAUSE. I didn't want to bother you in front of everyone, but I would like to take the quest. To marry her.

KING CARLTON. Hmm . . . marry who, Sir Crab . . . ?

SIR KRAUSE. Krause.

KING CARLTON. You . . . would like to marry Sir Krause?

SIR KRAUSE. No, sir. I would like to marry Princess Jacqueline.

KING CARLTON. Well, Sir Galahad has *already* taken up the quest, a wonderful man for my wonderful daughter . . . but I do like a good competition. Yes, please take the quest. A royal competition.

King Carlton chuckles. He is simply tickled with himself for dreaming up this little game.

KING CARLTON. Oh yes! A battle of the ages for the beautiful Jacqueline's hand! Head to the monastery; that is where your first task lies.

The handservant returns—again—with a bottle of champagne and a monstrous layer-cake.

QUEEN VICTORIA. Now, what is this?

HANDSERVANT. The champagne and cake his highness requested.

King Carlton and Queen Victoria turn to the cake and then share a quizzical gaze into each other's eyes.

QUEEN VICTORIA. I say let 'em eat cake.

KING CARLTON. Take it to the feasting room.

Handservant steps toward the door out. Queen Victoria raises a finger to get the servant's attention.

QUEEN VICTORIA. Ah-bah-bah!

Handservant turns around. Queen Victoria takes the bottle of champagne out of the servant's hand. Queen Victoria waves the handservant out of the room. Handservant exits.

KING CARLTON. I'm sure the knights will enjoy it, such a wonderful gift from me. Shall we adjourn?

Queen Victoria pops the bottle open. Sir Krause crosses to the King's seat at the Square Table. He puts a hand on the back of the chair.

QUEEN VICTORIA. We shall.

King Carlton and Queen Victoria exit together, sharing swigs of the champagne bottle as Sir Krause caresses the throne, laughing evilly.

An Honest Question

Act One, Scene 3

The Monastery within Our Lady of Ambiguous Malaise in the eastern hills outside Rumplegoose Castle, later that day. FRIAR WESLEY sits on a chair in a simple, beautiful room full of stained glass windows lining the wall. There are two candles and a bowl of fire in front of him. Lady Heron enters, carrying a scroll. She crosses herself as she enters.

LADY HERON. The King and Queen express their deepest gratitude for your agreement to provide this task on such short notice.

FRIAR WESLEY. It is an undeserved blessing to serve in the court of Slekochovakia.

LADY HERON. I have here the message you are to give the knights as they pass through on the quest—

Lady Heron hands Friar Wesley a scroll.

LADY HERON. —you recall your instructions?

FRIAR WESLEY. Yes, I do.

LADY HERON. Thank you, Friar.

Lady Heron wanders to exit the hall, absentmindedly running into Sir Galahad as he enters.

LADY HERON. Sorry!

Sir Galahad watches Lady Heron exit.

FRIAR WESLEY. Sir Galahad—please, come, sit down.

Sir Galahad sits at Friar Wesley's feet.

SIR GALAHAD. Friar, what is my task?

FRIAR WESLEY. Your task is simple—you must light this candle and then receive my blessing.

Friar Wesley gestures to the candle to his left.

SIR GALAHAD. That's it?

FRIAR WESLEY. But I must first ask you a riddle before I give you the splint.

SIR GALAHAD. As you wish, Wesley.

FRIAR WESLEY. I will give you this splint only if you answer me this riddle with honesty.

SIR GALAHAD. Okay.

FRIAR WESLEY. Who is your true love?

A beat. Sir Galahad has no answer to this question. He laughs.

SIR GALAHAD. That's a good riddle, Friar.

FRIAR WESLEY. It is indeed. But I will only give you this splint if you answer me with honesty.

SIR GALAHAD. Well . . . I don't think I have a true love. If you want me to say Princess Jacqueline, honest to God, that's not my answer.

FRIAR WESLEY. Sir Galahad, my son, you have not answered me with honesty. I will only give you this splint if you answer me with honesty. Who is your true love?

Sir Galahad raises a finger and gestures to Friar Wesley.

SIR GALAHAD. Oh—yeah—I get it. We're in church. God. My true love is God.

Friar Wesley chuckles.

FRIAR WESLEY. A wonderful answer, Sir Galahad, but that is not the answer to this riddle. Remember, riddles are not always to be answered with honesty, but this one is. Who is your true love?

Another beat. Sir Galahad replays what Friar Wesley just told him as a smile spreads across his face. He thinks he may be onto something.

SIR GALAHAD. I need to answer with honesty, huh . . . ?

FRIAR WESLEY. I expect honesty for your answer.

SIR GALAHAD. You expect honesty . . .honesty . . .honesty.

Another pause as Sir Galahad assures to himself he must be right.

SIR GALAHAD. Honesty. My true love is honesty.

Friar Wesley beams.

FRIAR WESLEY. You have answered my riddle with honesty indeed!

Friar Wesley dips the splint into the fire pit to set it on fire and offers it to Sir Galahad.

FRIAR WESLEY. Sir Galahad, I invite you to light this candle and receive my blessing.

Sir Galahad takes the splint and lights the candle. He hands the flaming splint back to Friar Wesley, who blows it out.

FRIAR WESLEY. Sir Galahad, though this task was quick and the riddle was silly, my prayer for you is that you remain honest in your journey—honest before God, honest to those you love, and honest to yourself as well. The road may take turns you do not expect, but that is how this life moves. Make do with the twists and turns, and you'll find yourself taking a far better road. Blessings to you, my son.

SIR GALAHAD. Thank you, Friar Wesley. Might you know what *twist* my quest is about to take?

Friar Wesley pulls out the scroll and unrolls it.

FRIAR WESLEY. Ah! Yes I do! Lady Heron just stopped by moments ago—"Head to Cape Emerald and recover evidence of topiary from the lush seaport."

Friar Wesley tucks the scroll back in his robe as he looks at Sir Galahad square in the eye.

FRIAR WESLEY. I will be honored to serve as your loyal subject, Sir Galahad.

SIR GALAHAD. Thank you, Friar Wesley. See you soon.

FRIAR WESLEY. At mass on Sunday?

Sir Galahad is not much for mass.

SIR GALAHAD. Uh . . . we'll see.

Sir Krause enters the room and rams himself into Sir Galahad, though Sir Galahad believes this was mere accident.

SIR GALAHAD. *(Surprised.)* Sorry! Oh—hello, Sir Krause!

As Sir Galahad steps left, Sir Krause steps right—their movements mirror each other.

SIR KRAUSE. Galahad.

SIR GALAHAD. Krause.

SIR KRAUSE. Galahad.

SIR GALAHAD. Krause.

SIR KRAUSE. Galahad.

SIR GALAHAD. Here for confession, Sir Krause?

SIR KRAUSE. Yes, confession, I'm here to confess my brilliance.

SIR GALAHAD. Of course. And hey—I won't see you around for a while. I'm taking up the quest for Princess Jacqueline's hand in marriage. I'm off to Cape Emerald, actually. The second task is to find evidence of topiary for the king.

SIR KRAUSE. Oh. Okay.

Sir Krause flashes a devilish grin.

SIR KRAUSE. Good luck.

SIR GALAHAD. *(Confused.)* . . . Yes.

Sir Galahad exits.

FRIAR WESLEY. Sir Krau—

Sir Krause quickly takes a seat at Friar Wesley's feet.

SIR KRAUSE. You can yadda-yadda the spiel, what do I have to do? I'm here for the quest.

FRIAR WESLEY. Indeed you are. Your task is simple—you must light this candle and then receive my blessing.

Friar Wesley gestures to the unlit candle to his right. Sir Krause rashly takes the splint from him, dips it in the fire and lights the second candle.

SIR KRAUSE. Bless me. Actually, I don't have time for that.

Sir Krause starts to exit.

FRIAR WESLEY. *(Calmly.)* Sir Krause—

SIR KRAUSE. Right.

Sir Krause hastily crosses himself and exits.

Questionable Life Choices

Act One, Scene 4

The lawn outside Merlin's House, which is a simple hut in the hills near Rumplegoose Castle, the next day. Sir Galahad wanders down to the hut and knocks on the door.

SIR GALAHAD. Merlin? *(Knocks again.)* Merlin!

A woman giggling is heard from inside the hut.

MERLIN. *(Offstage.)* Wait here, my lass.

WOMAN. *(Offstage.)* Where are you going?

MERLIN. *(Offstage.)* Just have another swig while you wait.

WOMAN. *(Offstage.)* What's in this drink?

MERLIN. *(Offstage.)* Sugar. Lots and lots of sugar.

More female giggling. MERLIN emerges from the hut.

MERLIN. Ah! Sir Galahad! What a surprise!

SIR GALAHAD. I'm sorry, is this a bad time?

Merlin looks over his shoulder into his house.

MERLIN. Nonsense. *(Sarcastically.)* I always have time to interrupt a rendezvous.

SIR GALAHAD. So . . . may I come in?

MERLIN. *(Abruptly.)* No. Nope. No. No-no.

SIR GALAHAD. Is someone in there?

MERLIN. No, dear boy, it's just such a beautiful April evening . . . Why converse inside when we could do the same outdoors?

SIR GALAHAD. Um—

Merlin gestures to a fire pit, with a couple of stumps set around. Sir Galahad takes a seat on one of the stumps.

SIR GALAHAD. Sure.

MERLIN. If you're here for a love potion, dreadfully sorry—they take weeks to make and I can't let you have any of my stash.

SIR GALAHAD. Love . . . potions?

MERLIN. Undetectable to the human conscience. "True love" at its finest. Side effects may include mood swings and drowsiness. Oh, and increased appetite.

SIR GALAHAD. No—no, Merlin, I don't want a love potion, I wanted to apologize to you. I kinda took off and never said goodbye when I left.

MERLIN. Oh. You left?

SIR GALAHAD. Merlin, that was five years ago.

MERLIN. Five years? *(Chuckles.)* Well, when you live 826 of them, what's another five?

SIR GALAHAD. Eight hundred twenty-six? Wow, you don't look a day over . . . uh . . .

MERLIN. Nonetheless, I am happy to see you again. And thanks to my potions, I stopped aging 102 years ago. Helps keep life lively, no?

SIR GALAHAD. And you are doing well?

MERLIN. I'd like to think so. I'm getting wiser by the years, and with that wisdom comes a certain draw that brings the young maidens down to see old Merlin. Their smoke signals keep me busy.

SIR GALAHAD. Oh, like you can tell what someone's saying with a smoke signal?

MERLIN. Actually, my boy, you can. You can always tell what the lass is saying by the wood she chooses to burn. You see, if she picks a log of oak, then she simply acknowledges that she saw your smoke and would like to consider your advances. Hickory is a flat rejection. But when she burns aspen or pine, *(Chuckling.)* that's when you figure out where and when the events will transpire.

SIR GALAHAD. I didn't need to know that.

MERLIN. Caleb, it's life lesson time, so listen up: life is short—

SIR GALAHAD. You're 826—

MERLIN. Life. Is. Short. Trust nobody, step on everyone in your way, and throw them off a cliff even if they win. You got it?

SIR GALAHAD. Uh—Merlin? Are you okay?

MERLIN. I'm just a man who knows what he wants and I always get it. *(Points inside.)* Like her. You're never going to believe who it is I have in there—

SIR GALAHAD. *(Grossed out.)* Okay. Why don't we change the subject? Perhaps you've heard, the king has sent me on a quest for Princess Jacqueline's hand in marriage.

MERLIN. Princess . . . Jacqueline. Oh my. That sounds complicated. *(Not missing a beat.)* And you would like my assistance?

Merlin is conflicted.

SIR GALAHAD. Well, I—yeah. I'm trying to get to Cape Emerald in search of new topiary.

MERLIN. Cape Emerald? This expedition could be rather perilous, don't you think?

SIR GALAHAD. I don't care. I'll die for the princess and for Slekochovakia if I must.

MERLIN. *(To himself.)* Oh dear. *(Insincerely.)* That's—that's the sound of a dedicated warrior! This all sounds too exciting. I need to keep an eye on you. I'm coming along.

SIR GALAHAD. Really? Uh—I just wanted your help figuring out how to get there.

MERLIN. Nonsense.

Lady Heron enters.

MERLIN. You need someone by your side, and I have nothing better to do. I have a way of making everything work out for me. Us.

SIR GALAHAD. Great. I think.

MERLIN. Now, if you'll excuse me, I must take care of one business item before we leave.

Merlin gets up and enters his hut, slamming the door behind him.

LADY HERON. Sir Galahad?

SIR GALAHAD. Andrea. Any messages for me?

LADY HERON. Ha! I wish. No, I have one for Merlin—is he around?

SIR GALAHAD. He just went inside. We're about to leave together—he's, uh, invited himself to join my quest for the princess's hand.

LADY HERON. *(Sarcastically, grinning.)* Oh. Lovely.

Merlin emerges again from the hut.

LADY HERON. You know, Sir Galahad, it might not be the end of the world if you skipped the whole perilous quest thing and stuck around here.

MERLIN. Well unfortunately for all of us, there's no talking this legendary knight out of an epic quest for the beautiful Jacqueline's hand—he even said he would die for her if that's what it would take.

Lady Heron is surprised to hear Sir Galahad would use the phrase "die for her".

MERLIN. Fancy seeing you here again, Lady Heron!

LADY HERON. King Carlton sends you a message.

MERLIN. Ah. What has his majesty sent to me?

LADY HERON. The king requests his . . . ehm . . . "prescription."

MERLIN. Here it is.
Merlin tosses an unmarked sack to Lady Heron.

LADY HERON. Great.

Sir Galahad looks into Lady Heron's eyes with empathy, recognizing her discontent.

SIR GALAHAD. Are you all right?

LADY HERON. I'm fine.

SIR GALAHAD. Okay. We look forward to your updates from the kingdom, Lady Heron.

Sir Galahad smiles. Lady Heron returns the smile in kind.

LADY HERON. Yes, of course.

Merlin is no longer conflicted.

MERLIN. Yes. Yes, this will all work just fine.

SIR GALAHAD. Good. Merlin, let's go!

MERLIN. Cape Emerald awaits!

Sir Galahad and Merlin exit.

LADY HERON. Wow. He'd . . . die for her.
Lady Heron lets these words sink in again. As they wash over her, a tear involuntarily rolls down her cheek. She immediately cleans it up.

LADY HERON. This is fine.

Queen Victoria rushes in.

QUEEN VICTORIA. Lady Heron! There you are!

LADY HERON. My queen . . . What are you doing out here?

QUEEN VICTORIA. The king and I have a crisis! I had to run after you—we need all hands on deck!

Queen Victoria looks into Lady Heron's eyes and sees the residue of her tears.

QUEEN VICTORIA. Goodness me, what is in your eyes?

LADY HERON. Oh . . . allergies. I get really bad allergies this time of year.

Lady Heron fakes a sneeze.

QUEEN VICTORIA. You shall see the Duke of Benadryl posthaste. But later. After we deal with the crisis.

LADY HERON. What is going on?

QUEEN VICTORIA. It's a secret. I can't tell you yet.

LADY HERON. Um . . . why not?

QUEEN VICTORIA. I'm sorry, my dear, but it must remain my little secret for now. Let's just call it Victoria's secret.

LADY HERON. *(More or less to herself.)* That's kinda catchy . . .

QUEEN VICTORIA. Hmm?

LADY HERON. Oh, nothing. Secret crisis, you said. We better be off to deal with it. We can't have King Carlton all agitated and overwrought by Victoria's secret, now can we?

Bored On a Boat

Act One, Scene 5

A rowboat somewhere in the middle of the sea, four days later. Sir Galahad and Merlin sit facing each other with nowhere to hide. Merlin has a journal and feather quill, narrating what he is writing.

MERLIN. Ship log: Day three of the voyage. The elusive territory known as Cape Emerald is in fact not a seaport, but instead, a tiny island several days south of the grand peninsula, toward Africa. The knight has been experiencing intense migraines and covers his ears. The captain has no idea how he contracted these ailments. I speak to him constantly—attempting to more fully understand these symptoms. Yet he speaks so little. I cannot say I understand.

Sir Galahad sighs as Merlin continues. The lights dim as fog filters across the stage, signaling a fantasy interlude. In his fantasy, Sir Galahad steps out of the rowboat onto the sea.

SIR GALAHAD. Princess Jacqueline . . . the headstrong beauty of Slekochovakia . . .

Merlin stops his ship logging upon hearing this.

MERLIN. Oh dearest me. He's fantasizing about her.

Merlin exits. Ambient wedding music begins to play. Princess Jacqueline enters in a wedding dress, moving beautifully. A small congregation of extras filters in and is seated. Merlin enters. At no point in the fantasy sequence does Sir Galahad see Merlin or notice his antics.

SIR GALAHAD. I'm going to marry her someday . . . and on that day . . . her hair will be as beautiful as a flock of goats descending from a mountain!

PRINCESS JACQUELINE. I'm not sure how to take that.

SIR GALAHAD. I'm pretty sure it's a compliment.

PRINCESS JACQUELINE. Are you sure . . . ?

SIR GALAHAD. It's a compliment. I've heard, anyway. It's my fantasy—just go with it.

PRINCESS JACQUELINE. *(Shrugs.)* Okay.

Merlin sighs, frustrated. He exits.

SIR GALAHAD. Her father, there to walk her down the aisle.

King Carlton enters and takes Princess Jacqueline by the arm.

KING CARLTON. Sweet Jacqueline, are you ready to marry your knight in shining armor?

PRINCESS JACQUELINE. Of course, Father!

SIR GALAHAD. And then the bridesmaids will enter with their beautiful bouquets of frozen ham . . .

A couple BRIDESMAIDS enter, each carrying a frozen ham.

PRINCESS JACQUELINE. Uh, Sir Galahad, have you even been to a wedding before? There are a lot of things wrong with this one. Everyone knows in a traditional Slekochovakian wedding, the bridesmaids carry rubber chickens. This is just basic kingdom etiquette. And I don't come out for a while, I'm the last one in the chapel.

Bridesmaids pass Princess Jacqueline.

PRINCESS JACQUELINE. And no one, I repeat, no one—comes in front of the bride.

SIR GALAHAD. We'll work on it. This is my fantasy.

PRINCESS JACQUELINE. *(Sighs.)* Fine, whatever.

SIR GALAHAD. And then, just as Jacqueline gets a little nervous . . .

Princess Jacqueline tenses up.

SIR GALAHAD. I'll waltz into the chapel.

Sir Galahad crosses the surface of the sea, wandering down the aisle to join hands with Princess Jacqueline. He stops when he is just out of the Princess's reach.

PRINCESS JACQUELINE. Sir Galahad? What's wrong?

MERLIN. *(Offstage.)* All right—in you go!

Merlin shoves Lady Heron on stage, emerging in Sir Galahad's line of sight behind Princess Jacqueline.

SIR GALAHAD. Andrea—

Princess Jacqueline turns around to see Lady Heron. Princess Jacqueline contorts her face.

PRINCESS JACQUELINE. Ew, what is *she* doing here?

SIR GALAHAD. I—I don't know. This is really weird.

LADY HERON. Yeah, I was just minding my own business and somehow, here I am! At the forefront of your mind.

PRINCESS JACQUELINE. This is *your* fantasy, Galahad—make her go away. I do not want my messenger, of all people, messing up our perfect fantasy wedding—*flawed* as it may be.

SIR GALAHAD. *(Nodding.)* Andrea—please?

LADY HERON. Yeah—how do I get out of here?

Lady Heron exits.

PRINCESS JACQUELINE. That was weird.

SIR GALAHAD. Yeah. So weird.

PRINCESS JACQUELINE. What happens next?

SIR GALAHAD. Right! So then Friar Wesley shows up and the entire congregation will rise when they see him enter.

PRINCESS JACQUELINE. *(Chuckles.)* You're ridiculous.

Friar Wesley enters, the gathered congregation rises as he takes his spot on the altar behind Sir Galahad and Princess Jacqueline.

FRIAR WESLEY. You have done well to make it this far, Sir Galahad.

SIR GALAHAD. Thank you, Friar Wesley. Princess Jacqueline and I are unhappy together.
Princess Jacqueline glances twice at Sir Galahad.

SIR GALAHAD. I mean happy, very happy together.

FRIAR WESLEY. Sir Galahad of the Square Table, do you take Princess Jacqueline of Slekochovakia to be your—

Merlin enters. He casts a spell with his hands.

MERLIN. "Yoga instructor"!

FRIAR WESLEY. Sir Galahad of the Square Table, do you take Princess Jacqueline of Slekochovakia to be your yoga instructor?

SIR GALAHAD. I do.

FRIAR WESLEY. And Princess Jacqueline of Slekochovakia, do you take Sir Galahad to be your—

Merlin casts a spell with his hands.

MERLIN. "Traveling band videographer."

FRIAR WESLEY. Do you take Sir Galahad to be your traveling band videographer?

PRINCESS JACQUELINE. I do.

FRIAR WESLEY. I now pronounce you man and yoga instructor. Sir Galahad, you may now seek your namaste. Now I gotta run—

SIR GALAHAD. Where are you off to?

FRIAR WESLEY. I'm a busy man, Sir Galahad. I'm conducting your funeral in some other knight's fantasy, actually. Blessings to you both.

Friar Wesley exits with purpose. Princess Jacqueline turns to Sir Galahad.

PRINCESS JACQUELINE. So, I know I'm your yoga instructor now and you're my band videographer, but it seems like we should kiss.

Sir Galahad surveys Princess Jacqueline.

SIR GALAHAD. Yes ma'am.

They kiss.

MERLIN. Ay-yai-yai. Okay, get back here, you.

Merlin exits, immediately re-enters with Lady Heron. Sir Galahad pulls away from the princess when he sees Lady Heron.

PRINCESS JACQUELINE. Sir Galahad?

SIR GALAHAD. *(Angrily.)* This is my fantasy, Andrea—why are you here again? Please. Go away!

Lady Heron exits with a silent nod.

PRINCESS JACQUELINE. So . . . Finish that kiss?

SIR GALAHAD. *(With hurried urgency.)* So then after the wedding, we'll have our reception under the moonlight in the castle courtyard.

Merlin snickers, satisfied.

PRINCESS JACQUELINE. Could we have it somewhere else? My hay fever is truly awful this time of year—

SIR GALAHAD. My fantasy, Jacqueline!

PRINCESS JACQUELINE. Right. Go on.

Princess Jacqueline sneezes. Lady Heron enters with a scroll.

SIR GALAHAD. And then Lady Heron will proclaim to the kingdom—

PRINCESS JACQUELINE. Lady Heron?

LADY HERON. *(Reading off scroll.)* "Bananas, chocolate, onions, pasta, carr—"

Sir Galahad and Lady Heron make eye contact and both laugh as Lady Heron switches scrolls.

LADY HERON. *(Through laughter.)* For the first time as yoga instructor and traveling band videographer, Mr. and Mrs. Caleb and Jacqueline Galahad!

Princess Jacqueline crosses angrily to Lady Heron.

PRINCESS JACQUELINE. What are you doing here?

LADY HERON. Good question. What am I doing here?

PRINCESS JACQUELINE. Why am I angry? Should I be angry?

Sir Galahad processes his thought aloud.

SIR GALAHAD. I don't . . . think so? Tell you the truth, I'm not so sure why she keeps popping up myself.

LADY HERON. I can't seem to find my way out of your mind.

Princess Jacqueline thinks quickly and comes up with a rash explanation.

PRINCESS JACQUELINE. Oh, I know why! She was the last woman you saw before you left. I have nothing to worry about. You have nothing to worry about. Our day, when it comes, will be perfect.
Princess Jacqueline kisses Sir Galahad on the cheek. Sir Galahad looks off into the distance toward Lady Heron.

SIR GALAHAD. Yeah. Perfect.

LADY HERON. Caleb . . .

Sir Galahad leaves Princess Jacqueline's side and walks on the surface of the sea toward Lady Heron.

SIR GALAHAD. Andrea . . .

Before Sir Galahad can take her hand, Lady Heron points offstage.

LADY HERON. *(Abruptly.)* Do you see that huge sandbar you're headed for?

Sir Galahad turns around in alarm.

SIR GALAHAD. Oh, crap!

All characters in the fantasy exit abruptly in both directions as fog dissipates. Sir Galahad hops back into the rowboat and paddles frantically. He stops after a few seconds and stares off into the distance.

MERLIN. *(Snidely.)* Bad dream?

SIR GALAHAD. Just a dream. Just a silly dream.

MERLIN. Ah, well. Your headache seems to be cleared.

SIR GALAHAD. I have a new one now.
Sir Galahad points off into the distance.
SIR GALAHAD. Merlin! Is that Cape Emerald?

MERLIN. My beard, I daresay it is! Leave it all to me, we shall sail ashore immediately!

Merlin rows the boat offstage as the lights dim.

Exactly Two Radishes

Act One, Scene 6

The Hall of the Square Table in Rumplegoose Castle, later that day. King Carlton paces back and forth as Queen Victoria, Lady Heron, CHEF TORTE, and a few other handservants look on. Torte turns to Lady Heron.

TORTE. *(Aside.)* Well. This should be good.

LADY HERON. Indeed.

QUEEN VICTORIA. Carlton, please explain to the servants what is going on here.

KING CARLTON. The execution of that interior designer fellow went off without a hitch! Why just afterward, I said to the—

QUEEN VICTORIA. About the wedding planner!

KING CARLTON. Ah, yes. Our wedding planner for dear Jacqueline's wedding has quit so we sent her to the dungeon where she awaits my judgment. What a silly, pig-headed, very dead woman!

LADY HERON. So you want me to send a message to Sir Galahad and Sir Krause that the quest is postponed because there is no longer a wedding?

KING CARLTON. No, of course not.

LADY HERON. . . . because I was just kidding.

KING CARLTON. We need a wedding planner, Lady Heron, and you are responsible for finding one.

LADY HERON. Of course, your highness. I'll see what I can do. I take my leave.

Lady Heron exits and returns immediately with LESLIE GODZILLABRIDE, a #girlboss type, conventionally beautiful and dressed in a 21st-Century business suit—which makes her look rather out of place in the medieval scene. Others are shocked at Lady Heron's speed.

KING CARLTON. Your efficiency is astounding, Lady Heron. You are all dismissed.

Torte and other servants disperse offstage.

LADY HERON. Your bidding, as always, is my command. Here is the first accomplished wedding planner I was able to find without the internet.

LESLIE GODZILLABRIDE. It is an honor to meet you, your highness. *(Bows deeply.)* The name is Leslie Godzillabride.

QUEEN VICTORIA. It certainly sounds like we're in good hands.

LESLIE GODZILLABRIDE. I get results. A bride in every chapel and a cost at every corner.

KING CARLTON. My deepest gratitude, Lady Heron. This woman sounds nearly as wonderful as I! I have full faith in you, Lucy—

LESLIE GODZILLABRIDE. I have no time for your silly niceties. I will begin immediately. And the name's Leslie Godzillabride, your highness.

KING CARLTON. And remember, secrecy is of the utmost importance! Princess Jacqueline will not know about this wedding until she walks down the aisle—

Princess Jacqueline enters, eating directly from a bag of sugar.

PRINCESS JACQUELINE. Good morning, Mother. Good morning, Father. *(To Leslie.)* Good morning, lady I don't know.

QUEEN VICTORIA. Jacqueline! We were worried sick! Where have you been?

PRINCESS JACQUELINE. Eating sugar. I haven't gone anywhere, if you're asking. Might I ask why there is a peasant standing in front of you?

LESLIE GODZILLABRIDE. Peasant? Did she just call me a peasant? *Leslie lunges toward Jacqueline.*

QUEEN VICTORIA. Ms. Godzillabride!

King Carlton crosses to Princess Jacqueline and puts his arm around her, turning her around, away from the action.

KING CARLTON. Oh, you precocious daughter of mine! Someday you may be as intelligent as your father, but for now, you're just our little princess. *King Carlton pats PRINCESS JACQUELINE on the head.*

KING CARLTON. Now go, enjoy the day, my daughter.

PRINCESS JACQUELINE. Um, all right. Hey, have you heard anything about my quest from any of the knights?

KING CARLTON. Quest . . . erm . . . what quest?

PRINCESS JACQUELINE. Father! You were there at the Square Table when not one knight would take up the quest for my hand.

KING CARLTON. Look at you, having another one of your flights of fancy. I recall no such thing. Less sugar, princess. Now, go, enjoy the day.

Princess Jacqueline is skeptical and vaguely offended, as she should be.

PRINCESS JACQUELINE. Um . . . okay.
Princess Jacqueline exits. Focus shifts to Queen Victoria speaking to Leslie Godzillabride about her duties.

KING CARLTON. Lady Heron, I need you to send messages to both Sir Galahad and Sir . . . the other one at Cape Emerald.

LADY HERON. My pleasure.

King Carlton hands two scrolls to Lady Heron, who takes them and exits.

QUEEN VICTORIA. Your first task is to order a cake from the royal baker. The princess would like Death by Chocolate, topped with exactly two radishes, as is tradition.

LESLIE GODZILLABRIDE. Which poison does the baker fancy? There are many delectable options the guests and groom would never suspect: arsenic, asbestos, cyanide, strychnine . . .

QUEEN VICTORIA. No! No! Of course not. Our chef is familiar with Death by Chocolate. More of a figurative name, really.

LESLIE GODZILLABRIDE. Oh, okay. I guess that's just your little secret then?

QUEEN VICTORIA. While you are planning the wedding, you may work in this room right here. And if you so much as step one toe out of line, we will throw you to the dungeon. You may room with the prior planner.

LESLIE GODZILLABRIDE. She can have the room to herself. I will have this wedding shaped up in no time.

Queen Victoria hands Leslie Godzillabride a scroll.

QUEEN VICTORIA. To get things started, I have a list of people you must speak to at once.

Leslie Godzillabride opens the scroll, which extends to the floor.

LESLIE GODZILLABRIDE. My, my, what a list! I admire your thoroughness. We will get along famously! I will head off to the baker at once.

Leslie Godzillabride exits, crumpling the scroll and chucking it far away. Princess Jacqueline enters, this time eating a whole baguette.

KING CARLTON. Jacqueline, dearest, why does this room interest you so? Please, enjoy the day.

PRINCESS JACQUELINE. I think you and Mother are hiding something from me.

KING CARLTON. And why on earth would you think that?

PRINCESS JACQUELINE. Father, I know something's up. What's going on?

QUEEN VICTORIA. Dear, your father and I are planning a big surprise for you very soon!

PRINCESS JACQUELINE. Really? I mean, I am quite accustomed to what we do for my birthday most years, but a surprise would be most exciting! Nineteen is a big year.

It is apparent that neither King Carlton nor Queen Victoria had any idea Jacqueline's birthday was coming up.

KING CARLTON. It's your birthday soon?

PRINCESS JACQUELINE. Yes. The twenty-fifth.
A beat.

PRINCESS JACQUELINE. You did know that, right?

King Carlton begins to form what he wants to say as Queen Victoria speaks up instead.

QUEEN VICTORIA. Why of course, dear. I say let 'em eat cake.

Leslie Godzillabride enters, physically pushing Torte into the room toward King Carlton and Queen Victoria.

LESLIE GODZILLABRIDE. I'm not even going to give this insubordinate worm the dignity of my time explaining his insufferable acts. I trust that you will personally execute him this instant. And now for the florist.

Leslie Godzillabride marches offstage.

TORTE. Your highnesses!

Torte bows.

QUEEN VICTORIA. What happened to you?

TORTE. I'm honestly not sure, my queen. I looked for the radishes to put on the cake for Princess Jacqueline—

PRINCESS JACQUELINE. Ooh, this is about my birthday! Radishes? Oh—it's a wedding-themed birthday! I don't want to hear any more of it—I'll be off!

Princess Jacqueline joyfully covers her ears and exits.

QUEEN VICTORIA. *(Sternly, to Torte.)* She just saved you.

Torte is unfazed.

TORTE. Right. Anyway, it just finally occurred to me: I don't care what the legends and traditions say. Radishes taste awful on cakes. So I thought . . . what about strawberries? So I placed exactly two strawberries on the cake, intending to coat them in icing to look like radishes but then this woman just barges in and physically picked me up and pushed me in here. Eh—anyway—would you like to taste the cake I was making?

QUEEN VICTORIA. Yes, of course.

Torte pulls the cake out from behind his person and hands King Carlton and Queen Victoria each a slice. They eat.

QUEEN VICTORIA. Oh, Torte, you never disappoint.

TORTE. Good.

QUEEN VICTORIA. I do not care what Ms. Godzillabride tells you; make this cake for Jacqueline's wedding. But, do make sure the strawberries look like radishes. Just do some of that icing-thing with them. It's very important.

Leslie Godzillabride marches back in.

LESLIE GODZILLABRIDE. Hey you! Tortellini! What are you still doing here? Get back to the kitchen now! There's bread to be made! March! March! March!

Torte exits, with a little jump on each "March!"

LESLIE GODZILLABRIDE. Now, you will be happy to know I dismissed the florist. Her attempt at light medium pink roses did not hit my standard, so she had to go. We cannot stand for anything less than Godzillabride excellence. A bride in every chapel and a cost at every corner, remember.

QUEEN VICTORIA. Well, it's not—

LESLIE GODZILLABRIDE. *(Sharply.)* Thank you for agreeing with me. I think I will now have a little chat with Friar Wesley. Good day.

Leslie Godzillabride exits.

QUEEN VICTORIA. Ms. Godzillabride—

LESLIE GODZILLABRIDE. I said good day!

Prolonged Sounds of Warning

Act One, Scene 7

Cape Emerald, a classic case of false advertising. What Sir Galahad and the other knights had surmised would be a thriving seaport town is actually just a deserted island somewhere in the middle of the sea. Sir Galahad and Merlin wander the shore in search of something—anything. Merlin hums a funny tune. The only sign of civilization is a sign that literally reads, "Dead End".

SIR GALAHAD. Well. This must be a dead end.

MERLIN. How do you know?

Sir Galahad points to the sign.

MERLIN. Of course! Pay attention to the signs, silly me!

SIR GALAHAD. Well. It's as good as we have to be for now, with the rowboat crashing and all.

Flotsam from the rowboat wreckage washes in from the sea.

MERLIN. Ah, what fun is a *"sailor's voyage"* without a little run-in with the rocks every now and then?

SIR GALAHAD. Well, I mean . . . How did we get off course so quickly? You took the oars from me and then—

MERLIN. *(Hastily dismissive.)* It was jolly good fun. Now, no use figuring out how we got here, point is we're here. I'm sure we'll find the emeralds somewhere.

SIR GALAHAD. You mean topiary. We're looking for topiary.

MERLIN. Don't be ridiculous. For what reason would a King send you for topiary?

SIR GALAHAD. A very silly one.

Three ethereal island beauties—CIRCE, PARVATI, and AMANDA—emerge from the brush and come into Merlin and Sir Galahad's lines of sight. They move seductively toward the two men, which quickly catches Merlin's attention.

MERLIN. Though I suspect these young ladies may be able to shed some light—among other things—on our journey. We shall approach them at once.

SIR GALAHAD. I don't think that's going to be necessary—

Circe, Parvati, and Amanda have now reached Sir Galahad and Merlin. They stop and look over their guests. Sir Galahad intuits there is no soul behind any of these beings' eyes. His own internal alarm bells start ringing.

SIR GALAHAD. Um . . . Merlin, I kind of have a bad feeling—

MERLIN. Hello! My name is Merlin, Court Wizard of Slekochovakia, and this is my associate, Sir Galahad of the Square Table. We request that you spend some time getting to know us and maybe pointing us in the direction of some, ah—what were we looking f—topiaries!

SIR GALAHAD. Merlin—

MERLIN. Show us to those bushes!

Circe, Parvati, and Amanda speak in airy, mysterious voices and move as though this is a choreographed dance they have done for thousands of years (because it kind of is).

CIRCE. Welcome to Cape Emerald. I am Circe—

PARVATI. Parvati—

AMANDA. Amanda.

MERLIN. Alas! The ladies are quite all right! They even speak!

CIRCE. My sisters and I have lived here many years. You are weary—

PARVATI. You have come a long way—

AMANDA. You need rest.

CIRCE. Come—

PARVATI. Stay—

AMANDA. Feast.

CIRCE. We must pick fruit for the feast.

PARVATI. Come with us—

AMANDA. Please come.

MERLIN. Well count me in for coming, ladies. Are you coming, Caleb?

SIR GALAHAD. I'm still pretty tired. I think I just want to lay down for a while...

Circe gestures offstage. Another ISLAND BEAUTY enters, bringing a picnic blanket and cauldron in and sets the items down. The island beauty exits. Sir Galahad observes the blanket and cauldron, briefly letting his guard down.

SIR GALAHAD. Well that's neat. *(To Merlin.)* You enjoy yourself . . . I guess.

MERLIN. Are you sure you don't want to accompany me?

SIR GALAHAD. Yes.

MERLIN. Suit yourself . . . Ladies?

Circe, Parvati, and Amanda take Merlin by the arms as they go off on their sidequest. Merlin has a stupid grin painted across his face. Sir Galahad lies down on the picnic blanket next to the cauldron.

SIR GALAHAD. Oh, I need this so much.

Sir Galahad is left alone for a moment, but he hears muffled struggle noises. He bolts up and draws his sword.

SIR GALAHAD. Merlin. *(Shouts.)* Merlin?!

MERLIN. *(Offstage.)* Oh, now that is quite an interesting way to pick a coconut.

Sir Galahad mumbles "he's fine" to himself and lays back down. A few more moments of hearing muffled struggle noises and indeed, Sir Galahad realizes he heard something, but it wasn't Merlin. He decides to look inside the cauldron.

SIR GALAHAD. Who's this? Jeffrey?

Sir Galahad pulls Sir Traber out from inside the cauldron, bound and gagged. Sir Galahad pulls out the gag from Traber's mouth.

SIR TRABER. Oh thank God.

SIR GALAHAD. What's going on?

SIR TRABER. Awful things.

SIR GALAHAD. How did you get here?

SIR TRABER. Could you cut me loose first?

SIR GALAHAD. Yeah, definitely.

Sir Galahad pulls out his sword and cuts the rope that binds Sir Traber together. Traber sits up.

SIR GALAHAD. What happened to you?

SIR TRABER. Geez, where do I start?

SIR GALAHAD. Anywhere.

SIR TRABER. Well, as you know, King Carlton appointed me to lead the expedition to Cape Emerald—

SIR GALAHAD. Mhmm.

SIR TRABER. And I got here after discovering it's an island wasteland. King Carlton wasn't kidding when he said we had full coast access—it's in the middle of the sea! He sent me looking for . . .

SIR GALAHAD. Topiaries?

SIR TRABER. Topiaries! Instead, I found the sirens. Er . . . rather, they found me.

SIR GALAHAD. Sirens?

SIR TRABER. Yeah. They're beautiful women, but they're dangerous. Dangerous women indeed.

SIR GALAHAD. What did they do to you?

SIR TRABER. They said I was such a worthy man and that they were going to feast with me.

SIR GALAHAD. And then what happened?

SIR TRABER. I can't remember—we feasted, and then they started singing. I fell asleep, and next thing I knew, I was bound and gagged and inside that cauldron. Praise the saints you were here to find me—I think I was to be the main course of your feast. Why—why are you here, Sir Galahad?

SIR GALAHAD. Funny enough, I have been sent here by King Carlton as well. I took up the quest for Princess Jacqueline's hand in marriage.

SIR TRABER. And . . . he sent you here?

SIR GALAHAD. Yeah, I'm supposed to bring him back some topiaries. This is the second task.

SIR TRABER. What is he planning to do with all those topiaries?

SIR GALAHAD. You're asking the wrong guy, Traber.

SIR TRABER. So then . . . what about Lady Heron?

SIR GALAHAD. What about her?

SIR TRABER. You told me the other day that she talked to you.

Sir Galahad's face lights up softly.

SIR GALAHAD. Yeah, she did.

Merlin is heard in the distance flirting with Circe, Parvati, and Amanda.

SIR TRABER. I want to talk about this later—I don't think this is a good time right now.

Sir Traber gestures as Circe, Parvati, Amanda, and Merlin enter, carrying an assortment of fruits and a potted topiary plant.

CIRCE. Sir Traber—

PARVATI. What a lovely surprise.

AMANDA. We were not expecting another guest.

Sir Galahad rises.

SIR GALAHAD. I will accept full responsibility for this—I did not realize Sir Traber was not invited to this little . . . shindig. If you'll just excuse me, we will be off.

MERLIN. Where are you going?

SIR GALAHAD. Far away from here. Thank you for your hospitality, we—

Circe forcibly grabs Sir Galahad by the arm.

CIRCE. Don't go.

PARVATI. Please stay.

AMANDA. We love guests.

MERLIN. And, look what they conjured up on our little fruit-picking adventure!

Merlin gestures to the plant in Parvati's hands. Sir Galahad inspects the topiary and snaps a branch off of it.

SIR GALAHAD. Well, wouldja look at that.

CIRCE. We have brought you your bush, Sir Galahad.

PARVATI. You're so brave and so handsome.

AMANDA. Please, repay us by just staying to eat.

Amanda reveals full plates of food on the picnic blanket with a wave of her hand. Sir Galahad eyes the food and the sirens, mesmerized. He shrugs.

SIR GALAHAD. I guess we could stay for a bite.

CIRCE. Come—

PARVATI. Dally not—

AMANDA. The feast is now.

Circe, Parvati, and Amanda each take Sir Galahad, Sir Traber, and Merlin by the hand and sit down on the blanket. They eat in silence.

Sir Krause enters.

Circe, Parvati, and Amanda look at each other and silently decide that now is the time to strike. They rise from their seats on the blanket. Circe, Parvati, and Amanda stand in place and sing as they have trapped the men.

SIR KRAUSE. Hello, Galahad.

Sir Galahad rises and turns to see Sir Krause standing behind him. Sir Galahad cocks his head, more than a little confused as to why this guy has just shown up on the beach. Krause yawns.

SIR GALAHAD. Sir Krause? Uh . . . What are you doing here?

SIR KRAUSE. You're the legendary knight. You tell me.

The sirens continue their song. Merlin falls asleep. Sir Galahad yawns.

SIR GALAHAD. Legendary, maybe, but I'm not a mind reader.

Sir Krause shoves Sir Galahad.

SIR KRAUSE. You think you're the only knight worthy to marry Princess Jacqueline. You just assume you can walk into Slekochovakia and become my king! You are nothing. I spit on you.

Sir Krause picks up the topiary plant.

SIR KRAUSE. And now joke's on you, I have your topiary—and I'm going to win.

Sir Krause laughs wickedly as Sir Galahad yawns. Sir Traber falls asleep.

SIR GALAHAD. What's going on?

SIR KRAUSE. Did you not hear me, idiot? *(Egging himself on.)* You think you're the only knight worthy to marry Princess Jacqueline? You just assume—

SIR GALAHAD. No, I heard you—*(Through a yawn.)* I'm just wondering why I'm so tired.

Sir Krause yawns; mumbling angrily but incoherently. Circe, Parvati, and Amanda approach Sir Galahad and Sir Krause. Sir Galahad and Sir Krause have fallen under their spell and lay down asleep after mumbling a few more unintelligible things to each other. Circe, Parvati, and Amanda continue to sing as the lights dim.

END OF ACT ONE.

Rescue at Sea

Act Two, Scene 1

Cape Emerald, the next morning. Sir Krause, Sir Galahad, Merlin, and Sir Traber are bound and gagged. The sirens work like clockwork in an eerie dance-like motion: Parvati stirs the cauldron, Amanda squirts lemon juice on the four men, and Circe sprinkles seasoning onto them. The men remain fast asleep. Merlin could be snoring obnoxiously. Lady Heron enters, sopping wet. She is mortified at the sight of the sirens preparing to eat her colleagues, but she plays cool.

LADY HERON. Excuse me.

A beat. Lady Heron taps Parvati on the shoulder.

LADY HERON. Hi—

Parvati does not budge. Lady Heron approaches Circe.

LADY HERON. My name's Lady Heron, but you can call me Andrea. Excuse me?

Not a single siren makes eye contact with Lady Heron. They simply stop what they are doing and leave together. Lady Heron draws her dagger and cuts Sir Krause loose from his binding. She removes his gag.

LADY HERON. Sir Krause—*(Tapping him lightly.)* Sir Krause!

Sir Krause stirs awake.

SIR KRAUSE. Lady Heron—

LADY HERON. Listen, I'm not sure how long I have, so I have a message for you from King Carlton.

Lady Heron hands Sir Krause a scroll. Krause takes the message as he rises and looks around, eyeing the topiary plant. He picks it up.

SIR KRAUSE. I'll be going then.

Sir Krause rushes off stage with the topiary.

LADY HERON. Sir Krause! *(Sighs.)* Dangit!

Lady Heron looks down and sees Sir Galahad bound. She smiles to herself as she cuts him loose and removes his gag, tapping him lightly as he wakes.

LADY HERON. Sir Galahad—Caleb. Sir Caleb Galahad.

Sir Galahad smiles.

SIR GALAHAD. Yes, those are my names.

LADY HERON. What happened here?

Sir Galahad suddenly notices his surroundings.

SIR GALAHAD. Don't trust those women—they're crazy!

RESCUE AT SEA

LADY HERON. It's all right; they're not here right now.

SIR GALAHAD. They're sirens!

LADY HERON. Sirens, huh? Well—glad I just . . . saved you. Other than that—(Grins.) how's the trip?

SIR GALAHAD. Well . . . first thing, I figured out that Cape Emerald is not a seaport—at all.

LADY HERON. You and me both. I had to swim here.

SIR GALAHAD. *(Laughs.)* Really?

LADY HERON. Look at me, Sir Galahad. I'm soaked.

SIR GALAHAD. Huh. Look at that. Are you okay?

LADY HERON. I'm all right. Listen, I have a message for you from the king. Take this.

Lady Heron hands Sir Galahad a scroll.

SIR GALAHAD. Thank you.

LADY HERON. Now, let's free the others . . .

Lady Heron brings her dagger down to Merlin's ropes, but decides otherwise.

LADY HERON. You can free Merlin, I'll get Traber.

Sir Galahad nods his head. They cut Merlin and Sir Traber free, ungag them, and wake them.

MERLIN. *(Mumbled.)* Circe—

SIR GALAHAD. Merlin?

Sir Traber realizes he was tied up.

SIR TRABER. Oh my gosh, again?!? Come on!

LADY HERON. They're gone, you still have time to escape! We need to move quickly—

SIR GALAHAD. Where's Sir Krause?

LADY HERON. I cut him loose first, and he took off.

Circe, Parvati, and Amanda enter, creeping silently toward Lady Heron. Nobody notices them.

SIR GALAHAD. Took the topiary with him, didn't he?

LADY HERON. Yeah, he did.

SIR TRABER. *(With contempt.)* Sir Krause.

SIR GALAHAD. Apparently, he's an evil mastermind now. So that's new.

LADY HERON. I should've thought ahead and woken you first.

SIR GALAHAD. Don't worry about it at all, Andrea. I have faith—

Sir Galahad feels around on his person.

SIR GALAHAD. Yeah—we're gonna be okay—

Sir Galahad pulls out a branch.

SIR GALAHAD. I slipped this into my pocket before the feast!

LADY HERON. Wow—good thinking. Or you're just really lucky.

Lady Heron grins.

The sirens grab Lady Heron by the shoulder and let out blood-curdling screams. Sir Galahad, Sir Traber, and Merlin clutch their ears while Lady Heron is unfazed. She casually pulls out her dagger.

LADY HERON. So—woman to woman here . . . I have this dagger—and I'm pretty good with it—

Points her dagger toward the sirens and steps toward them.

The sirens share a look, pause, and then scatter into the jungle, screaming in terror. Lady Heron turns to leave.

SIR TRABER. What the heck?

LADY HERON. *(With a laugh.)* I don't really know what happened, either!

MERLIN. Ah, the classic weakness of the seductress is a woman who knows her own strength.

LADY HERON. Oh, the more ya know! Guess I must be a strong woman.

SIR GALAHAD. Or at least self-aware.

Lady Heron twirls her dagger and puts it back in her sheath. She waves to Sir Galahad.

LADY HERON. So . . . I guess I'll be going now. Have a good quest, boys—

Lady Heron turns to leave, and stops in her tracks.

SIR GALAHAD. Andrea—

Lady Heron turns around.

LADY HERON. What's that?

SIR GALAHAD. Oh—ah—never mind. I can't remember.

LADY HERON. Well, if you remember, tell me next time?

SIR GALAHAD. Of course I will.

LADY HERON. See you later, Sir Galahad. And Traber. And . . . Merlin.

Lady Heron exits toward the beach. When she leaves, a splash is heard.

SIR TRABER. So—I *gotta* know about you and Lady Heron—can we please talk about her now?

SIR GALAHAD. Nah, I don't think so.

Sir Galahad indicates Merlin.

SIR TRABER. Ugh, fine.

SIR GALAHAD. We just need to get off this island somehow. Our rowboat crashed—

SIR TRABER. So did mine.

SIR GALAHAD. What are we going to do?

As Sir Galahad and Sir Traber contemplate how they might get off the island, the sirens return with spears. Shouting with demonic guttural noises, the sirens charge at Sir Galahad, Sir Traber, and Merlin.

MERLIN. Boys, take my arm.

SIR GALAHAD. Why?

MERLIN. Trust me.

As Circe rams into Sir Galahad's side with a spear, he and Sir Traber grab Merlin's arm as the lights black out abruptly.

The Trial of Torte

Act Two, Scene 2

The kitchen of Rumplegoose Castle, earlier that day. Chef Torte is hard at work mixing cake batter. The castle kitchen has been outfitted with an inexplicably modern oven—perhaps a gift from the equally inexplicably modern Leslie Godzillabride. Leslie Godzillabride enters the kitchen in military fashion, ready to pick a bone with him.

LESLIE GODZILLABRIDE. Let's get down to business here; is this cake ready or not? I have this wedding planned for the entire kingdom, and it had better be outstanding!

TORTE. I don't know what to tell you, Ms. Godzillabride. You keep coming back here and my answer is still the same: You can't rush cake—even with this fancy *gas* oven.

LESLIE GODZILLABRIDE. *(Sniffs.)* Do you smell that?

TORTE. Smell what?

LESLIE GODZILLABRIDE. It smells like sass in my kitchen.

TORTE. Hmm, that's weird. All I smell is bread.

LESLIE GODZILLABRIDE. I want you to listen, and I want you to listen close:

(Leans in.) When I smell sass in my kitchen, people turn up places. Do you want to turn up somewhere?

TORTE. No thanks—

LESLIE GODZILLABRIDE. Good.

TORTE. What you smell—I don't think that's sass. It's more of a . . .casual indifference, really. And also bread. Nobody's turning up anywhere.

LESLIE GODZILLABRIDE. We'll see about that. Now give me twenty hard stirs of that batter!

TORTE. Ms. Godzillabride, I'm the chef here—

LESLIE GODZILLABRIDE. And I'm the wedding planner and I demand excellence from everyone. Now work!

TORTE. Right away, Ms. Godzillabride. Do you mind . . . leaving me be for a bit? I think I work better when you—*(Catches himself.)* people aren't around.

LESLIE GODZILLABRIDE. Give me time. Now stir!

Leslie Godzillabride marches right out of the kitchen. As she marches off, Princess Jacqueline enters, eating a head of lettuce. Torte is immediately confused, but looks back down to his batter and stirs.

PRINCESS JACQUELINE. Torte?

Princess Jacqueline takes a gargantuan bite of lettuce as Torte looks up again, watching her chew.

TORTE. Your highness. What brings you to visit such a—*(Dripping with* *sass.)* lowly baker as I?

PRINCESS JACQUELINE. You know something.

TORTE. Excuse me?

PRINCESS JACQUELINE. My mother and father are keeping a secret from me, and I want to know what it is. I think I see radishes which means wedding cake which means wedding planner which means wedding which means someone's keeping a secret.

TORTE. You could say that.

PRINCESS JACQUELINE. Really?

TORTE. No. (Mocking KING CARLTON.) Now go, "enjoy the day."

PRINCESS JACQUELINE. Come on, Torte. It's for the princess.

TORTE. I'd tell you, but I think your mother would have to kill me.

Leslie Godzillabride enters, marching across room, muttering to herself.

LESLIE GODZILLABRIDE. They couldn't find middle C if it came up and bit them—that choir is gone!

TORTE. Surely you are being harsh.

LESLIE GODZILLABRIDE. I think not.

TORTE. You can say that again.

Leslie Godzillabride stops in her tracks and crosses to Torte.

LESLIE GODZILLABRIDE. Watch it, Torte. You are on notice. I must find a singer for Princess Jacqueline's wedding immediately—aagh!

Leslie Godzillabride exits, marching. Princess Jacqueline drops the head of lettuce, mortified.

PRINCESS JACQUELINE. Wedding? *(Calling out.)* Mother! Father!

TORTE. Stop—no—

Alarmingly quickly, King Carlton and Queen Victoria enter. Princess Jacqueline was not expecting them to arrive at their speed.

QUEEN VICTORIA. Yes, dear? Something wrong?

PRINCESS JACQUELINE. Um . . . well, I certainly didn't expect you and Father to come to the kitchen so quickly.

KING CARLTON. Ah, what can we say? Just turning over a new, responsible leaf before our daughter is married.

QUEEN VICTORIA. Carlton!

PRINCESS JACQUELINE. I know that you have been planning a surprise wedding for me.

KING CARLTON. And how on earth would you possibly know that?

If looks could kill, Queen Victoria has just murdered Torte.

PRINCESS JACQUELINE. For starters, there's been a wedding planner roaming the castle for the past week.

King Carlton and Queen Victoria look at each other and decide they are done lying to their daughter. The inexplicably modern oven in the background dings and Torte removes a cake from it and slides another in.

QUEEN VICTORIA. We just wanted to give you what you wanted, dear.

KING CARLTON. We sent the bravest knight on the quest to claim your hand in marriage.

QUEEN VICTORIA. And we even sent another one, as well.

PRINCESS JACQUELINE. *(To herself.)* This is not good—

KING CARLTON. Why is that?

PRINCESS JACQUELINE. No reason.

QUEEN VICTORIA. We need you to be married posthaste, dear Jacqueline.

PRINCESS JACQUELINE. Yeah, I know, Father is dying of a not-particularly-well-explained disease.

Queen Victoria is taken aback.

QUEEN VICTORIA. Well then. I suppose we do not need to have that conversation, either.

TORTE. I don't mean to interrupt, but I finished this cake, if any of you would like to try it.

PRINCESS JACQUELINE. Absolutely!

QUEEN VICTORIA. I say let 'em eat cake.

Torte hands slices to King Carlton, Queen Victoria, and Princess Jacqueline.

PRINCESS JACQUELINE. Mmmmm . . . these radishes are awfully sweet today!

QUEEN VICTORIA. Absolute perfection. Well done, Torte.

King Carlton has nothing to say about the cake but clearly really enjoys it, as he makes animalistic noises of approval. Lady Heron enters and contemplates the absurdity that the entire royal family is in the kitchen eating cake with their hands.

LADY HERON. There you are! I have a message for you, King Carlton. Jacqueline, if you would, please . . . *(Mocking King Carlton.)* "enjoy the day."

PRINCESS JACQUELINE. If it's about the wedding, I know.

LADY HERON. Oh. All right, then.

KING CARLTON. Give me some good news, Lady Heron. Have Sir Galahad and Sir . . . Crow——?

LADY HERON. Krause.

KING CARLTON. Krause. Have they accomplished everything I sent them to do?

LADY HERON. So far, so good. They just found evidence of topiaries at Cape Emerald.

KING CARLTON. Splendid! And is the territory everything I had hoped it would be?

LADY HERON. Remind me what you hoped for.

KING CARLTON. Why, it would be the flagship of glory for dear Slekochovakia! That we, a landlocked kingdom within the Holy Roman Empire, would find our way to full coast access on the Mediterranean. Lush with gold, I imagine. The entire western world would look to Cape Emerald and see the victory that King Carlton won at auction.

LADY HERON. It's not. Not even a little.

QUEEN VICTORIA. But what is the message, Lady Heron?

LADY HERON. Yes, a technical detail kind of message from me . . . as I proofread your messages to Sir Galahad and Sir Krause, I happened to realize that you forgot to specify exactly what the knights are to do for the final task.

KING CARLTON. They know not what to do at the House of Dragons?

LADY HERON. No.

KING CARLTON. Is it not obvious? Have I not made myself abundantly clear? As plain as the nose on my face?

LADY HERON. Uh, no. Not even kind of.

QUEEN VICTORIA. Lady Heron, take notes. This is important.

Lady Heron draws her quill and grits her teeth.

LADY HERON. With pleasure.

KING CARLTON. They must each slay a dragon, of course! And they must do it blindfolded! Yes, a most intriguing wrinkle. Not only are they blindfolded, but they must also navigate their way through the labyrinth of the house to slay the dragon. Now, I have achieved no such feat in my lifetime, but I daresay it would be rather admirable if my successor could claim such a thing. It's not easy, you know—

QUEEN VICTORIA. Carlton, dear! Focus!

LADY HERON. Why yes, naturally. How easy for your highness to miss the small matter of killing the dragon.

KING CARLTON. A small matter indeed. But I wish the knights will take that task as a token of my benevolence—that I, King Carlton the fourth, granted the future king a chance to kill a dragon, blindfolded. The legends will be endless; every Slekochovakian historian will write about my reign and legacy. What fun!

LADY HERON. Anything you would like to add?

KING CARLTON. Since they are on their way to the House of Dragons now, the knights will slay a dragon and return home tonight. The wedding will be held tomorrow.

LADY HERON. So, you are saying . . .

KING CARLTON. My darling Jacqueline shall be married in the morning.

Lady Heron finishes writing the message.

LADY HERON. Got it.

PRINCESS JACQUELINE. Oh dear. I need some fresh air.

Princess Jacqueline exits. Queen Victoria follows Jacqueline out of the room.

QUEEN VICTORIA. Oh, Jacqueline dearest.

KING CARLTON. Ms. Godzillabride!

Leslie Godzillabride enters.

KING CARLTON. The wedding will now be tomorrow. So, do—something about that.

King Carlton exits. Leslie Godzillabride grins—she was born for this.

LESLIE GODZILLABRIDE. All right, troops, assume the formation!

Several handservants enter, joining Lady Heron and Torte in a single-file line. All salute Leslie Godzillabride.

LESLIE GODZILLABRIDE. We have a wedding to put on in less than a day. Are we ready?

All handservants ad-lib, "Ma'am, yes ma'am!"

LESLIE GODZILLABRIDE. *(To Lady Heron.)* Send a message to Sir Galahad and Sir Krause about the confirmed wedding time.

LADY HERON. Ma'am, yes ma'am!

LESLIE GODZILLABRIDE. Are we clear?

LADY HERON. Ma'am, yes ma'am!

LESLIE GODZILLABRIDE. And please stop calling me ma'am.

THE TRIAL OF TORTE

LADY HERON. Sir, yes s—

If looks could kill, Leslie Godzillabride has now murdered Lady Heron. Lady Heron dashes offstage.

LESLIE GODZILLABRIDE. Now that we've taken care of her . . . who's next? I don't know any of your names. Don't just stand there! You know what you have to do—go, get out of my face and do whatever your sorry selves should be doing!

Handservants disperse. Leslie Godzillabride crosses to Torte.

LESLIE GODZILLABRIDE. Why aren't you moving? Go, get working!

TORTE. This is my kitchen. You go.

LESLIE GODZILLABRIDE. *(Sniffs.)* It still smells like sass. Do something about it. Now.

Leslie Godzillabride marches out. Torte sniffs. He smirks.

TORTE. *(Under his breath.)* All I smell is bread.

Quiet Evening in the Forest

Act Two, Scene 3

A *clearing in the forest between Rumplegoose Castle and the House of Dragons, a few hours later. Sir Galahad, Sir Traber, and Merlin enter. Sir Galahad and Sir Traber are quite disoriented from teleporting. Sir Galahad clutches his side with one hand, severely wounded, but finds the strength to angrily throw a stick at Merlin.*

MERLIN. What was that for?

SIR GALAHAD. We spent three days in that stupid rowboat—three days I listened to you yammer on about God knows what when we could have just teleported to Cape Emerald?

Sir Galahad throws another stick at Merlin.

SIR GALAHAD. Do you want me to fail this quest?

MERLIN. Yes—come now, you are hurt, I will heal you.

SIR GALAHAD. Don't change the subject. I didn't even want you to come along with me on this quest, and the only time you've helped me has been when your life was on the line, too.

Sir Traber tries to talk Sir Galahad down.

SIR TRABER. Merlin's right, Galahad. You're hurt pretty badly—that siren must have gotten to you as we disappeared. At least let him heal you.

SIR GALAHAD. Fine.

Sir Galahad sits down. Merlin and Sir Traber crouch by his side.

MERLIN. Now, hold still. This should be no harder than when I fixed my sweet Grandmother Edna's feet. Though she did have a nasty fungus. It lingered for years—no, decades . . .

SIR TRABER. But you know magic. You should have helped her.

MERLIN. I tried charming them, but then they became anything but charming. I remember—

SIR GALAHAD. Please. I don't want to think about old lady feet.

MERLIN. As you wish, Sir Galahad. Now, this may hurt a bit.

Merlin waves his hand across Sir Galahad's side. As he does, Sir Galahad cringes a bit, but pulls his hand away from his side. He's healed.

SIR TRABER. Now, why didn't you do something like that to ward off the sirens?

MERLIN. Because, dearest Jeffrey, the magic of estrogen is infinitely stronger than any I could conjure.

Merlin looks off into the distance.

MERLIN. Speaking of—excuse me, boys. Smoke signal!

Merlin exits, following a smoke signal.

SIR TRABER. Well . . . Lady Heron?

SIR GALAHAD. Right.

SIR TRABER. Is there something going on? You kind of seem like you're into each other.

SIR GALAHAD. Really? I mean, back before the meeting she told me she wanted to have dinner at the tavern.

SIR TRABER. And . . . ?

SIR GALAHAD. I told her no.

SIR TRABER. Why?

SIR GALAHAD. I may be a legendary knight, Sir Traber, but women are a fierce force of nature. For God's sake, I hadn't even *spoken* to her before.

SIR TRABER. You've never spoken to Princess Jacqueline, either.

SIR GALAHAD. True.

SIR TRABER. But what do you think of her?

SIR GALAHAD. Lady Heron?

Sir Traber nods.

SIR GALAHAD. I like being around her. She's pretty. She knows how to use a dagger. She's going to make somebody happy someday.

SIR TRABER. *(Nodding, with a slight laugh.)* You and her might be the only sane people in this kingdom, too.

SIR GALAHAD. So are you! The three of us—

SIR TRABER. Maybe Torte.

SIR GALAHAD. *(Smiles.)* Yeah, Torte. Well—anyway, Lady Heron's just . . . a servant, and the King and Queen want me to marry Princess Jacqueline.

SIR TRABER. But they're as boring as . . . white rice.

SIR GALAHAD. Really? White rice?

SIR TRABER. Uh . . . yeah?

SIR GALAHAD. You really need to work on your similes, dude. Half of being a hero's about being quippy like that. Always on your toes and ready to turn a phrase—

Sir Traber smirks.

SIR TRABER. You're starting to sound like our king.

SIR GALAHAD. *(Clears throat.)* Right. Anyway—royalty is royalty. Authority is authority. I made a promise to the King and Queen. So I will marry Princess Jacqueline. Lady Heron—I just have to forget about her.

Lady Heron enters from the distance, Sir Traber rises as Sir Galahad falls silent.

SIR TRABER. Speak of the devil—Lady Heron!

LADY HERON. Sir Traber! Sir Galahad—I am so glad I found you.

SIR TRABER. Do you have a message?

LADY HERON. Yes! For Sir Galahad straight from the crown—the wedding will be tomorrow!

SIR TRABER. Wait, that doesn't even make sense! We're miles away from . . . Wait—where are we?

LADY HERON. *(Incredulously.)* . . . What are you talking about? The House of Dragons is right here—

Lady Heron points offstage.

LADY HERON. And the castle is over there.

Lady Heron points in the opposite direction.

SIR TRABER. You don't say! Well, that makes things easier, doesn't it?

Merlin returns as Sir Galahad sits back down. Merlin has pine needles and other elements of nature stuck into his robes that he picks out as he rejoins the group. Lady Heron notices Sir Galahad has been awfully quiet.

MERLIN. So sorry about that, lads, but when there's smoke, there's a lady waiting for a nice afternoon—

Merlin notices Lady Heron.

MERLIN. Lady Heron! What a wonderful surprise!

LADY HERON. *(Paying no attention to Merlin.)* What's wrong, Sir Galahad?

SIR GALAHAD. Oh, nothing. I'm . . . pretty tired.

MERLIN. No doubt thinking about how wonderful it will be when this is all said and done! 'Tis a lovely thing, marriage. Why, my sweet Grandmother Edna with hideous bunions once said—

Lady Heron reads—correctly—that Sir Galahad must be having second thoughts.

LADY HERON. The wedding.

SIR GALAHAD. All of this—it's a lot to take in.

LADY HERON. You don't want to marry Jacqueline at all, do you?

SIR GALAHAD. It's . . . complicated. It's a lot to take in. My head's kinda spinning.

MERLIN. 'Tis nothing but a case of cold feet. Speaking of feet—

SIR GALAHAD. Stop! Just stop with your grandmother's feet! I just wish I knew for sure that she's the one, you know?

MERLIN. My grandmother? Why, she's been dead for centuries!

Sir Galahad completely ignores Merlin.

SIR GALAHAD. But that's of no matter. I suppose I'll just have to lean into it. It's complicated. I'm sure you understand.

Lady Heron nods.

LADY HERON. I do.

SIR GALAHAD. Was there any other word for me? Do you have any idea what I'm actually supposed to do for this final task?

LADY HERON. Yes, a small matter: for your third task, you must slay a dragon blindfolded!

SIR GALAHAD. Are you serious?

LADY HERON. About . . . which part?

SIR GALAHAD. All of them.

Lady Heron laughs with empathy.

LADY HERON. It's all true.

Sir Galahad nods, quietly accepting his fate.

SIR TRABER. Since the wedding's now tomorrow, we probably need to get going.

SIR GALAHAD. Yeah. You'll be at the wedding, Andrea?

LADY HERON. *(Smiling.)* Good luck, Sir Galahad.

Lady Heron begins to walk away.

SIR GALAHAD. Andrea!

Lady Heron turns toward Sir Galahad, as she did on the beach before.

LADY HERON. What's that?

SIR GALAHAD. Thank you. You saved my life. Twice, I think. Thanks.

LADY HERON. Was that what you wanted to tell me earlier?

SIR GALAHAD. Yeah, it's what I wanted to say. So—thanks. You saved my life.

LADY HERON. You're welcome! I'm sure you'd have done the same. You're a good knight, Sir Galahad. I'll see you at the castle.

Lady Heron exits. As she exits, Sir Galahad and Sir Traber notice two GUARDS standing at the door of the ornate House of Dragons.

SIR TRABER. Are you ready to do this?

SIR GALAHAD. Yeah—I have to marry Princess Jacqueline and that's gonna be that.

Sir Galahad, Sir Traber, and Merlin approach the guards.

GUARD 1. Who goes there?

SIR GALAHAD. I am Galahad, knight of the Square Table!

GUARD 2. What is your purpose in being here?

SIR GALAHAD. I come to complete a task in order to marry the Princess Jacqueline.

GUARD 1. Do you have a warrant?

SIR GALAHAD. A what?

GUARD 2. No mortals are allowed in here without a warrant.

GUARD 1. Or a house key.

GUARD 2. Yes, could be a house key.

GUARD 1. Could be a set of keys.

GUARD 2. Yes, a set of keys might work.

GUARD 1. Might be knowing the security code.

GUARD 2. Ah, yes, the security code would be good.

GUARD 1. Could be enchanted feet.

An awkward silence as Merlin opens and closes his mouth several times like a beached fish.

GUARD 2. No, not the enchanted feet.

GUARD 1. Right. Won't work.

GUARD 2. Never would.

GUARD 1. We torture trespassers.

GUARD 2. Yes, we do.

SIR GALAHAD. How are we going to get in?

SIR TRABER. No clue.

SIR GALAHAD. Merlin?

Merlin stops fiddling around in his pocket under his robe.

MERLIN. What?

SIR GALAHAD. I can't get into the home of the dragons because I don't have a key, a warrant, or the security code!

MERLIN. I suppose you could just use mine.

Merlin pulls out a key and opens door.

SIR GALAHAD. What? You waited until now to tell me you had a key?

GUARD 1. Good luck.

GUARD 2. Have fun.

Sir Galahad, Sir Traber, and Merlin enter the house. Lady Heron enters with purpose, not looking up.

LADY HERON. Sir Galahad, I want to tell you—

GUARD 1. Excuse me, ma'am—

Lady Heron looks up, alarmed.

GUARD 1. —you will need a warrant or a house key to be near the House of Dragons.

GUARD 2. And a reminder, lass, we do torture if necessary and proper.

LADY HERON. It's never necessary or proper to torture anyone!

GUARD 1. Need not be necessary or proper. We just torture anyway.

GUARD 2. So, what's your name?

LADY HERON. I am Lady Heron, personal messenger of Slekochovakia's royal family.

GUARD 1. Well, if she's the royal messenger she must have a message for us.

LADY HERON. Err . . . Yes, in fact—I do!

GUARD 2. Go on, spit it out.

LADY HERON. Queen Victoria herself has personally told me to, uh . . . express her gratitude for your faithful service.

GUARD 1. Alas! The Queen cares for lowly guards such as ourselves!

GUARD 2. Tell her immediately of our gratitude.

LADY HERON. I shall do so right this instant!

Guards exit into the doorway as Lady Heron sighs in relief.

Lady Heron takes a moment to compose herself. She hears the birds chirping in the forest as she smiles softly. The lights dim.

Kill the Beast

Act Two, Scene 4

Deep in the labyrinth-like setup of the House of Dragons, the next morning. A dragon's roar is heard offstage. Sir Krause stumbles across the stage, blindfolded. Sir Krause trips over a bench in the otherwise empty castle room.

SIR KRAUSE. Are you serious? What the . . . whatever.

Sir Krause removes his blindfold.

SIR KRAUSE. Who even knows if I need this?

SIR TRABER. *(Offstage.)* Easy—step. Step. A little to the left. Okay, you're good.

SIR KRAUSE. And Galahad's cheating. This is ridiculous.

Sir Galahad enters, blindfolded and swinging his sword, with Sir Traber guiding him through.

SIR TRABER. Okay, we're here—*(Sees Sir Krause.)* and we caught up to Sir Krause! Where is your blindfold?

SIR KRAUSE. Who will know if I don't have my blindfold on when I kill the dragon?

SIR TRABER. I will.

Sir Krause points his sword at Sir Traber.

SIR KRAUSE. Well that's nothing a little sword couldn't handle, now is it? I will be king, you know.

SIR TRABER. Of course, your highness.

SIR KRAUSE. Shut up.

SIR TRABER. Shall we settle this now?

Sir Traber draws his sword.

SIR TRABER. Caleb, back me up.

Sir Galahad removes the blindfold and draws his sword.

SIR GALAHAD. It's two against one, Sir Krause. We will kill you if we fight today.

Sir Krause shrugs.

SIR KRAUSE. You probably will. Fine—I'll wear the stupid blindfold if it means that much to you.

Sir Krause places his blindfold back on.

SIR GALAHAD. No—you know what, Krause? Enough is enough.

Sir Krause removes the blindfold.

SIR GALAHAD. I say we settle this quest like gentlemen. Clearly, the princess cannot marry the both of us.

SIR KRAUSE. Clearly.

SIR GALAHAD. So, let us see who slays the dragon first. Winner gets to marry Jacqueline; the loser . . . just quits. We're done.

SIR TRABER. Are you sure, Galahad?

SIR GALAHAD. Trust me.

SIR KRAUSE. Fine. Let's do this.

SIR GALAHAD. May the best man marry the princess.

SIR KRAUSE. Yes.

Sir Traber helps Sir Galahad with his blindfold as Sir Krause puts his own blindfold back on. They both take awkward, ungainly steps in opposite directions but make it offstage. Sir Traber remains on stage hoping and praying Sir Galahad returns. Once they are both out of the audience's sight, dramatic music plays, complete with ominous dragon roars. They return from opposite directions and remove their blindfolds. Sir Galahad has blood all over his sword and his armor, while Sir Krause does not. Sir Traber runs to congratulate his friend.

SIR TRABER. Galahad—you did it!

Sir Galahad removes his blindfold.

SIR GALAHAD. I did it! I just killed a dragon blindfolded—what? I beat you,

Sir Krause. It's over now.

Merlin enters, trying to sneak back in.

SIR GALAHAD. Merlin? Where have you been?

MERLIN. Oh, what a goose am I! I—er, got lost in this house overnight.

SIR GALAHAD. Lost? How could you be . . . ?

MERLIN. *(Hastily interrupting.)* Couldn't find you anywhere.

Sir Galahad and Sir Traber don't believe this lie for a second.

MERLIN. Eating. I was eating. And goodness, what happened to you? You're absolutely drenched in blood!

SIR GALAHAD. I just slew a dragon—blindfolded.

Merlin looks down at his own arms and flashes a bright, folksy smile.

MERLIN. The goosebumps! Sir Galahad, you have genuinely impressed me!

SIR GALAHAD. And now it's time for me to marry a princess.

MERLIN. But . . . you can't.

SIR GALAHAD. Excuse me?

MERLIN. You're in love with Lady Heron. This only works out if you're in love with Lady Heron.

SIR GALAHAD. W-what are you talking about, Merlin?

SIR KRAUSE. Well this is interesting. The legendary knight doesn't care about marrying the princess, now does he?

SIR GALAHAD. Krause, come on! I beat you fair and square. I will marry Princess Jacqueline and never look back. Whatever feelings I have—

SIR KRAUSE. I'd be happy to book your wedding band for you and Lady Heron if you just let me marry Jacqueline today. *(Guffaws.)* You and that messenger. Such a simple girl for such a demigod legend, don't you think?

Sir Galahad draws his sword.

SIR GALAHAD. Don't you dare.

SIR KRAUSE. *(Draws sword.)* I already have.

SIR GALAHAD. Lady Heron is kind—and smart—and beautiful—and . . . she's so much more than just a messenger!

SIR KRAUSE. Ugh, what will the legends ever say about you now—? The hero knight just *deserves* a princess don't you think?

SIR GALAHAD. Do you "deserve" Princess Jacqueline? Did *you* even love her?

SIR KRAUSE. That worthless blonde? Surely you jest!

MERLIN. Sir Krause was indeed in love, but never with Slekochovakia's delicate flower. He fell in love with the power of the throne and beating you.

SIR KRAUSE. Hush, you speak of things you know not! Sir Galahad, your quest ends here. As does yours, crazy old man! And Sir Traber . . . you don't matter here. Just go home.

Sir Traber draws his sword.

SIR TRABER. Not a chance. We shall settle this like gentlemen of the Square Table.

MERLIN. Yes, there is only one way for knights of the Square Table to resolve turf, territory, and ego issues . . . as decreed long ago in the Ancient Book of Slekochovakian Red Tape.

SIR KRAUSE. Why, yes indeed! The square dance!

Lively square dance music begins, but is abruptly cut off.

SIR GALAHAD. No, not a square dance. We can duel.

SIR KRAUSE. Then let us duel, Galahad.

Sir Krause charges at Sir Galahad. They fight. Sir Galahad, who is a much more adept swordsman than Sir Krause, disarms him. Sir Krause goes to get his sword, which Sir Galahad has kicked offstage.

SIR TRABER. Now, Sir Galahad, run! Quickly!

Sir Traber runs offstage but comes back when he realizes Sir Galahad hasn't followed him.

SIR TRABER. Hurry! Don't you want to marry Princess Jacqueline?

Sir Galahad waffles for a second or two until he is interrupted by Princess Jacqueline's voice.

PRINCESS JACQUELINE. *(Shouting, Offstage.)* Sir Galahad!

Action freezes. Fog filters in to signify we are once again entering Sir Galahad's thoughts. Princess Jacqueline and Lady Heron enter from opposite sides of the stage.

PRINCESS JACQUELINE. Time is running out, Sir Galahad, tick tock. Tick tock.

LADY HERON. Personally, I know for a fact you don't want to marry the princess.

PRINCESS JACQUELINE. And I know for a fact you don't want to break your word to the king. My father is dying, Sir Galahad, there will be a new king very soon.

SIR GALAHAD. Don't put this kind of pressure on me!

LADY HERON. Who cares about this kingdom? You don't want to be tied to a throne all day, do you? You belong adventuring with me—there's a reason you left Slekochovakia all those years ago.

PRINCESS JACQUELINE. Listen to me for a second, Sir Galahad. Money. Servants. Power. The kingdom.

SIR GALAHAD. I have got to do this. I'm marrying Jacqueline today. It's what I have to do.

LADY HERON. You've never spoken to her in your life! You can't possibly love her, let alone marry her! Besides, *(Matter-of-factly.)* you like me.

SIR GALAHAD. Yes, I do—gahhhhh.

PRINCESS JACQUELINE. Sir Krause would be a terrible king. You know in your heart of hearts you deserve a princess, and I deserve a legendary knight.

LADY HERON. Yeah, it'll suck if Sir Krause is king. But we're going to run away together, we'll go everywhere! Prance, Gentlemandia, Just Okay Britain. Marrying the princess today would be a disaster—you'll be thinking about me for the rest of your life.

Merlin breaks his freeze.

MERLIN. *(Exasperated.)* How is this even a decision for you?!

SIR GALAHAD. Whoa, what are you doing here?

Merlin clears his throat and composes himself.

MERLIN. Listen to Lady Heron, love and happiness don't always come as a package deal when marrying royalty.

SIR GALAHAD. I—Yes, I believe you, but you're honestly starting to sound very, very suspicious—

MERLIN. You love Lady Heron. This. Only. Works. If you love Lady Heron.

SIR GALAHAD. I do. *(Realizes he just vocalized that.)* I think I do. . . . But what are you doing here, Merlin?

LADY HERON. Come to me. All the riches in this kingdom will pale next to our love.

PRINCESS JACQUELINE. Listen to me, handsome king-to-be.

SIR GALAHAD. Enough. These voices in my head—

Lady Heron and Princess Jacqueline nod, speaking their lines as they exit.

PRINCESS JACQUELINE. You can't undo your decision today, so don't blow it.

LADY HERON. You'll regret it for a lifetime if you do . . .

Sir Galahad nods as the fog dissipates.

SIR GALAHAD. That's the only thing I know for sure. *(Shouting.)* Traber! Merlin! Let's get back to the castle!!

Sir Galahad, Sir Traber, and Merlin run offstage. Sir Krause enters with his sword drawn.

SIR KRAUSE. Well, I didn't take this quest just to be left behind. First knight to the altar wins!

Sir Krause charges after Sir Galahad, Sir Traber, and Merlin..

Backward Kingdom

Act Two, Scene 5

The courtyard of Rumplegoose Castle, about twenty minutes later. Several pews are set up around the yard to form an elegant makeshift outdoor chapel. Friar Wesley stands at the altar. Queen Victoria and King Carlton are seated in the front pews. Lady heron, Lady Soberick, and Leslie Godzillabride are bridesmaids holding bouquets of rubber chickens. A few NOBLES and KNIGHTS are scattered throughout the pews, but it is an underwhelming crowd.

FRIAR WESLEY. *(Somewhat to himself.)* Dearly beloved, we are gathered here today to await the princess putting on her dress.

PRINCESS JACQUELINE. *(Offstage, in frustration.)* It won't zip!

QUEEN VICTORIA. Don't fret, Mother's coming, dear!

Queen Victoria takes her sweet time getting up and exiting to tend to Princess Jacqueline's dress.

LESLIE GODZILLABRIDE. Everything is ruined! The bride no longer fits into her dress. There's no sign of a groom. We have insufficient guests—I may as well escort myself to the dungeon. Nothing's gone right.

LADY HERON. *(Echoing.)* Nothing's gone right.

LADY SOBERICK. What's that?

Lady Heron realizes she just said that out loud.

LADY HERON. Oh—uh, nothing.

LADY SOBERICK. Are you sure?

LADY HERON. Uh, yeah. This is fine.

Lady Soberick would attempt to further probe Lady Heron, but Leslie Godzillabride interrupts the thought by continuing her rant.

LESLIE GODZILLABRIDE. Twenty minutes past the appointed hour, and we have neither a bride nor a groom! And the cake? Where is the cake?

Torte enters, coolly and collected.

TORTE. It's just coming out of the oven, and after an appropriate amount of time, I will ice it.

Leslie Godzillabride glares and beats her bouquet of rubber chickens against her hands. Torte goes red in the face.

TORTE. Please don't hurt me.

Torte rushes back to the kitchen. Queen Victoria enters and crosses to the altar.

QUEEN VICTORIA. Hear ye, hear ye. The lovely and most beautiful Princess Jacqueline has been squeezed into her dress!

Lady Heron grits her teeth. King Carlton exits.

LADY HERON. All right. Congratulations, Sir Galahad. Let's just get this out of the way.

QUEEN VICTORIA. Not yet! We still need a groom.

Right on cue, Sir Krause enters with a war whoop of glee. Sir Galahad, Sir Traber, and Merlin enter close behind.

SIR KRAUSE. I got here first! I win! Take a seat, losers. You just take a seat right now because your quest is over! That entire quest you took was for nothing! King Krause is taking the throne and I get Princess Jacqueline all to myself!

Sir Krause takes his spot at the altar, laughing manically. Sir Galahad has lost the quest to Sir Krause.

SIR KRAUSE. You sit down, Sir Galahad. I'm marrying Jacqueline. Bring out the bride, Queen Vicki, I'm ready.

SIR GALAHAD. I just have one thing left to say to you, Sir Krause.

SIR KRAUSE. What?

SIR GALAHAD. I wish you the best in all of your endeavors, all of them: Your relationship with Princess Jacqueline, being king of Slekochovakia—

SIR KRAUSE. You just lost, like a *loser*—why are you so happy about this?

Sir Galahad and Lady Heron make eye contact. They share a smile back and forth at each other.

SIR GALAHAD. Good luck, Sir Krause.

SIR KRAUSE. Uh, thank you. Bring in the bride now. Friar.

Friar Wesley nods and motions. Wedding music begins. All rise as Princess Jacqueline enters in a white dress, arm in arm with King Carlton. She makes her way up to the altar with Sir Krause.

FRIAR WESLEY. Dearly beloved, we are gathered here today to witness and celebrate the joining of Princess Jacqueline of Slekochovakia and Sir Krause, esteemed knight of the Square Table.

A beat.

FRIAR WESLEY. Sir Krause, do you take Princess Jacqueline to be your lawfully wedded wife? To love and to cherish, to have—

SIR KRAUSE. *(Interrupting.)* Yeah, yeah, yeah. I do.

FRIAR WESLEY. And Princess Jacqueline, do you take Sir Krause to be your lawfully wedded husband—

PRINCESS JACQUELINE. *(Also interrupting.)* I don't!

The assembled crowd is confused and aghast, complete with audible gasps.

SIR KRAUSE. What is this, Princess Jacqueline? *(Holds her forcibly.)* Say "I do." I am your husband now. I am your king. You respond to me, Jacquie.

Merlin rises.

MERLIN. That's enough of that.

Merlin snaps his fingers and Sir Krause falls to the ground, dead.

SIR GALAHAD. *(Alarmed.)* Did you just kill Sir Krause?

MERLIN. Yes, yes I did. Next question.

LESLIE GODZILLABRIDE. The nerve!! You killed the groom without my permission! And you, Princess Jacqueline—how dare you? You were to be married today! How dare you say no to the man we gave you!!

PRINCESS JACQUELINE. To be fair, he is dead now.

MERLIN. Never mind, Ms. Godzillabride, is it?

LESLIE GODZILLABRIDE. Don't you look at me like that.

MERLIN. I can unravel this puzzling twist.

SIR GALAHAD. Uh—what?

Merlin and Princess Jacqueline walk toward each other and kiss, causing a gasp across the entire congregation. They hold each other's hands after the kiss.

MERLIN. Sir Galahad, I must come clean to you. I was not always the most—present—on your quest.

SIR GALAHAD. Yes.

SIR TRABER. Now that's an understatement. You disappeared like three times after we came back from the island!

MERLIN. Right before you came asking for my help on my quest—a certain young lady had come to my hut for company.

PRINCESS JACQUELINE. I was just heartbroken when none of the knights wanted to marry me the moment I proposed the quest. So I went to visit Merlin.

MERLIN. One thing led to another and another thing led to a love potion, and then, she and I began an affair.

PRINCESS JACQUELINE. He made me forget . . . I instantly fell for this mystery man—can't even really explain how, it just happened.

Merlin hands Princess Jacqueline a flask.

MERLIN. Have another swig, wouldya?

LADY HERON. *(Mouthed, to Princess Jacqueline.)* Don't drink that.

Princess Jacqueline nods. She does not drink from the flask.

SIR GALAHAD. A love potion? This all came down to love potions? You sick, twisted son—

MERLIN. I guess I felt bad about it until I realized that you never wanted this—you were merely doing the quest as a favor to our king and queen. Noble as you are, everyone has their own agenda. It really all worked out perfectly for me.

SIR GALAHAD. But—Merlin, you were with me that whole time—and you knew I—you never once just told me the truth?

MERLIN. I don't know why you trusted me, I *explicitly* told you not to.

SIR GALAHAD. What?

Merlin clears his throat.

MERLIN. "Life is short. You have to look out for number one because no one else will. Trust nobody, step on everyone in your way, and throw them off a cliff even if they win."

SIR GALAHAD. So . . . Sir Krause then . . .

MERLIN. None of your concern. He was unfortunate collateral damage.

SIR GALAHAD. You're disgusting.

MERLIN. I'm just a man who knows what he wants and I always get it. *(Points to Princess Jacqueline.)* Like her. Come on, Princess, let's roll out.

Merlin grabs Jacqueline's arm. Lady Heron rises.

LADY HERON. Merlin, I believe I speak for every decent human being assembled in this castle courtyard today—you are the worst. Just the worst. Princess Jacqueline is a human being. Do you want to go with him?

PRINCESS JACQUELINE. I . . . I don't know what to think.

LADY HERON. Let go of her!

Merlin drops his hold on Princess Jacqueline.

MERLIN. Suit yourself. Guess I'll be going alone, then.

SIR TRABER. You can't get away with this! Love potions should be illegal.

Sir Traber points to Sir Krause's body.

SIR TRABER. Murder should be illegal!

SIR GALAHAD. Hey—King Carlton—quick question, given the recent events, uh . . . Would there happen to be a law against murder in Slekochovakia?

KING CARLTON. Hmmm . . . Well—ah—

SIR GALAHAD. Yes. Yes, there is.

KING CARLTON. Yes! Murder . . . is an outrage!

Sir Galahad gives King Carlton a thumbs-up.

KING CARLTON. Uh . . . ?

Sir Galahad rolls his eyes.

SIR GALAHAD. Guards! Escort Merlin to the dungeon this instant!

MERLIN. What?

Guards 1 and 2 enter and take Merlin by the arms.

MERLIN. Unhand me! I'm a very old and defenseless man! *(Screams.)* Nooooooo!!!!

The guards exit, dragging Merlin away. The crowd cheers. Sir Traber leans over to Sir Galahad.

SIR TRABER. Do they know he can teleport?

KING CARLTON. But to think that my own daughter would find a way to sneak away from the loving arms of her dutiful parents? How did you possibly do such a thing?

PRINCESS JACQUELINE. Uh . . . it really wasn't that hard, Father, trust me. I'm sorry, Father. You do know that Mother will continue to be queen alone after you pass? It's an okay thing.

KING CARLTON. Well, I suppose that's true, but—

PRINCESS JACQUELINE. I'm very sorry you're disappointed, Father. We can talk about this later. I—I need to eat something.

Princess Jacqueline exits, wiping away a single tear.

LESLIE GODZILLABRIDE. *(Furious.)* I cannot believe I planned this whole wedding for the entire kingdom and now it is utterly and completely ruined! Ruined, ruined, ruined!

SIR TRABER. How are you, Caleb?

SIR GALAHAD. I'm okay. Yeah. This is fine.

SIR TRABER. Fine? Seriously?

Sir Galahad nods.

SIR TRABER. You risked your life God knows how many times—to please a king and queen you can't stand—to marry a beautiful princess who you've never spoken to—who never planned to marry anyone because of Merlin . . . who is the worst—

SIR GALAHAD. The worst.

SIR TRABER. Also you lost to Sir Krause, may he rest in . . . peace? Uh, how on earth can you be fine right now?

SIR GALAHAD. When you put it that way, it sounds like I failed. But I didn't fail . . .no, not at all.

Sir Galahad looks across the room at Lady Heron. Sir Traber shakes his head with a smile.

SIR TRABER. So it was real, huh?

Sir Galahad rises and gets Lady Heron's attention.

SIR GALAHAD. Andrea—can I talk to you?

LADY HERON. Yeah, sure!

Sir Galahad looks around the gathered crowd.

SIR GALAHAD. Let's get away from these people.

Lady Heron points to the area of the courtyard they had their first conversation a week or so earlier. She smiles.

LADY HERON. How about there?

Sir Galahad and Lady Heron cross to the secluded area of the courtyard. Sir Traber beams as he watches this unfold.

LADY HERON. Full circle.

SIR GALAHAD. Yeah I guess we have come full circle. I have a message for you. I didn't write this down, so just—uh—bear with me here.

LADY HERON. I will.

SIR GALAHAD. Andrea, I've had a lot to think about for the past couple days—really taking a moment and thinking about my life, and basically I had two choices: I had to decide whether I should come in and marry the headstrong beauty of Slekochovakia full speed into a life ruling over this kingdom because that's the plan when you're a legendary knight—or whether I would be honest. To some extent, my decision was made for me, but I know this was the best path I could have taken. I wouldn't have wanted it any other way. So right now I'm going to be honest with myself, honest with you, and honest with all these people around us: Merlin was right.

LADY HERON. *(Alarmed.)* About . . . ?

SIR GALAHAD. *(Clarifying.)* I never wanted to marry Princess Jacqueline. Sure, I guess I wanted to honor the king and queen because I said I would, but what I never considered was—why? It occurred to me, everything that's gone on . . . Obeying the crown is only good when you can trust it. And I don't trust the crown. I don't want anything to do with Slekochovakia. This is—and always will be—a backward kingdom.

LADY HERON. You and I weren't made for this kingdom at all, were we?

SIR GALAHAD. Exactly! That's why I let Sir Krause win. I don't belong in Slekochovakia and neither do you. I don't know where we belong, but it's certainly not here.

Lady Heron grins, tearing up a little. Sir Galahad smiles.

SIR GALAHAD. So before we go, I want to take you up on your offer.

LADY HERON. What are you talking about?

SIR GALAHAD. Let's get dinner at the tavern. Right now.

LADY HERON. *(Beaming.)* All right.

Sir Galahad and Lady Heron walk away, hand in hand. Before they get offstage, Lady Heron breaks from his hand and holds up a finger.

LADY HERON. Wait!

SIR GALAHAD. Hmm?

Lady Heron grins. She kisses Sir Galahad on the lips. He loves it.

SIR GALAHAD. Now there's a first.

LADY HERON. *(Surprised.)* Man, from all the legends, I'd have guessed—

SIR GALAHAD. I don't write the legends, Andrea. I live 'em.

LADY HERON. It's time you and I start living some new ones.

Lady Heron takes Sir Galahad's hand.

LADY HERON. Together.

Sir Galahad and Lady Heron walk together offstage.

SIR GALAHAD. Is the food at the tavern any good?

LADY HERON. I have no idea!

Sir Galahad and Lady Heron exit.

LESLIE GODZILLABRIDE. All my efforts in shambles! Ruined!

KING CARLTON. Not necessarily—Ms. Godzillabride, there's something I wanted to ask you. Now, the Queen and I have been thinking . . .

LESLIE GODZILLABRIDE. *(Under her breath.)* Well there's a first.

KING CARLTON. Our general consensus is that you are a very talented—*(Awkward pause.)*—woman.

LESLIE GODZILLABRIDE. And it took you this long to figure that out? Please!

KING CARLTON. Your work ethic is exceptional. We would like to keep you around our castle for a little while, but not in exactly the same role, since there are no more weddings to plan.

LESLIE GODZILLABRIDE. My purse is open. My ears are listening. What will I be doing?

KING CARLTON. You see, Lord Diehm will be taking a temporary leave of absence, and as you know, he is the commander of the army. Thus, the position must be filled immediately, and we thought of you for the job. All military command and control of Slekochovakia. What say you?

LESLIE GODZILLABRIDE. I'll do it!

King Carlton and Leslie Godzillabride continue to discuss logistics. Torte enters with the grand cake, topped with exactly two strawberries. Princess Jacqueline enters, tracking the cake like a bloodhound.

TORTE. *(Falsely enthusiastic.)* For the first time as a couple, Mr. and Mrs.—

Torte looks around and sees nobody celebrating.

TORTE. Uh—did I miss . . . something? . . . Whatever.

Torte sets the cake down in front of himself and begins eating it with his hands. Sir Traber sits down beside him and joins him. Princess Jacqueline sits and joins the chef and the knight with the cake. Friar Wesley crosses to Queen Victoria.

FRIAR WESLEY. Your highness. What are we going to do with all these people now that the wedding's kind of . . . not?

QUEEN VICTORIA. I say let 'em eat cake.

THE END

THE THOUSAND YEAR ROSE

est. 2016

PETER FENTON

This play is dedicated to all of the Vivians of the world and the Kimmi Larkins who draw goodness out of them. May those of us who walk confidently through life be generous with our spirits.

Author's Preface to The Thousand-Year Rose

I f there's one thing I've learned from bartending, it's that while anyone can do anything once, and frankly, anyone can *succeed* at anything once, I would say the truest testament to a person's skill comes from their ability to do the thing a second time. A highly skilled artist (cocktail or otherwise) can riff on a formula to make it uniquely their own or even throw out the existing draft to create a whole new one from the ground up, but still, the best answer to the question, "Can you make an Irish Coffee?" is the ability to show up with two frothy mugs that look and taste identical (and delicious!) . . . which brings me to *The Thousand-Year Rose*.

As I write this preface in the summer of 2021—because God only knows how much longer the thing will stay intact—I still have the rose we used on the opening night performance in the Wheaton College Jukebox Theater production on October 28, 2016, which is five years to the day before this book was first published. It's sitting in a simple glass vase, along with the remains of petals of the roses we used in the other performances—it's a very *Beauty and the Beast* kind of setup I have on that end table in my apartment. The rose is extravagantly dead and faded, to the point where my gut tells me if I were to touch it wrong, the rose would surely collapse into dust. It's moved with me four times now and continually serves as a visual reminder of how far I've come since writing this work. I do have the softest spot in my heart for *The Thousand-Year Rose*. I'll go on record and say it is not my favorite thing I've ever written, but this play's very existence and the memories attached to writing it represent some wonderfully formative, significant developments for both my writing career and my personal growth.

If you've noticed the original completion dates attached to this play and the previous one, you will find there was a seven-year gap between the writing of the first and second works in my library. I spent those seven years iterating and re-iterating *Good Knight and Goodbye*, this silly story I came up with at fourteen years old, and here I was, about to turn twenty-one, still trying to squeeze something out of that intellectual property that had long since dried out.

Coming fresh off of directing that rocky film adaptation of *Good Knight and Goodbye* in my sophomore year of college which had culminated in a film festival where mine was the only work not to receive an award, that whole experience had left me in a raw mental state. I really wasn't ready to put myself or my work back out there for a while. My ego couldn't handle it. I learned the hard way that when you hang your entire identity on the success of a single entity—a project, a relationship, a belief system—if that single entity caves in, so will your entire concept of self.

I entered my junior year in the fall of 2015 determined to fashion the back half of my college experience as a second chance—a second chance to discover who God really made me to be and to discover what I was going to do about it. In one of my interpersonal communication classes, my professor taught us about this concept of understanding the self, the Johari Window, developed by psychologists Joseph Luft and Harrington Ingham. (Which I will point out, I've always found it hilarious that the word "Johari" is nothing more than a combination of the psychologists' first names, Joe and Harry.)

According to the Johari Window, there are four essential dimensions of the self, which in my college notebooks, I had made little nicknames for: We have the "No Surprises Here" self, which comprises what is understood and known by both you and by others; the "Dark and Mysterious" self, the secret elements known to only you and hidden from others; the "Absent-Minded" self, which are the parts of a person known to others but not known to you;

and the "Unlockable Character" self, which encompasses everything that is true but not yet known to anyone—the self or others.

This idea that there were layers to myself that were neither known to me nor known to others was fascinating, and even the idea that others had a unique (and truthful) perspective into understanding what already existed in me was exhilarating. After a bit of soul-searching on my own and some tough questions about who I really am were explored with loved ones, I came to grips with patterns of facts about how I'm wired: I would not be satisfied pursuing a "normal" career right out of college like conventional teaching, preaching, academia, or counseling . . . I'm a writer. I've known that since I was fourteen.

So, after all of that discovery-of-self rigmarole, you may want to say to me, "Cool story, Pete, but what does any of this have to do with *The Thousand-Year Rose?*"—and to that, I would reply, "Everything."

I walked through the back half of college looking for opportunities to learn about the dimensions of myself that I'd been choosing not to see. Opportunity came knocking at the end of junior year when my eighth grade English teacher and lifelong mentor, Mrs. Fisher (the same Mrs. Fisher who directed the world premiere of *Good Knight and Goodbye*), sent me an email to let me know that at the end of the 2016-17 school year, she was retiring after some forty years of teaching middle school English and directing the school plays. She wondered if I still wanted to make good on the promise I made years earlier to write her final play. Now that I was in the right headspace to create something completely new, I took on the challenge.

Writing *Rose*—no matter how good or bad the end product would be—meant that after everything I'd gone through with *Good Knight and Goodbye* and all of the complicated feelings attached to it, I chose to let that one be a first play and I chose to move on from there to write something new. Building a career as a writer is not so much about creating the masterpieces so much as it is about showing up and being willing to take the next step. A second play's existence meant I put one foot in front of the other to make another step toward being a writer. After all, if you're going to call yourself a writer, one thing you should probably do is *write*.

That's what I think when I think of the story before you. Mrs. Fisher asked me, "Can you write a play?"—and here I was, a blank page, about to see if what I'd done seven years earlier could be replicated. If the truest test of "Can you do this thing?" is whether you are able to do it again, this was it. And that's exactly what I did.

The Thousand-Year Rose had its world premiere Halloween weekend in 2016 as a Jukebox Theater production on a makeshift stage in the basement of the Billy Graham Center at Wheaton College. I was crying again at the end of a production I directed, but this time it was different. There were just sixty-four people in the audience, but each one chose to be there to support our show, and I felt the love and support of everyone in that room—my cast, their parents, my parents, my roommates, other classmates, Wheaton faculty—there were no awards attached to this one, but this was a win. A redemption arc if I've ever experienced one. *Rose* then made its way to the Conestoga Valley Middle School stage in spring 2017 as a fitting curtain call for Mrs. Fisher's teaching career.

Enjoy *The Thousand-Year Rose*, my friend.

Planter's Warts

Act One, Scene 1

A flower garden in what appears to be a sea cave. At center stage, there is a raised stone pot filled with soil. An elegant rose is carved or painted on the side of the pot.

It's nighttime. Crickets chirp, lights are dim. A hooded GARDENER meanders the garden, humming a tune in a minor key to himself as he plants seeds methodically. It appears he has done this for a thousand years . . . because he has. The Gardener stops humming after a couple of moments. He continues making his rounds through the garden as he speaks to nobody in particular.

GARDENER.
On this night, a heart is shattered
For all things good had disappeared.
E'en so, a garden grows in the cave—
While the rose waits a thousand years.

Three storybook-style witches, pointy hats and all—ABIGAIL, CIERA, and VIVIAN—enter stumbling, cackling with delight. Abigail has a locket around her neck and a treasure map in her hands. The Gardener ignores them.

ABIGAIL. We found it! I can see the treasure now—and it's all going to be mine!

Vivian smiles.

VIVIAN. I don't exactly see treasure here, so much as I see . . . flowers.

ABIGAIL. It's a figure of speech, Vivian. Control yourself.

Vivian's smile disappears.

VIVIAN. *(Mumbled.)* Sorry, Abi.

ABIGAIL. What was that?

VIVIAN. Sorry, Abi.

ABIGAIL. Good. It's about time you treated your big sister with respect.

Vivian tugs at a bandanna tied around her wrist.

VIVIAN. I'm 27—

ABIGAIL. But you're the youngest.

CIERA. How horrid! Vivian ruined our day again!

ABIGAIL. Oh, Ciera, honey, I won't let a little disrespect from Vivian spoil our day of getting the legendary treasure and taking over the world. At least not today. Now, Vivian, make yourself useful for once—hand me the plans—

Vivian was never given the plans. Meanwhile, Ciera loses interest.

VIVIAN. What?

ABIGAIL. That "what?" makes it sound like you don't have them. Did you lose my plans, Vivian?

Abigail looks around on her person for the plans—because she knows she lost them.

VIVIAN. You told me it was too important for me to keep, so you—

ABIGAIL. Silence! Ciera—

CIERA. *(Now paying attention.)* What?

ABIGAIL. Vivian lost the plans.

CIERA. Oh. Is that bad?

ABIGAIL. Absolutely.

VIVIAN. Abi, you said you'd give them—

ABIGAIL. I don't want to hear your excuses, Vivian, I gave you one chance—

VIVIAN. Will you let me finish?

ABIGAIL. One chance! To prove to me that you're ready—and you failed!

VIVIAN. *(Hastily.)* You said you'd give the plans to Ciera.

Abigail glares at Ciera. Ciera's eyes light up. She pulls out a piece of paper folded in her belt.

CIERA. Oh! You mean these plans?

ABIGAIL. Never mind, Vivian. I found the plans.

Abigail clears her throat as she unfolds the paper.

ABIGAIL. *(Reading aloud.)* "The Three Witches of Hanenbough's Plan to Find the Treasure of The Thousand-Year Rose and Take Over the World, Step One: Follow the mysterious treasure map we got from that old man to find the secret garden in the underground cave on the sea caves to northwestern edge of the city where the treasure is fabled to be buried."

VIVIAN. Check.

ABIGAIL. Vivian. Could you not?

VIVIAN. S-sorry, Abi.

ABIGAIL. Good. I sense a genuine submission to my authority. You're getting better already. "Step Two: Steal a man's shovel and start digging." Now where do we find this . . . Man?

VIVIAN. There's a man over there—

Vivian begins to gently approach Gardener, but Abigail intercepts, approaching him with intensity. Gardener makes no eye contact with the witches.

ABIGAIL. Hello. My name is Abigail. I am a witch—and my sisters are also witches. We're going to take your shovel now.

The Gardener says nothing as he continues to work.

ABIGAIL. Sir, perhaps you do not comprehend. I am a witch, and my sisters are also witches. We could end you if we wanted to, but for now, we just want your shovel.

The Gardener continues to not say a word. Abigail raises her eyebrows at Ciera and Vivian. They extend their arms toward Gardener, preparing to cast a lethal spell on the humble Gardener. Ciera and Vivian look to Abigail, who flashes a devilish grin.

ABIGAIL. Now!

The witches push forward to cast their spell. Powerful magical sound effects are abruptly cut off when the Gardener, without looking away from his work, waves his hand. The earth shakes and the witches fall over. Abigail stands up and dusts herself off.

ABIGAIL. You—you're a wizard.

GARDENER. I am a humble gardener.

A beat.

GARDENER. You seek the lost treasure of Desrosier, sealed by the Thousand-Year Rose.

VIVIAN. Yes!

ABIGAIL. Vivian—this is where I talk. So where do we start digging?

GARDENER.
On this night, a heart is shattered
For all things good had disappeared.
E'en so, a garden grows in the cave—
While the rose waits a thousand years.

ABIGAIL. Wonderful. He speaks in riddles. Thanks for nothing, humble gardener.

VIVIAN. I mean, we did all the work of finding this place—we should at least look for the treasure.

ABIGAIL. *(Insincerely.)* Gee, thanks! What would I ever do without you?

VIVIAN. That was uncalled for.

ABIGAIL. You were uncalled for.

Ciera has wandered over to the front of the stone pot. Evidently, there is an X marking a spot.

CIERA. Wonder what this X means . . .

Ciera steps onto the X, triggering a violent crack of thunder and flashes of crimson lightning. The Gardener jerks his body up supernaturally, with his eyes locked on Ciera. The witches are taken by complete surprise.

GARDENER. Someone sets their feet before the Thousand-Year Rose.

The Gardener crooks his finger toward Ciera from where he stands.

GARDENER. It will not bloom for you.

As if nothing happened at all, the Gardener resumes his work. The witches are understandably confused.

ABIGAIL. Uh . . . *(Laughing nervously.)* What?

While Gardener is indeed responding to Abigail, his communication remains asynchronous.

GARDENER.
  At dawn, the rose shall bloom
  When the pure of heart draw near
  The wicked may seek its beauty,

But the treasure they'll ne'er find here.

ABIGAIL. Can't he just tell us what the deal is? None of this poetry garbage...

VIVIAN. *(Somewhat to herself.)* The pure of heart . . . He's saying the rose will bloom for a pure heart.

ABIGAIL. What are you mumbling about, Vivian?

VIVIAN. Oh—uh, nothing.

ABIGAIL. Vivian—

VIVIAN. It's pretty simple, I think. He says one day at dawn, the rose will bloom, when the pure of heart draw near . . . So I think . . .

ABIGAIL. Let me think here . . .

A beat. Abigail's face lights up.

ABIGAIL. I know! Ladies, come with me. We're heading into town!

CIERA. What are we doing?

ABIGAIL. Humble gardener over here says we need someone with a pure heart to make this stupid flower bloom. So we're going into the city to find someone with a pure heart. And then we kidnap them. The rose will bloom, we'll get the treasure, leave Vivian in the dust, and take over the world!

VIVIAN. Leave me in the what now?

ABIGAIL. Pull yourself together, Vivian. I'm kidding. Let's go.

Abigail, Ciera, and Vivian start walking out of the garden.

CIERA. Wait—but the rose didn't bloom for me.

ABIGAIL. Yes.

CIERA. But . . . I have a pure heart, don't I?

ABIGAIL. We're witches, Ciera. Do I really need to answer that question?

Abigail, Ciera, and Vivian exit. The Gardener continues his work, now reciting his poem in full.

GARDENER.
On this night, a heart is shattered
For all things good had disappeared.
E'en so, a garden grows in the cave—
While the rose waits a thousand years.
At dawn, the rose shall bloom
When the pure of heart draw near
The wicked may seek its beauty,
But the treasure they'll ne'er find here.
For the treasure is a beating heart
Held fast in grips of fear.
When the gales thrash the ocean
And the rolling thunder leers—
E'en so, a garden grows in the cave
While the rose waits a thousand years.

The Gardener resumes humming his minor key tune as the lights fade out.

Dank Mythology

Act One, Scene 2

It's nearly the end of a European Folklore class at a liberal arts college in the Chicagoland area, the next morning. The grandfatherly PROFESSOR DAVIS stands at a lectern, frequently checking a clock behind him. The sharp-witted and sassy KIMMI LARKIN sits next to her "basic" roommate ELIZABETH as a few STUDENT EXTRAS sit in the classroom.

PROFESSOR DAVIS. That's all the time we've got for today—don't go yet! I graded your midterms in record time.

Professor Davis takes a stack of graded papers and hands them back to students.

PROFESSOR DAVIS. Pass that down to Mr. Schultz—Ms. Spradlin—

Professor Davis crosses to Kimmi and hands her back her essay.

PROFESSOR DAVIS. Excellent work, Ms. Larkin—

Kimmi surveys her exam, satisfied. Elizabeth leans over to see what she got.

ELIZABETH. Ninety-seven? Geez, Kimmi, you sure you're not the archaeology major here?

KIMMI. Calm down. I just got lucky again.

Elizabeth grins.

ELIZABETH. Well, that's a lie.

Kimmi matches Elizabeth's grin with a laugh.

KIMMI. Yeah, it is.

Professor Davis returns Elizabeth's paper to her.

PROFESSOR DAVIS. Ms. Peaches—

Elizabeth takes the paper and sets it in front of her.

KIMMI. Not good?

Elizabeth flicks her exam over to Kimmi.

KIMMI. What are you talking about? You got an A.

ELIZABETH. *Minus.* It's not . . . terrible, but I'm an archaeology major. You're what? English?

KIMMI. Communication.

Elizabeth shrugs, dismissive.

ELIZABETH. Talking good. Writing good. It's all the same.

Kimmi rolls her eyes. They've had this conversation before.

ELIZABETH. Okay, maybe you're more diligent or studious or whatever you wanna call it, but this is my turf, y'know? I should've just studied theater.

KIMMI. You still could, right? We're only . . . juniors. Okay, maybe you don't have time anymore. Maybe you could still do a minor?

ELIZABETH. Ughhh, and I can't think of anything you're not good at.

KIMMI. I'm a terrible liar.

ELIZABETH. Okay, besides that.

KIMMI. Water polo.

ELIZABETH. Funny.

KIMMI. Hey, you're going to be a great archaeologist—someday. I know it. Don't sweat it, life's so not about papers. It's about doing things. I just happen to be good at the papers.

Elizabeth is not amused by Kimmi's attempt at a life lesson. By this point, Professor Davis has passed out all the papers and has returned to the front of the classroom.

PROFESSOR DAVIS. See you all on Monday! Have a great weekend!

Elizabeth and Kimmi start to exit.

PROFESSOR DAVIS. Ms. Larkin! A word?

Kimmi turns to Elizabeth, who is pressed for time.

ELIZABETH. See ya later.

KIMMI. Yeah, see ya!

Elizabeth exits. Kimmi turns to her professor.

KIMMI. Yeah, what's up . . . Doc?

PROFESSOR DAVIS. I've been thinking . . . I know you're a communication major, but I need a research intern this summer and I believe you might be the perfect fit.

KIMMI. Oh?

PROFESSOR DAVIS. What are you doing this summer, Ms. Larkin?

KIMMI. Just the usual—*(Sarcastically.)* A little spelunking, a little soul-saving, or maybe if I'm lucky, I'll return to my sick gig in the vibrant casual dining scene of the Boston suburbs.

PROFESSOR DAVIS. Sick . . . gig?

KIMMI. A seating hostess. At Chili's.

Professor Davis chuckles.

PROFESSOR DAVIS. You'll have to forgive me, Ms. Larkin. I suppose I spend so much time with dank mythology I don't quite know what young people are saying these days.

KIMMI. I believe you, no one's said dank since 2016.

PROFESSOR DAVIS. Dank?

KIMMI. Oh—uh—yeah when something was really cool. They'd say it was dank. Like if this were 2016, I might say without a twinge of irony, something like . . . "This research internship is gonna be super dank, yo."

That sounded really weird and dumb, I'm gonna stop talking now.

Professor Davis chuckles again.

PROFESSOR DAVIS. Well, in any case, I could really use your help. It pays . . . Not a whole lot, but it's a job. What do you think?

KIMMI. Omigosh, what about Liz?!

PROFESSOR DAVIS. Hmm?

KIMMI. You should ask Elizabeth. I know she's looking for a summer job.

PROFESSOR DAVIS. No, no, Ms. Larkin, your take on human nature is exactly what I need for this opportunity. It's an offer for Kimberly Larkin.

KIMMI. You can just call me Kimmi, Doc.

PROFESSOR DAVIS. . . . "Kimmi".

KIMMI. Actually—you can stick with Ms. Larkin. But this internship sounds super interesting. So, like, what are you doing?

PROFESSOR DAVIS. I trust you've heard of Hanenbough? It's in Ireland.

KIMMI. Uh . . . No?

PROFESSOR DAVIS. And how?

KIMMI. I went to an American public school?

PROFESSOR DAVIS. Do you have a minute?

Assuming a "yes" in response as he asks the question, Professor Davis picks a book off the lectern and turns to Kimmi.

KIMMI. I'm . . . all ears, Doc.

Professor Davis holds the book, but doesn't really read out of it. He has a lot of practice telling the story, freely talking with his hands. Celtic undertones accompany Professor Davis as he tells the legend.

PROFESSOR DAVIS. Once upon a time, Hanenbough was the crown jewel of the western coast of Ireland. It was like a holiday every single day in this port city: people of all nations flocked to see the beautiful sights and to meet the lovely people. Not a single person lacked anything in food, clothing, or spirit. The people of Hanenbough were always happy to share.

Rich medieval TOWNSPEOPLE enter and some poor TOURISTS enter from the other side.

PROFESSOR DAVIS. But certain as life itself—no things are meant to last. Thieves and vandals invaded from the south. They destroyed the city, robbed every man, woman, and child of what was rightfully theirs, killing anyone who stood against them. The massacre of the city and its people took place just over forty days before anything began to change.

THIEVES enter and attack the townspeople and the tourists, striking them dead and stealing most of their gold. A few remain alive, and those that remain are terrified.

PROFESSOR DAVIS. In the thousandth hour, one man gained the courage to save what was left of the city. This young man was a recent immigrant to Hanenbough from France by the name Desrosier.

The Gardener appears without his hood. He is a young Frenchman.

PROFESSOR DAVIS. He snuck from house to burning house, scavenging treasures from his fellow people of Hanenbough that the thieves would never have found. He acquired an enormous hoard of treasure.

The Gardener helps the townspeople and tourists up and puts their coins into a sack. Each person exits as he helps him or her up. The final townsperson he saves gifts him with a rose. He tucks it into his robe.

PROFESSOR DAVIS. Desrosier searched the coast for a place to bury the treasure and trekked deep within one of the sea caves. They say he was a wizard, that he cast an enchantment on the entire cave to grow a hospitable garden—in a place that had never seen a ray of the sun!

The Gardener casts a spell. A lush garden surrounds him. The Gardener pulls out the rose and places a spell on it with a perfectly timed flourish of the hand.

PROFESSOR DAVIS. He planted a single rose next to the buried treasure and bewitched it with a powerful spell: the rose would wait to bloom for a thousand years—

KIMMI. That seems a little excessive.

PROFESSOR DAVIS. —thereby sealing the treasure completely until there came the right type of person.

The Gardener exits, along with the garden. The Celtic undertones fade out.

KIMMI. The "right type of person"?

PROFESSOR DAVIS. Precisely! The rose would only bloom when somebody with a pure heart stands in front of the rose. Only then would the seal be broken and the treasure could be found. Desrosier drew a map to the treasure, hid the map inside a locket, and left the locket somewhere in plain sight in

Hanenbough. He returned to the cave and never left.

KIMMI. So there's some French dude's skeleton just chillin' down there with the treasure?

PROFESSOR DAVIS. There's a number of theories, but legend has it that Desrosier walks the garden to this day, waiting for the thousandth year when the pure of heart returns and the rose shall thence bloom.

KIMMI. Huh. Cool story. So "thence". . . What does this have to do with me?

PROFESSOR DAVIS. Years ago, I traveled to Hanenbough. After weeks of excavating, I found the mysterious locket and I followed the map deep into a cave. I saw everything, Ms. Larkin. This treasure is real.

KIMMI. Wow . . . that's insane! Wait! Did you already find the treasure?

PROFESSOR DAVIS. Unfortunately, no. It was not quite the thousandth year when I discovered the garden. That same night, a pack of thieves attacked me and stole the locket. After further research, I have deduced with a high degree of certitude that the thousandth year is—of course, this year.

KIMMI. Huh. So you want me to come with you this summer—

PROFESSOR DAVIS. So this summer, I hope to recover the map and then the map will guide us to the treasure. What do you think?

KIMMI. But you've already been to the cave and seen it, right?

PROFESSOR DAVIS. Last I was there was—oh, I don't know, 30 years ago. I don't know if I recall exactly where the rose is. But what do you think?

KIMMI. I think I'm late to class, but I'll definitely think about it!

PROFESSOR DAVIS. Oh! Dreadfully sorry—please, get to class. Take the weekend and think it over. Let me know what you decide.

KIMMI. Yeah, I'll think about it. See ya, Doc!

Professor Davis exits. Kimmi pulls out her cell phone and makes a call as she begins to leave the classroom.

KIMMI. Hey, Dad. I'm good, how are you? Dad, have you ever heard of Hanenbough? It's in Ireland.

The Pure of Heart

Act One, Scene 3

The bustling, open-air market in the port of Hanenbough, six weeks later. There are several little shops or stalls set up including a baker's stand. One shop in the center sells rare jewelry. Various shoppers and townspeople walk through the market. Abigail, Ciera, and Vivian prowl around, trying to keep a low profile. Abigail casually shoplifts a baguette from the baker's stand.

ABIGAIL. This is getting ridiculous.

CIERA. Are there any good people out here?

ABIGAIL. There are good people out there somewhere. And we're going to find them.

Abigail scans the crowd as she eats her baguette.

ABIGAIL. It's hopeless. All these people are dreadful. We're getting coffee.

Abigail and Ciera walk away. Vivian stops at the JEWELER'S stand.

VIVIAN. . . . Now what do we have here?

JEWELER. Rare jewelry—I've bought, traded, sold, and discovered all these items from China to Chile. Feel free to look around; I'll answer any of your questions. And if you've got any jewelry to sell or trade . . . I'm always interested.

VIVIAN. Thanks.

Vivian browses through the jeweler's hoard. She picks up a necklace and admires it. Abigail turns around and sees Vivian dallying.

ABIGAIL. What do you think you're doing, Vivian?

Vivian sets the necklace down as Abigail makes a beeline for her.

VIVIAN. Oh . . . it's nothing—

ABIGAIL. You know we can't afford any of this! Come on, Ciera's probably lost by now.

The Jeweler clears her throat.

JEWELER. If you have anything you would like to sell or trade—I'm always interested.

Vivian glances down at the bandanna tied around her wrist before abruptly hiding it. Abigail unhooks the locket from her neck. She shoves it in the Jeweler's face.

ABIGAIL. Here. Whaddiya want for it? Fifty? A hundred?

JEWELER. May I?

Jeweler inspects the locket and pops it open.

JEWELER. I could give you thirty.

ABIGAIL. Thirty?

JEWELER. Look, it doesn't shine. It just looks like a rock on a chain. There's an ugly flower etched onto the side of it. I'll take it, but it's no more than thirty.

VIVIAN. Abigail, I don't think this is a good idea. We might need it for—

ABIGAIL. Shut up. Just give me thirty and take the locket.

The Jeweler hands Abigail thirty euros and places the locket inside a box. Abigail and Vivian meet up with Ciera and exit. DIANA, PAREZCO, a STAGE MOM, a CHILD ACTOR, and a few other actors from the local theater enter the market carrying buckets of change.

DIANA. Support the arts!! Save the Suzanne!! Get us a new roof!

Diana shakes her bucket of change.

DIANA. Save the Suzanne!!

Parezco approaches a shopper at the baker's stand.

PAREZCO. You there! You look like an appreciator of the arts!

DIANA. Let's keep the Suzanne alive now, shall we? Support the theater! Give some change!

The shopper puts money into Parezco's bucket. While the shopper is distracted, Parezco reaches into their pocket and steals their wallet.

PAREZCO. No, no, my dear—thank you. I am . . . the master of impressions. I am . . . Parezco!!

DIANA. Spare us some change!! Save the Suzanne!!

STAGE MOM. My boy needs a place to learn the craft!! Save my beautiful boy!!

CHILD ACTOR. Mom, stop.

Parezco approaches Diana.

DIANA. Save the Suzanne!!

PAREZCO. Are we done yet, sweetheart?

Diana's enthusiasm deflates a bit at Parezco's patronizing tone.

DIANA. Nope. Boss-man says we're not done until noon. Now, come on! We're going to Killarney Street. Save the Suzanne!!

Professor Davis enters and approaches the Jeweler's stand as Diana leads the entire company from the theater offstage.

JEWELER. Well, if you have any questions . . . just speak up.

PROFESSOR DAVIS. Thank you.

Professor Davis thoroughly examines the Jeweler's collection. Kimmi enters with CAPTAIN SEAMUS BOGGS, who carries her multiple suitcases.

KIMMI. Oh, thank you so much—you really didn't have to carry my bags for me. Really.

CAPTAIN BOGGS. Don't mind a bit, Kimmi. I just get all worried seein' a girl like you comin' to a town alone—err, like this'un.

KIMMI. Oh please, what's wrong with the town?

CAPTAIN BOGGS. Ol' Hanenbough's got a bit of a . . . reputation.

KIMMI. Well, having a *reputation* doesn't mean it's bad. My little, Kelly, got a reputation for giving the best—never mind, it's a long story. What I'm saying is Hanenbough could have a reputation for chocolate-covered pretzels for all we know.

CAPTAIN BOGGS. Oh, funny y'say that! Bonnie's on Main Street—ask fer the whisky flavored ones. They're to die for's all I'm sayin'.

KIMMI. Really now . . . ?

CAPTAIN BOGGS. But I'm jus' surprised yer comin' to Hanenbough what with all the thieves—

Kimmi has to clarify what Boggs said, due to his accent.

KIMMI. Thieves?

CAPTAIN BOGGS. Thieves. You've heard the legend, haven'cha? They teach Americans that'un?

Kimmi laughs.

KIMMI. Oh yeah, they *totally* teach Americans that one . . . Hanenbough was a beautiful city full of beautiful people and then the bad people burned it to the ground but then some French guy saved some treasure and planted a garden.

CAPTAIN BOGGS. Yep, the beautiful days of Hanenbough . . . they're ancient hist'ry.

KIMMI. I'd hardly call a thousand years ancient history.

CAPTAIN BOGGS. Poor Hanenbough never recovered and nobody's cared to recover it. Nobody comes on holiday to Hanenbough's all I'm sayin'. Anywho . . . Who ya stayin' with?

KIMMI. My professor—Frank Davis.

Captain Boggs' face lights up.

CAPTAIN BOGGS. Frankie?

KIMMI. Uh, yeah—

CAPTAIN BOGGS. Oh Frankie an' I go way back. He's stayin' this summer, set up a little study in my upstairs apartment—I'm his lan'lord!

KIMMI. That's super weird.

CAPTAIN BOGGS. Two bedroom, free wi-fi, full workin' toaster—she's a beaut'.

KIMMI. Oh, perfect! How am I supposed to get there? I mean, I've got an address, but it *(Chuckles.)* literally means nothing to me.

Captain Boggs notices Professor Davis at the Jeweler's stand. He points to him.

CAPTAIN BOGGS. Hardly think that'll be necessary.

KIMMI. Oh, Doc! Thank you, Captain—?

CAPTAIN BOGGS. Boggs, Seamus Boggs! Good day to you, Kimmi Larkin! *(Shouting.)* Twelve fifteen ferry down t'airstrip—leavin' ten minutes!

Captain Boggs exits. Kimmi waves from the distance.

KIMMI. *(Shouting.)* Doc!

Kimmi runs over to Professor Davis, who looks up from a piece of jewelry.

PROFESSOR DAVIS. Ms. Larkin!

Kimmi and her professor share a brief hug.

KIMMI. I'd say it's been too long, but I guess you just gave me my final a week ago.

PROFESSOR DAVIS. And what a week it's been! How was your flight?

KIMMI. Bumpy takeoff, crying baby, therapy pig on the seat next to me . . . you know, you win some, you lose some. I'm just happy I made it. Oh! I just met your . . . landlord? Seamus Boggs.

PROFESSOR DAVIS. Yes! We will head to his house at once—

JEWELER. Pardon me, miss—I love your necklace.

KIMMI. Oh, really? Thanks.

The Jeweler gets a closer look at Kimmi's necklace.

JEWELER. I really like it. Would you make a trade for it?

KIMMI. I'd love to.

Kimmi turns to Professor Davis.

KIMMI. Mind if I—?

PROFESSOR DAVIS. Go ahead. We're in no rush.

Kimmi combs over a couple of pieces of jewelry. Abigail enters, with Ciera and Vivian following closely behind.

ABIGAIL. Fine, okay? You want the stupid locket back. Let's take it back.

VIVIAN. Maybe we don't need it, I don't know.

Vivian points to Kimmi.

VIVIAN. Besides, there's someone there right now—

Abigail sticks her finger in Vivian's face.

ABIGAIL. Vivian—it is not polite to point. Now, you mean her?

Abigail points at Kimmi.

ABIGAIL. She's no threat.

Abigail raises her eyebrow and takes a closer look at Kimmi.

ABIGAIL. But . . . she could be pure of heart. Creep with me.

Abigail, Ciera, and Vivian creep a little closer to eavesdrop.

KIMMI. Hey, this might be a long shot, but . . . do you have anything from around here?

JEWELER. Do you mean Ireland—or Hanenbough?

KIMMI. Hanenbough, if you have it.

The Jeweler digs around inside her box.

JEWELER. Mmm . . . you probably don't want this . . . I just made the trade a couple minutes ago. This here locket . . .

The Jeweler pulls out the locket. Kimmi and Professor Davis lock eyes when they hear "locket."

KIMMI and PROFESSOR DAVIS. Locket?

JEWELER. It's really old and weathered; it's got an ugly rose etched onto it . . .

PROFESSOR DAVIS. She'll have a look at it.

JEWELER. Really?

The Jeweler hands the locket to Kimmi. Professor Davis takes the locket from Kimmi and inspects it closely. He smiles, as if having solved a puzzle.

KIMMI. Whaddiya think, Doc?

PROFESSOR DAVIS. I think you want this locket, Ms. Larkin.

KIMMI. I'll take it.

JEWELER. I'm surprised. That thing's so ugly. Gosh, I'd feel really bad taking your necklace over that.

Kimmi removes her necklace and hands it to the Jeweler.

KIMMI. No thanks—I really like the locket. Pleasure doing business.

The Jeweler shrugs.

JEWELER. Your funeral.

Kimmi takes the locket from Professor Davis. When she picks it up, there is a flash of red lightning and a violent roar of thunder.

KIMMI. Omigosh!

PROFESSOR DAVIS. Bizarre. Ms. Larkin—somehow, by some miracle—this is the locket! The map should be inside.

Kimmi pops the locket open and there is no map.

KIMMI. Doc, there's nothing in here.

PROFESSOR DAVIS. Really?

Professor Davis inspects the inside of the locket.

KIMMI. How do you know this is the locket, and not just—y'know, someone's ugly locket?

PROFESSOR DAVIS. I owned it once, Ms. Larkin. This is the locket—legend says it can only be opened by the pure of heart.

KIMMI. Again—seems a little excessive of this Desrosier guy.

Kimmi pops open the locket again.

KIMMI. See, I mean, I got it open.

Kimmi puts the locket around her neck. Professor Davis and Kimmi ad-lib and start to gather her suitcases. Abigail eagerly hits Ciera and Vivian in excitement.

CIERA. Ow!

ABIGAIL. Didya see that? Didya see that? Look—the old coot over there says the locket can only be opened by a pure heart—and that girl right there just opened it like it was nothing! I could never get that thing open! Ladies, these things don't just happen. It's a sign! We're going to kidnap her.

CIERA. Okay, great! When?

ABIGAIL. Now!

Abigail runs toward Kimmi and Professor Davis, cackling. Ciera and Vivian follow her. immiK whips her head around and sees the witches ambushing her.

KIMMI. What the—*(Panicked.)* Doc?!?

As Professor Davis tries to collect Kimmi's belongings, Abigail, Ciera, and Vivian grab Kimmi and run her offstage with gleeful cackles. It takes Professor Davis a moment to fully process what just happened.

PROFESSOR DAVIS. Hold on, Ms. Larkin! I-I'm coming!!

Professor Davis runs after the witches. Kimmi's luggage is left onstage as market shoppers eye it up and encircle it like vultures.

Forsaking Duty and Jet Lag

Act One, Scene 4

A dilapidated back alley in Hanenbough, moments later. The street is deserted. Abigail, Ciera, and Vivian continue from right where we left off in the previous scene, abducting Kimmi. As they make it to center stage, Kimmi pushes the witches away and breaks free.

KIMMI. *(Shouting.)* Help!!!

Abigail cackles.

ABIGAIL. You'll never be helped here. It's Hanenbough, the city of thieves.

KIMMI. Oh, so you want to like rob me or something? I'm probably the worst person in this city to rob—I have nothing. Literally nothing. I'm a college student.

ABIGAIL. Okay—we can calm this down a touch. An ambush and abduction is far from a proper greeting, I get that. But you, my dear lass, have something we need.

Abigail puts her arm around Kimmi's shoulder.

ABIGAIL. Let's have a civil conversation, you and I—

A physically fit grandmother, MARYANN, and her precocious, shy teenage grandson SCOTT enter to see Kimmi push Abigail's arm off her shoulder and back away.

KIMMI. N-no—get away from me, you freak! I'll scream—again!

ABIGAIL. It would certainly do you or I no good if you were to meet an untimely demise, here in a lonely back alley where no one will find your body...

Maryann crosses to Abigail and Kimmi, speaking up.

MARYANN. Now, what on earth—?

KIMMI. Grandma!

Kimmi runs over to Maryann and hugs her.

CIERA. Aw, she has a grandma.

Kimmi turns outward and speaks loudly enough that the witches hear her.

KIMMI. I'm so glad I am now reunited with my grandmother, who is a—

Kimmi quickly looks up and down Maryann and comes up with a quick lie.

KIMMI. Krav Maga instructor?

Abigail snaps her fingers.

ABIGAIL. Huddle!

Ciera and Vivian form a huddle with Abigail.

ABIGAIL. Krav Maga. Okay—Krav Maga, that's scary.

VIVIAN. There is no way that lady teaches Krav Maga. None. She's obviously lying—

ABIGAIL. *(Cutting her off.)* We can't chance that, Vivian. We'll keep an eye on her, wait till granny's gone, then we attack. Plan?

VIVIAN. *(Begrudgingly.)* Plan.

CIERA. Plan!

ABIGAIL. Okay, break!

Vivian and Ciera break the huddle as Abigail addresses Kimmi.

ABIGAIL. I'll get you, my pretty.

Abigail, Ciera, and Vivian exit. Kimmi hugs Maryann again.

KIMMI. Phew! Thank you, thank you! That was so scary.

MARYANN. Who was that?

KIMMI. I don't know. But I'm so glad I'm rid of them, y'know? My name's Kim—wow—Kimmi. Kimmi Larkin. That's what I call myself. Sorry, I'm a little—*(Overwhelmed noise.)*, y'know.

MARYANN. Don't worry about that for a second, Kimmi. I'm Maryann Foley and this is my grandson, Scott.

KIMMI. Hi.

Kimmi and Scott briefly shake hands.

SCOTT. *(Flatly.)* Hi.

Professor Davis enters, exhausted.

PROFESSOR DAVIS. Ms. Larkin... I ran as fast... as I... could...

Professor Davis collapses. Kimmi rushes to his side.

KIMMI. Doc, Doc, I'm fine. This is fine. Everything is fine. Ten minutes in Ireland and I have no luggage, three strange women want to hurt me, and my professor's covered in sweat.

Kimmi feels for her locket.

KIMMI. It's all okay, though, I still have the locket!

PROFESSOR DAVIS. How did you break away from the thieves?

KIMMI. Just a little quick thinking on my feet and I even made a few friends. Internship's off to a great start.

PROFESSOR DAVIS. Well thank God you're all right. Okay, my apartment is just this w—

Professor Davis aborts his thought midsentence when he makes eye contact with Maryann.

PROFESSOR DAVIS. —well hello! Who is this?

Maryann and Professor Davis are immediately smitten with each other. Maryann steps toward the Professor.

MARYANN. I'm Maryann Foley. And what's your name there, handsome?

PROFESSOR DAVIS. Frank Davis. *Professor* Frank Davis.

MARYANN. My, my! A professor! Oh, lordy. I want to know what brought an academic like you to this dusty old town.

SCOTT. This is gross.

KIMMI. And like, kinda sweet.

SCOTT. But mostly gross.

Kimmi and Scott nod in agreement.

PROFESSOR DAVIS. Well—I'd love to tell you about it if you—if you have a minute.

MARYANN. I have all the minutes left in my life, professor.

PROFESSOR DAVIS. Care to take a walk?

MARYANN. I know a place with the best chocolate-covered pretzels in Ireland.

PROFESSOR DAVIS. I only ask that you take me there! Ms. Larkin—I'll see you to the apartment—later.

Professor Davis and Maryann take each other's arms and exit. Kimmi and Scott are left alone with each other in awkward silence. They feel like they shouldn't leave each other and Kimmi has literally no idea where the apartment is. Kimmi finally decides to break the ice.

KIMMI. So... Scott Foley?

SCOTT. That's my name.

KIMMI. Tell me about yourself, Scott Foley.

SCOTT. Uh... I'm in eighth grade. I like... video games. And... soccer, I guess.

KIMMI. Oh! That's cool! I played soccer in high school. I was a forward—no, it was field hockey. I definitely played field hockey.

SCOTT. Those are, uh, two really different sports.

KIMMI. I mean, when you get down to it—there's a ball, there's a netted goal. You try to get the ball into the netted goal. Lacrosse is the same way.

A beat.

KIMMI. Basketball, too...

SCOTT. Heh—yeah.

Kimmi and Scott return to an uncomfortable silence. After another moment, Kimmi speaks up again.

KIMMI. Well, Scott Foley, do you know anything about the legend of the Thousand-Year Rose?

Scott feigns disinterest.

SCOTT. Are you kidding me? That story's been told to me since I've been in diapers.

KIMMI. Which was how long ago?

SCOTT. *(Snapping indignantly.)* I'm fourteen.

A beat. Scott realizes his abrasiveness.

SCOTT. Sorry. Uh, so, some French guy planted a seed in a cave, buried the treasure, and hid the treasure map in a locket. It's all made-up.

KIMMI. Good. So, my professor and I are spending the summer looking for the treasure map. We've already found the locket.

Scott's eyes light up. He breaks his feign.

SCOTT. Wait! So you mean . . . ?

KIMMI. Yep! The legend is real. I actually—have the locket right here.

Kimmi unhooks the locket and gives it to Scott. Scott opens the locket.

SCOTT. Hey, uh—there's something written inside it.

Scott gives the locket back to Kimmi.

KIMMI. Oh really? Whoa, this is crazy! It's got some ancient mystical language going on here on the inside—get a look at this, Scott!

Scott takes the locket from Kimmi.

SCOTT. This isn't some ancient language, Kimmi, it's French!

KIMMI. You read French?

SCOTT. *(Proudly.)* Je parle aussi.

KIMMI. There's a little more to you than meets the eye, Scott Foley. Anyway . . . what's it say?

SCOTT. It's a little hard to read . . . but I think it says something about a theater.

KIMMI. Maybe that's where the map is!

SCOTT. How can you be sure?

KIMMI. I don't know for sure, but how will we know unless we go find out? C'mon! We're going to a theater!

Kimmi exits. She immediately re-enters.

KIMMI. Where is the theater?

SCOTT. It's just two blocks that way—

Scott points offstage.

SCOTT. —but—uh—shouldn't we wait for the . . . responsible adults?

KIMMI. Please. Let's go!

Kimmi and Scott run offstage.

ABIGAIL. *(Offstage.)* . . . Now!

Well after Kimmi and Scott's exit, Abigail, Ciera, and Vivian burst onto the scene, cackling and encircling where they think Kimmi should be until ABIGAIL stops.

She raises her finger and Vivian and Ciera come to a halt.

ABIGAIL. She's not here!

VIVIAN. Well maybe we should've hid where we could still see her instead of just—

ABIGAIL. Oh hush will you!

VIVIAN. Yeesh.

Ciera points off into the distance.

CIERA. Hey—I think I see a girl running for her life—

ABIGAIL. After her!

Abigail springs into a running motion with Ciera and Vivian trailing.

Stage Fright

Act One, Scene 5

Outside the Grand Suzanne Theater of Hanenbough, ten minutes later. Kimmi and Scott arrive in front of the curtain before the scene officially begins.

KIMMI. All right, here we are! *(Reading the sign.)* The Grand Suzanne Theater of Hanenbough—

SCOTT. It's the only theater in town and the Suzanne's been around forever. It was built around the ruins of a Roman amphitheater.

KIMMI. Neat. So how do we get in? Do we just—sneak in?

SCOTT. Yeah, I don't have money for a ticket.

KIMMI. I don't either.

SCOTT. Which is a problem.

KIMMI. Which is a problem!

Scott sees the flyer on the door, which reads:

"*MAINSTAGE GROUP AUDITIONS—2:00 p.m.*

STAGE FRIGHT

ENTRANCE AROUND BACK"

SCOTT. Yeah . . . huh. Looks like they're holding auditions for . . .their next show.

A CASTING DIRECTOR enters with a clipboard in one hand and latte in the other. He addresses Kimmi and Scott.

DIRECTOR. You guys are lost, go on around back. First door on the left.

KIMMI. What?

DIRECTOR. Didn't your agent tell you anything?? Auditions are through the back door.

KIMMI. *(Flattered.)* So you think I'm an actress?

The Director rolls his eyes.

DIRECTOR. Yes, you have the music in you. Head around back, first door on the left. *(Mutters.)* Actors.

The Director exits. As he exits, he drops a pen.

KIMMI. Okay, new plan—Scott, you low-key look for the map in the theater, and I'll cover by auditioning for the play.

Kimmi takes her cell phone out and hands it to Scott.

KIMMI. Actually—take pictures of me. Send them all to Elizabeth Peaches.

SCOTT. Okay.

KIMMI. Let's go!

Kimmi and Scott go around to the back of the building. Abigail, Ciera, and Vivian enter, somewhat running after them.

ABIGAIL. There! She must be auditioning for the play!

CIERA. Oh wow, she's an actress.

ABIGAIL. It's not even a good show that's coming up . . . *Good Knight and Goodbye*. Written by some kid, I heard.

VIVIAN. Have you even seen it? I enjoyed when I saw it in Glasgow.

ABIGAIL. No, Vivian, I haven't seen it. I have more important things to do with my life than frolic through Scotland like you did for four years.

VIVIAN. I was at university.

ABIGAIL. A waste of time—and look! I'm still in charge of you. But at least you learned your math. What's ten plus three?

VIVIAN. Thirteen.

CIERA. I sure wish we were actresses.

ABIGAIL. Oh, Ciera, honey, anyone can be an actress.

The Director returns to pick up the small item he dropped. The Director doesn't really make eye contact with the witches.

ABIGAIL. Excuse me, Mr. Director, sir. Where do two beautiful actresses and one Vivian go to audition for the play?

DIRECTOR. Are you sure you're an actress? How old are you?

ABIGAIL. Perhaps you do not comprehend: I am a witch. My sisters are also witches. We could end you right now, but all we want is an audition for the play.

The Director nods.

DIRECTOR. Witches. Suuuuuure. I see. Go around back, first door on the left. *(Muttering.)* Actors.

The Director exits.

CIERA. How old are you, Abigail?

VIVIAN. She's forty-s—

ABIGAIL. Vivian, your sock's untied. Let's go inside now, okay?

Abigail leads Ciera and Vivian to the back of the building. The set changes to reveal the grand main stage of the Suzanne, revealing a group of actors and actresses with scripts in hand.

As the curtain rises, the Director sits to one side of the stage at a table. Diana, Parezco, and Actress 1 wrap up reading a scene.

DIANA. *(Reading script.)* "Lovely, my dear. Just you wait and see!"

The Director waves his hands.

DIRECTOR. And scene. Thank you, who's next?

PAREZCO. Would you like me to read for the Queen? I do impressions, you know. I can impersonate anyone.

DIRECTOR. I'm aware, Parezco, master impressionist, how about you wait in the wings with everyone else?

Diana exits. Parezco returns to the group of actors. Kimmi and Scott enter with Abigail, Ciera, and Vivian close behind. They are each handed scripts.

KIMMI. Here we are!

DIRECTOR. Okay. Page 63. Why don't I have you—

KIMMI. Kimmi Larkin.

DIRECTOR. —read the part of Princess Jacqueline. And hmm... you're a little young, but why don't I hear you read for the King?

The Director looks down and points, making an imprecise choice.

DIRECTOR. And, uh... you back there...

ABIGAIL. Me?

DIRECTOR. Sure. You read the Queen. Page 63. Start with Carlton's line "My dearest..."

The Director sits back and sips some coffee. Kimmi, Scott, and Abigail get into place. Scott studies his lines intently as Kimmi looks up and makes eye contact with Abigail. Abigail murmurs a softly menacing laugh as she creepily waves to Kimmi.

Kimmi jabs Scott in the side as she speaks rapidly out of the corner of her mouth.

KIMMI. Scott, those thieves followed us here. Abort. Abort. Abort.

DIRECTOR. What are you waiting for? I haven't got all day. King, go.

SCOTT. Okay! I'm ready.

KIMMI. Scott!

SCOTT. *(Reading script.)* "My dearest Princess Jacqueline, why are you acting so suspicious? Please, enjoy the day."

KIMMI. No—Scott, we need to—

DIRECTOR. Read the scene!!

KIMMI. Um . . . okay.

Kimmi clears her throat.

Kimmi tries to use her inflection and body language to suggest to Scott that they are in grave danger, but Scott misses these signals entirely as he earnestly auditions for the role. Abigail, meanwhile, uses this time to taunt Kimmi and Scott. Hilarity ensues.

KIMMI. *(Reading script.)* "I think you and *'mother'* are hiding something from me."

SCOTT. *(Reading script.)* And why on earth would you think that?

KIMMI. *(Reading script.)* "Father, I know *'something's up.'* What's going on?"

ABIGAIL. *(Reading script.)* "Dear, your father and I are planning a *'big* *surprise'* for you *'very soon!'"*

Kimmi's face washes out with fear.

KIMMI. *(Reading script.)* "'Really?' I mean, I am . . . quite accustomed to what we do for my birthday most years, but a surprise would be most exciting."

ABIGAIL. *(Reading script.)* "It will be a *'marvelous'* surprise. I have been planning it for ages."

SCOTT. *(Reading script.)* "Then let's get on with it. We haven't got all day."

ABIGAIL. *(Reading script.)* "Lovely, my dear. Just you wait and see!"

Abigail tosses her script aside and cackles. Scott turns and sees who she is.

SCOTT. Run!

Kimmi and Scott begin to move quickly out of the way. Director is not having any of this—he rises, exasperated.

DIRECTOR. Stay on book!! All of you!

ABIGAIL. Freeze!!

Abigail spins around with a wave of her hand as a powerful gust of cold wind fills the room. The Director and every background actor currently onstage freezes. Vivian and Ciera push Kimmi and Scott back to center stage as the witches surround them. Diana, the Stage Mom, and Child Actor enter.

ABIGAIL. Marvel and be amazed at us!

CIERA. The three—

VIVIAN. Lost witches of Hanenbough!

Diana sneaks offstage, holding a cell phone to her ear.

ABIGAIL. Lost? Seriously, Vivian, that's what you came up with? You've gotta have more finesse with these things! That just sounds like we're some lousy hitchhikers.

STAGE MOM. *(Panicking.)* What do you want with us? Take my boy—I just want to live—

CHILD ACTOR. Moooooommmmm, stop.

Abigail throws her hand in the direction of Stage Mom and Child Actor. Another powerful gust of cold wind blows through the room and freezes them both.

ABIGAIL. That was annoying. Now, I have no intentions of ending any of your lives today.

KIMMI. Great. All right then, we'll be on our merry way. It's been wonderful to meet you all and it was nice having you try to rob me for an afternoon—

ABIGAIL. Rob you?

Abigail laughs.

ABIGAIL. This was never about robbing you. I'm sure you know all about Desrosier's treasure, and you certainly may know how a person may get the lost treasure.

KIMMI. Well, if it exists—

ABIGAIL. It absolutely exists. Vivian, show our new friends what you have.

Vivian unfolds the map.

KIMMI. Desrosier's map . . .

ABIGAIL. My sisters and I have been inside the cave of the Thousand-Year Rose. We met a man with a shovel. He speaks in riddles.

KIMMI. That's oddly specific.

ABIGAIL. And now that I know where the treasure is—

VIVIAN. *(Whispered.)* We.

ABIGAIL. —and that you're the pure of heart, you're the only thing standing between me and the treasure.

VIVIAN. *(Softly.)* Us.

ABIGAIL. So we will drag you to that rose and you will make that thing bloom which will make the treasure appear and then I take over the world.

KIMMI. And then what do you plan do with me?

ABIGAIL. I said I wouldn't kill you *today*.

Diana enters, dramatically hanging up her cell phone.

DIANA. *(Boldly.)* I have a question!

All eyes are on Diana as she crosses elegantly to Abigail.

STAGE FRIGHT

DIANA. Do you hear what I hear?

Diana smiles. Abigail concentrates and hears police sirens faintly in the distance.

ABIGAIL. You . . . called the police?

DIANA. Well, I never permit a felony to unfold before my eyes if I can do something about it. I am not a criminal—I'm an actress!

VIVIAN. I told you this would happen if we tried to get her in public—

ABIGAIL. Not now, Vivian!!

The police sirens get louder.

DIANA. Daresay we let them in? Oh, what a sight to behold!

Abigail and Diana make cunning eye contact with each other as the sirens continue to blare.

ABIGAIL. What fun is life without a little police chase? This isn't the last you've seen of us, Kimmi Larkin. Mark my words. Ciera! Vivian! We move!

Abigail, Ciera, and Vivian hightail it out of the theater.

DIANA. And the witches ran away. All is well for now.

DIRECTOR. Yeah, okay. Everyone take twenty. I'm too old for this—

Director, Parezco, and everyone else exits, leaving only Kimmi, Diana, and Scott onstage.

DIANA. The name's Diana Marie Bailey, by the way . . . Though you may have heard the name before. I'm a bit of a local celebrity here at the Suzanne.

KIMMI. Sorry, I haven't. I just got to town today.

SCOTT. M-my grandma's a big fan.

DIANA. Marvelous! And you are . . . ?

SCOTT. Scott. Scott Reed Foley.

DIANA. It's nice to meet you Scott Reed Foley, but I don't believe you two arrived at the Suzanne by chance today. What's your story?

KIMMI. I'm doing a research internship in Hanenbough this summer for my archaeology professor—we're researching Desrosier and the Thousand-Year Rose.

DIANA. Yes, I'm all too familiar with the legend of the rose. It's but a load of horse feathers.

KIMMI. Yes! I thought so, too, but then my professor and I found Desrosier's locket and now I guess I have witches hunting me down.

DIANA. Dearest me! May I see it?

Kimmi unhooks the locket and passes it to Diana. Diana opens it effortlessly.

DIANA. I say! This certainly looks like the real thing.

KIMMI. So then, we opened the locket and followed the inscription to the Suzanne. Do you think the Suzanne has any connection to the legend?

DIANA. Not off the top of my head. The Suzanne is old, but she hasn't been around forever.

KIMMI. It was a thought. Anyway, Diana—we can't thank you enough for calling the police and all. So—I guess we're on our way now. Thank you, Diana.

DIANA. Leave now? Alone? I live for adventure, the thrill and romance of it all, but traveling Hanenbough is dangerous let alone with witches placing a bounty on your head. There is safety in numbers, my dears. That's it—I'm coming with you!

KIMMI. Uh . . . aren't there more rounds of auditions today?

DIANA. Nonsense. I cannot stand idly by when I see a girl who could be my daughter put in danger. You need a mother's protection—both of you. I'll not have a bar of the treasure!

SCOTT. *(Attempted whisper.)* She says that now but that might change when we actually find the treasure.

KIMMI. *(Sidebar.)* That was very loud, Scott.

Kimmi turns to Diana.

KIMMI. We'll figure that out when we find it. We should get on the move!

SCOTT. Let's go find that professor, then—yeah?

DIANA. Masterful!

Kimmi, Scott, and Diana exit.

To Begin a Witch Hunt

Act One, Scene 6

The bustling, open-air market in the port of Hanenbough, about ten minutes later. There is a park bench in the vicinity. Abigail and Ciera enter, still in full sprint from their run from the theater. Vivian enters, having fallen behind.

CIERA. That was wicked!

ABIGAIL. Oh, I haven't had that much fun in *years*!

VIVIAN. Where are you going? We can probably catch them if we just wait outside the theater. They'll be right behind us!

ABIGAIL. Were you even paying attention, Vivian? The police are right behind us, you numbskull.

VIVIAN. It just seems counterintuitive when we know where they—

CIERA. Save yourself!!

Ciera and Abigail continue running through the marketplace, exiting the stage.

VIVIAN. *(Agitated.)* Fine! I guess I'll just do this myself.

Professor Davis and Maryann enter hand-in-hand. They sit on a park bench eating chocolate-covered pretzels. Vivian sees them out of the corner of her eye and panics.

VIVIAN. No I can't!

Vivian dives into hiding behind the baker's stand. Kimmi, Scott, and Diana enter.

KIMMI. Yo! Doc! Nice to run into you here, things have gotten super weird.

Vivian pokes her head out when she hears Kimmi's voice and ducks back into hiding. She crouches to get a better position to eavesdrop. Kimmi crosses to Professor Davis.

KIMMI. Did you know that witches, are, like, a thing? And they're looking for the treasure too? Doc? Doc? Hello—

PROFESSOR DAVIS. Ah! Ms. Larkin! I thought you'd be fighting jet lag back at the apartment.

KIMMI. Well . . . that was, y'know, the plan, but then you never actually showed me to the apartment and so Scott and I started looking for the map, we auditioned for roles at the community theater, scared some witches, and now here we are.

PROFESSOR DAVIS. Wonderful! I'll leave you to it.

KIMMI. But—Doc—I mean, c'mon Doc, don't you want to know what we did?

PROFESSOR DAVIS. Ms. Larkin, I will resume work tomorrow.

Professor Davis goes back to Maryann, as Kimmi tries to get his attention and he pays her none.

MARYANN. So you've never been married?

PROFESSOR DAVIS. I married my work—and at my age, retirement would be the death of me.

KIMMI. *(Snide.)* Hello?

MARYANN. Must get awful lonely in that big office . . . all those books . . .

KIMMI. Doc?

PROFESSOR DAVIS. The books are nice. But there's something . . . missing.

KIMMI. It's the map. We don't have the map.

MARYANN. Well you do have all your teeth.

PROFESSOR DAVIS. Brand-new pair of dentures!

MARYANN. I'd have never guessed!

PROFESSOR DAVIS. I find that . . . agreeable.

MARYANN. Well—I find you agreeable.

KIMMI. C'mon Doc—this is your life's work I'm doing here! Treasure, rose, map, locket, Cocoa Puffs—anything?!?

PROFESSOR DAVIS. If you want to keep working today—please do, keep searching for the treasure. I want you to learn to lead and discover things for yourself. And besides, Ms. Larkin, for the first time—

Professor Davis turns to Maryann and squeezes her hand.

PROFESSOR DAVIS. I feel closer to the treasure than I've ever been.

Maryann melts. Kimmi backs off and mutters under her breath.

KIMMI. Fine. Fine. We fly all the way to Hanenbough for what? For love. To fall in love. Of course.

PROFESSOR DAVIS. I'm entrusting the hunt to you for the day, Ms. Larkin. We will discuss this tomorrow. Now—Ms. Maryann—shall I take you to my apartment? I make a very nice Irish coffee.

MARYANN. Irish coffees are my favorite!

Professor Davis and Maryann exit. Kimmi shakes her head as she rejoins Scott and Diana.

SCOTT. Alright, Kimmi, Diana—what's the plan?

KIMMI. We need the map if we want to make any more real progress.

DIANA. And those horrid witches have it.

KIMMI. So we need to find the witches.

SCOTT. Are you crazy?

KIMMI. Depends on who you ask.

DIANA. Mmmm . . . if I were a horrid witch . . . where might I go to draw up my next plans?

KIMMI. The forest?

SCOTT. Maybe in that creepy old church . . .

Upon hearing this, Vivian bolts in the direction of the forest.

KIMMI. Creepy old church. Lovely. So where on earth is that?

DIANA. A creepy church in the forest? Call me daft, but I know exactly where that is!

SCOTT. Well, okay . . . let's go!

Diana leads Kimmi and Scott out of the market, toward the forest.

The Good Kind of Betrayal

Act One, Scene 7

The dense forest inland from Hanenbough, a few hours later. The sun is beginning to set in the distance. An abandoned cathedral overtaken by nature is seen in the background. Vivian stands at center stage, holding an apple.

VIVIAN. Okay—this is fine, Vivian. No, it's perfect: I'll get Kimmi myself and so Abigail can have what she wants and then nobody else has to get hurt. And maybe—just maybe—Abigail will—no. She'd never. But I have to do this. This is my shot. I have to get Kimmi. She'll be here any minute . . . so all I need is a plan. Now how should I go about this . . . ? A bear trap. No, she'll lose a leg. That'd be bad.

Vivian looks down at the apple in her hand.

VIVIAN. Maybe I'll just make her fall asleep . . . That feels a little more humane.

Vivian begins a motion to bewitch the apple with her hand, but stops herself.

VIVIAN. Well—gosh, I don't know. That just doesn't feel right either . . .

Vivian hears voices off in the distance.

VIVIAN. Hmm?

KIMMI. *(Offstage.)* No kidding—that is one creepy old church!

Vivian panics—she dives behind a tree as Kimmi, Scott, and Diana enter.

DIANA. Okay, fearless leader—how shall we go about finding these witches?

Vivian's heart races.

KIMMI. So I say we just split up, look around the trees here . . . but nobody go out of sight. We wouldn't want any of these witches to take us without a fair fight. Then we'll head into the church. Let's just take five minutes to look around out here—

DIANA. Five minutes sounds masterful!

Kimmi, Diana, and Scott search the trees all around. Vivian sneezes. Kimmi, Diana, and Scott's eyes each dart back and forth to each other.

DIANA. Did you just hear something?

SCOTT. No—I didn't.

KIMMI. Yeah, no, I—don't think so.

Diana crosses to the tree Vivian is hiding behind, walking around the base of the tree. Vivian moves around the tree in parallel to Diana's movement, causing Diana to completely miss seeing her.

DIANA. Mmm . . . I must be imagining things.

SCOTT. So . . . what's our plan? Say we find the witches here in the forest . .

. then what?

KIMMI. I don't really know. I guess we'll improvise some kinda action movie fight sequence or something.

VIVIAN. *(To herself.)* Oh god.

SCOTT. With what?

KIMMI. I went to a kick boxing class once.

Diana gestures to her purse.

DIANA. I have a portable hair dryer in here.

Kimmi shoots Diana an incredulous look as they both laugh.

SCOTT. You two are, uh, really chill about—fighting witches. Actual witches . . . who want to kill you.

Kimmi crosses to Scott.

KIMMI. Hey—what's up, dude? You feel okay?

Vivian smiles softly.

SCOTT. You're just—good at everything. And not afraid of anything. Which is cool, but I don't get it. All of this is terrifying.

KIMMI. Look, today has been bonkers. *(Laughs.)* Of course this is scary! Witches are hunting us. We're hunting witches. My professor fell in love with your grandma! That's not related, but it's still super weird. But what I sorta think—when something scary is happening: you can hide. You can attack. Or you can face it. And what I've found—hiding solves nothing. Attacking works only sometimes. You have to pick your battles and not hurt something or someone that didn't need to be hurt. But when something scary happens—and you face it for exactly what it is, with a level head and an open mind and you do good in the face of your fear—you'll be surprised what can happen.

VIVIAN. She's just . . . so kind.

DIANA. She's right, you know. And Kimmi and I will look out for you every step of the way.

VIVIAN. They all are . . .

Kimmi looks over at the tree.

KIMMI. Omigosh, what is that?

Kimmi crosses to the tree. Vivian tenses up in anticipation, but Kimmi just picks up a rock.

KIMMI. Just a cool rock. It's like kinda—flask shaped—

SCOTT. Flask . . . shaped?

KIMMI. Yeah, don'tcha see it? It's like—round. And curvy.

DIANA. Round and curvy . . . *(Playfully.)* Voluptuous, huh?

Kimmi, Diana, and Scott laugh.

SCOTT. What does that mean?

Diana whispers in Scott's ear. Kimmi laughs as she watches.

VIVIAN. Why do I even do what I do? *(Mocking tone.)* "It's because we're witches, Vivian." Abi, she's just . . . so mean to me, and Ciera's . . . nothing. What's wrong with me? Why can't I just kidnap her like I came here to do? I just wish there was some other way to . . . *(Involuntarily noisy.)* Ugggghhhhh

Kimmi, Scott, and Diana hear Vivian give away her position. They dart over to Vivian's side of the tree. Diana draws the portable hair dryer from her purse like a handgun and points it at Vivian.

DIANA. Where are the others?

Kimmi removes her earrings and hands her purse off to Scott as she strikes a fighter pose.

SCOTT. Kimmi, what are you doing?

Kimmi looks Vivian dead in the eyes—she's ready to go into battle.

KIMMI. I will fight you myself. You don't need to hurt any of these people here, they have nothing to do with—

VIVIAN. *(Calmly, but kind of shouting.)* I can explain!

Everyone is taken aback. Kimmi, Scott, and Diana all lock attention on Vivian.

VIVIAN. Look. None of you trust me. I get that. But please, please just listen to me.

KIMMI. Fine. You get two seconds—

VIVIAN. My name is Vivian and I am a witch. I'm here alone. My sisters want to take you, Kimmi, down to the secret garden so that you with your pure heart can make the rose bloom—which will make the treasure appear. And then they plan to kill you.

KIMMI. Yeah, we all know that. So we—

Kimmi steps toward Vivian, who shields her face.

VIVIAN. Please don't hurt me!

Kimmi steps back, realizing just how vulnerable Vivian is.

KIMMI. Vivian . . . uh, just woman to woman here: Is . . . everything okay?

VIVIAN. No, of course not. My sisters are horrible to me and I was planning to kidnap you out of blind loyalty but then—

Kimmi cocks her head.

KIMMI. "Was" planning?

VIVIAN. I know I don't actually want to. So I won't. This is probably the first time I can remember anyone's ever been nice to me.

SCOTT. The first time anyone has been nice to you is when Kimmi . . . chose to not beat the snot out of you?

KIMMI. Scott!!

VIVIAN. It's crazy, I know. But seeing you all . . . decent people . . . makes me know I don't want my sisters to find the treasure—I'd rather you find it. I'd even want to come with you. And maybe . . . learn to be a better . . . person?

SCOTT. Ooh. No way.

DIANA. That sounds like a lovely story, my dear, but you must understand how hard it would be for you to earn our trust. How on earth could you possibly?

VIVIAN. I have two reasons. I—I . . . No, you're right. This is pathetic, you'll never trust me, I'm a worthless, evil witch.

Vivian walks away. Kimmi follows her.
KIMMI. Vivian, no, come back. You're not worthless. You might be a witch 'cause you're, y'know, a woman who can do magic, but I can tell you're not evil. You have a reason we can trust you?

VIVIAN. Two.

Vivian pulls out the apple.

VIVIAN. This apple . . . I started to poison it with magic, but . . . I just didn't.

KIMMI. *(With a slight laugh.)* A witch with a poisoned apple?

DIANA. I say!

VIVIAN. I know. Anyway, I could've cursed it if I wanted to . . . but I won't. In fact . . .

Vivian chucks the apple deep into the woods.

VIVIAN. I don't have it. I'm not using magic. I will never attack you.

DIANA. We still don't trust you. Especially if you had the nerve to attack Ms. Kimberly with a cliché!

KIMMI. Di—

VIVIAN. It's fair. Sorry. That's not a great reason to trust me. But I think for my second reason . . . you might. Kimmi, I believe this belongs to your professor—

Vivian pulls out the map, others are in shock.

VIVIAN. I know this map leads straight to the treasure. I've been there. I've seen the cave already. But I think the person to find the treasure should be someone who deserves it . . . a pure heart. So . . . you take this, Kimmi. P-please find the treasure.

Vivian hands Kimmi the map.

VIVIAN. You can trust me. I'm on your side from now on. There's no going back.

KIMMI. Wow, Vivian. I don't know how to thank you—

VIVIAN. We can head straight to the cave now! I can lead you there, I got there once before and I can certainly help you get there, too!

KIMMI. Vivian—this just—this means so much that you'd do this for all of us.

VIVIAN. It's really nothing. I've been afraid to break away from my sisters my whole life. I just didn't know I needed to face that until . . . now. It's just three minus one. Which is two.

Diana clutches her necklace, moved.

SCOTT. She's pretty good at math.

Vivian smiles for the first time in a very long time.

VIVIAN. So I've been told. Let's head down to the cave now?

KIMMI. We can't yet! If we're literally going to find the treasure today—we have to get Doc! He won't want to miss this!!

DIANA. Here we go, my dears! I'll lead the way!!

CURTAIN CLOSES.

Abigail and Ciera enter in front of the curtain.

ABIGAIL. Now normally if Vivian disappeared like this, I'd be happy about it . . .but we haven't seen her in hours.

CIERA. Yeah, where did she go?

ABIGAIL. I don't know. It's not like her to run off like this. She better come back soon—as useless as she is, we need her.

CIERA. So what are we going to do?

ABIGAIL. We've got to pretend we've lost Vivian forever.

CIERA. Hooray!!

Ciera blows a limp party horn.

ABIGAIL. No. We need to find Kimmi Larkin and get her down to the garden ourselves. This is gonna get ugly.

Ciera yawns.

CIERA. I'm kinda tired...

ABIGAIL. I like the way you think. Okay—new plan: Take naps now, get ugly later. We go.

CIERA. Hooray!!

Ciera blows her party horn again.

Abigail and Ciera exit, cackling as the house lights come on.

END OF ACT ONE.

White Lies

Act Two, Scene 1

The open-air market in the port of Hanenbough, a couple of hours later. Darkness has fallen, some stands at the market have closed up for the night, though plenty of hanging lights keep the scene bright enough. Abigail and Ciera nap onstage as some townspeople mill in and out of the marketplace. Ciera wakes up and stretches her arms out, yawning. She jumps up and pokes Abigail.

CIERA. Abigail . . . Wake up!

Abigail makes tired grunting noises.

CIERA. Here we go!

Abigail rubs her eyes.

ABIGAIL. Okay. I'm up. Time to get the girl.

A beat as Abigail remains seated. She lifts her finger as she lets her thoughts settle for a second.

ABIGAIL. Coffee first. Then we get the girl. We go.

Abigail tries to stand up, but has a crick in her back.

ABIGAIL. Help me.

Ciera extends her arm to help Abigail up. As Abigail rises, Kimmi, Scott, Diana, and Vivian enter. Neither party sees each other at first.

VIVIAN. Diana, who was your favorite character you've ever played?

DIANA. Hmm . . . I've had many roles I've adored, but I do say Pride and Prejudice was my favorite.

SCOTT. Isn't that a book, though?

DIANA. Yes—lovely Jane Austen novel that someone adapted for the stage . . . It ran in Hanenbough just last summer.

SCOTT. Who were you?

DIANA. Mrs. Bennet of course! Fluttering about the mansion as a Victorian matron with five daughters . . . I felt right at home! The lovely actress who played Elizabeth was just like her . . . Though it was rather funny, as . . .

Diana continues telling her story to Scott. Kimmi sees Abigail and Ciera out of the corner of her eye. She nudges Vivian.

KIMMI. Omigosh—Vivian—they're here.

Vivian notices Abigail and Ciera—her heart races.

KIMMI. What are you going to do?

VIVIAN. Well—I . . . I guess I need to tell them the truth.

KIMMI. No! You can lie to them.

VIVIAN. I don't know . . . I'm trying to be a better person—

KIMMI. Have they ever been good to you?

VIVIAN. No. Okay, I can lie.

KIMMI. C'mon—you can do it!

Vivian steps toward Abigail and Ciera. A smug grin spreads across Abigail's face.

ABIGAIL. *(Sickeningly sweet.)* Vivian, my dear!

Kimmi ducks behind Diana and Scott. Diana continues her long-winded (albeit entertaining) story, inaudibly to the audience.

ABIGAIL. We were worried sick! We had no idea when you'd come back. But I see you got Miss Larkin all by yourself.

VIVIAN. Yes, I have Kimmi now. She came willingly.

ABIGAIL. A gold star for you, Vivian. So we have her, and we'll be on our merry way, then?

VIVIAN. Yeah—so I'm thinking . . . I'm thinking I'll ditch the others here and . . . I'll lure her down to the garden by myself and then, uh . . . then I'll tie her up and then I'll come get you. Yeah. That's the plan.

ABIGAIL. Hmm . . . Why?

VIVIAN. So you can nap.

ABIGAIL. So I can nap. For once I like the way you think, Vivian. You know your place. Excellent. We'll see you then.

VIVIAN. So . . . I'll be going, then.

ABIGAIL. You get going, then.

Vivian and Abigail share eye contact for just a little too long as Vivian turns around and walks away. Abigail watches Vivian like a hawk as Vivian returns to the group.

KIMMI. Everything okay?

VIVIAN. Yeah, I guess so. They'll leave us alone for a bit.

Diana finally wraps up her story.

DIANA. . . . So, that is precisely why I will never wear a corset again. But I loved that role so much. Quite fun!

KIMMI. Yeah, a corset sounds like a nightmare.

SCOTT. Where's the professor's house again?

KIMMI. Well . . . I have an address somewhere . . .

Kimmi pulls out a piece of paper.

KIMMI. Do y'know where this is?

SCOTT. Yeah, it's just a little ways east. Let's go!

Scott leads Kimmi and Diana out. Vivian turns around and sees Abigail still staring at her. Vivian awkwardly waves goodbye as Abigail creepily waves one finger at a time, cackling with Ciera. Vivian nervously joins the cackling as she exits. Parezco enters and mirrors Abigail and Ciera. Vivian runs offstage. As soon as Vivian exits, Abigail abruptly cuts off the cackling.

ABIGAIL. Vivian's lying to us. She's with them.

CIERA. How do you know that?

Abigail notices Parezco in her peripheral vision and jerks her head around.

ABIGAIL. Who do you think you are?

PAREZCO. I am the master of impressions . . . I am . . . Parezco!! I am . . . out of work. Here, take my card.

Parezco hands Abigail his card.

ABIGAIL. Get lost, bozo.

PAREZCO. Yeesh. Just tryin' to make a buck here. Oh—you're those witches? From the theater?

Abigail and Ciera nod vigorously.

PAREZCO. Right then.

Parezco runs offstage, Abigail cackles.

ABIGAIL. *Irregardless*, I don't like her plan. Even if she is still with us . . .

CIERA. Because you didn't think of it first?

ABIGAIL. No. It'll take too long. We have to get Kimmi on our own. We need a new plan . . . We might need to think outside the box . . . maybe consult some outside help . . . show them some magic . . .

Abigail thinks for a moment, looks around the streets. She pockets Parezco's card on her robes as a grin spreads across her face.

CIERA. Well who on earth would help us take over the world on such short notice?

ABIGAIL. I have an idea.

A beat as Abigail just grins. Ciera leans

CIERA. Uh . . . you're going to tell me, right?

ABIGAIL. In due time. There's too many prying ears here . . . Walk with me.

Abigail walks with purpose toward the Professor's apartment. Ciera follows her.

Reading the Map

Act Two, Scene 2

The loft apartment above Captain Boggs' house, the same time. Professor Davis and Maryann sit on a couch, sharing one Irish coffee, with two separate straws. Captain Boggs' sense of interior design is odd, to say the very least. KATHLEEN, the housekeeper, enters.

KATHLEEN. Another Irish coffee, professor?

Professor Davis does not break eye contact with Maryann.

PROFESSOR DAVIS. Yes, thank you, Kathleen.

KATHLEEN. Anything else you need? Ms. Maryann?

MARYANN. I need nothing else. Thank you, Kathleen.

Kathleen exits. Kimmi bursts into the room with Scott, Diana, and Vivian in tow.

KIMMI. We found the map, Doc! Like, as in now we have everything except the treasure and we're going to find it—like, today! You've got to come with us!!

PROFESSOR DAVIS. Bully.

Kimmi correctly reads her Professor's lack of enthusiasm.

KIMMI. Doc—I mean, I'd think you'd be really excited about finding the treasure you've been researching your whole life.

PROFESSOR DAVIS. You see, Kimberly—I am an old man.

KIMMI. Yes.

PROFESSOR DAVIS. I may have written a dissertation on the lost treasure of Hanenbough one time, when I was a young man . . .

KIMMI. Yes.

PROFESSOR DAVIS. But some things are a little less important now—I have an Irish coffee now, you see . . .

KIMMI. Ugh. C'mon, Doc! I'm still talking about the treasure! Like, literally, this is your life's work. You said you wanted to come to Hanenbough to find the treasure and you needed my help and I haven't seen you do a thing since we've gotten here!!

PROFESSOR DAVIS. You have been right about so many things, Ms. Larkin, but I'm afraid you are wrong about this one. It may seem to you that I've given up on the hunt for the treasure—and perhaps I have.

KIMMI. Then what are we doing here, Doc?

PROFESSOR DAVIS. The treasure is different than what you might expect: it might be something more than a box with a big lock buried underground. I've reached a point where I no longer need to find it, but you still do, Ms. Larkin. I believe it's your treasure to find now. It's all of yours.

KIMMI. But I thought we were a team—aren't we?

PROFESSOR DAVIS. On some level, we certainly are. But you've taken the reins and done it all without deferring to me. You've defied any expectation I had for you by winning people to your side and thinking on your feet. This is exactly why I wanted you, specifically you, Ms. Larkin, as my intern.

KIMMI. Stop, Doc, you're gonna make me cry.

MARYANN. Frank, we need to go with them. We need to be there when they find it.

PROFESSOR DAVIS. Yes, of course. How could we not?

DIANA. But we must move quickly . . .

Diana turns to Vivian.

DIANA. Your sisters will be in hot pursuit of us if they ever wise up.

VIVIAN. We've bought a little time because they still think I'm . . . with them, but they may catch on after a while.

SCOTT. That you're . . . not . . . capturing us, right? You're not capturing us, right?

VIVIAN. No.

KIMMI. C'mon, Scott! She gave us the map—she's with us.

DIANA. So where's this cave, then? You remember, don't you, Vivian?

VIVIAN. Mmm . . . sort of. I need the map in front of me.

KIMMI. Yes! Yeah, of course! Why didn't we do that first? Wait, where's the locket? Did I—

VIVIAN. Wasn't it in your bag?

Vivian picks up the locket out of Kimmi's bag and nonchalantly pops it open as she passes it to Kimmi. Vivian unfolds the map on the table as Professor Davis, Maryann, Kimmi, Scott, and Diana crowd around it.

VIVIAN. Okay—so Desrosier's cave is that X right there—

Vivian points on the map somewhere on the coast with a large, decorative X.

PROFESSOR DAVIS. Yes, yes of course!

VIVIAN. My sisters and I started from the old train station in town and followed the tracks on the line to Olcott until we reached the ruins of Castle Coca Féir—

KIMMI. Haystack.

SCOTT. What?

KIMMI. Coca Féir. It's an old Gaelic word for haystack. Coca Féir, haystack.

SCOTT. And you make fun of me for knowing French.

DIANA. Of course! Haystack Station. Right by Haystack Station are those ruins. I know that place, but it hasn't been operational since I was a little girl!

KIMMI. Why not?

DIANA. The whole little town around it burned to a crisp forty years ago, but the station still stands, uphill from the ruins of Castle Coca Féir. It's just used for storage these days.

KIMMI. Of what? Bodies?

A beat.

KIMMI. Anyway—I mean, okay, so we have to get to Haystack Station and that will be . . . close to the cave? Is that right?

VIVIAN. Yes. If we hop on a train and get off at Haystack Station, I can lead us down to the cave.

DIANA. I would certainly think so.

VIVIAN. But a last-minute train ticket? They get pretty expensive.

SCOTT. Ooh. Good point.

Captain Boggs bursts into the room, not looking up.

CAPTAIN BOGGS. Frankie!

KIMMI. Captain Boggs?

Captain Boggs looks up and notices everyone.

CAPTAIN BOGGS. Err—good ev'ning to you all—Kimmi—friends.

Kathleen enters with a mug.

KATHLEEN. Your 9:30, Captain Boggs—

KIMMI. Wait a sec', Doc—you have a maid??

PROFESSOR DAVIS. Well, technically she's Boggs' maid—

KIMMI. Wait a sec', Boggs—you have a maid??

CAPTAIN BOGGS. *(Matter-of-factly.)* A'course I do! She's basically family at this point.

KATHLEEN. And I tell him y'can't fire family.

Captain Boggs sits down on the couch next to Professor Davis.

CAPTAIN BOGGS. Boy, I tellin' ya, Frankie, things be'changing down at the port . . .

Professor Davis pays Captain Boggs no attention. Boggs turns to Kimmi.

CAPTAIN BOGGS. What's gott'into him?

KIMMI. He's in love. He's gotten lost in his own little world these days.

CAPTAIN BOGGS. Since yesterday?

KIMMI. He's found his lost treasure of Hanenbough. And we're about to find ours—Desrosier's Treasure.

CAPTAIN BOGGS. Desrosier? Oh no—ye're not actually going lookin' for that, are ya? Old Hanenbough—the thieves—the gold—the rose an' all that?

SCOTT. Yep!

CAPTAIN BOGGS. Oh Frankie's been researchin' that for years . . . Driven him mad's all I'm sayin'. But you're on the brink of finding the treasure, you say? Y'sure it's real?

KIMMI, SCOTT, DIANA, and VIVIAN. *(In unison, a little agitated.)* Yes, it's real.

KIMMI. Anyway, though, Boggs—your timing is perfect! Come with us!

CAPTAIN BOGGS. I don't do adventures anymore. Last time, I came home an' me wife was dead.

SCOTT. Oh. Wow. That's kind of . . . sad.

KIMMI, DIANA, and VIVIAN. *(In unison.)* Scott!!

CAPTAIN BOGGS. Runnin' the ferry down t'airstrip's close as I'm gonna get at my age. But there's a little bit of me that's wanted to get out there again on the open sea. Sometimes I think to meself a sea dog never really dies, now does he?

KIMMI. Wait! Boggs—this is perfect! Come along with us! I mean, we're not . . . sailing . . . but we can use your help! We're hopping on board a train to Haystack Station.

CAPTAIN BOGGS. Oh ya', could definitely get'cha free tickets if we needed. Susan loves me down there.

DIANA. My dear, who is Susan?

CAPTAIN BOGGS. The ticket lady, a'course!

KIMMI. So, you'll come with us?

CAPTAIN BOGGS. Wha'the hey, why not?

KIMMI. Then what are we waiting for? Let's get outta here!

Captain Boggs, Kimmi, Diana, Scott, and Vivian exit. Professor Davis and Maryann rise from their seats and prepare to leave.

MARYANN. Don't they know we need a little more warning before we up and storm out the door?

PROFESSOR DAVIS. I say! I suppose there's no time to waste when they're on the brink of something fantastic.

MARYANN. And so are we!

Maryann kisses Professor Davis on the cheek. They begin a full kiss until they are interrupted by an ominous knock at the door. The Professor and Maryann are perplexed.

PROFESSOR DAVIS. Come in.

The door creaks open on its own, triggering an electrical surge sound as the lights flicker wildly. A familiar cackle of witches is heard nearby.

Six Minutes

Act Two, Scene 3

The small open-air, graffiti-covered train station in Hanenbough in the dead of night, about an hour later. A flickering, dim bulb above a ticket window is the only distinguishable source of light. A CONDUCTOR paces back and forth in front of the train platform for the train bound to the nearby town.

CONDUCTOR. The eleven p.m. to Olcott leavin' in six minutes!

Stage Mom dashes from one end of the stage to the other, with several cases of luggage and possibly a fanny pack.

STAGE MOM. Don't you dare leave without my boy!! My precious son!!! My beautiful boy!!

The Stage Mom dives onto the train. The Child Actor walks in, rather embarrassed.

CHILD ACTOR. Moooooommmmm, stop.

The Child Actor hands the Conductor his and his mother's ticket and calmly gets onto the train. A figure enters in a trench coat, carrying nothing but a ticket. He hands it to the Conductor.

CONDUCTOR. Head right on in, sir—you have your pick of seat for the time being.

The figure turns—revealing an uncharacteristically nervous Professor Davis.

PROFESSOR DAVIS. I think I'll stay out for a second.

CONDUCTOR. Sir, the train leaves at eleven p.m. sharp, in six minutes—

PROFESSOR DAVIS. I need the fresh air.

CONDUCTOR. I hardly think standing outside the tr—

PROFESSOR DAVIS. *(With intensity.)* I'm not well. I need the fresh air. Please leave me be.

CONDUCTOR. . . . Okay. Yeah, you seem like you could use . . . the fresh air.

Conductor walks away from Professor Davis.

CONDUCTOR. Eleven p.m. to Olcott leavin' five minutes! All aboard in five minutes!

Kimmi, Scott, Diana, Vivian, and Captain Boggs rush into the station, toward the train platform.

PROFESSOR DAVIS. Kimmi!

The group stops in their tracks. Kimmi turns to face Professor Davis.

KIMMI. Uh, Doc? What—what are you doing here already? I thought you were . . . behind us?

PROFESSOR DAVIS. I took a shortcut.

KIMMI. Oh. Well, great—let's get on the train then! Did you get a ticket? Susan gave us a ton—

PROFESSOR DAVIS. No, I got one already.

Kimmi takes a step toward her Professor.

KIMMI. Are you doing all right, Doc? You look kinda—sick? Or something?

PROFESSOR DAVIS. No, no, I'm fine. Just getting old, I suppose.

KIMMI. No, not that—you are super old. I don't know, maybe I'm just seeing things. Could just be the weird light or something—

CAPTAIN BOGGS. I'm seein' 'em too, Kimmi. Ol'boy, looks like you seen a ghost'r something. I think you oughta lay down.

SCOTT. Where's grandma?

DIANA. Yes, where is she, that lovely thing?

SCOTT. I haven't seen you without her . . . well, since I met you.

PROFESSOR DAVIS. Your friends are certainly asking a lot of questions.

VIVIAN. Kimmi, I don't know your professor very well, but I don't know if that's really him. Could be—bewitched somehow. My sisters might be behind this—

KIMMI. Mm . . . Could be. But I don't know if it's . . . that.

Kimmi looks into Professor Davis' eyes.

KIMMI. What's wrong with you, Doc?

PROFESSOR DAVIS. Allergies. I get awful allergies this time of night. That's why I need the fresh air.

DIANA. Oh, how horrible! I'm certain one of us has a Benadryl—somewhere . . .

Diana rifles through her purse.

DIANA. I have a Peppermint Patty!

PROFESSOR DAVIS. Besides, Kimmi—you don't want to get on the train right now.

KIMMI. Uh . . . why not?

PROFESSOR DAVIS. I heard some punks broke in and made it . . . unsafe. The train's unsafe.

KIMMI. . . . "Punks"? Doc, you're making no sense at all right now—

DIANA. I'm thoroughly confused. Can you set your story straight, dear? First, you say you're coming with us, but now the train's unsafe? Which is it?

CAPTAIN BOGGS. I'll have a word with the conductor! Excuse me—good conductor sir—

Captain Boggs crosses to the Conductor.

CONDUCTOR. Yes?

CAPTAIN BOGGS. Have you heard of some—what'd he say?—*punks* breakin' into'the train?

CONDUCTOR. Heard nothing of it. Train's safe as it's ever been. *(Shouting.)* Eleven p.m. to Olcott leaving in three minutes! All aboard in three minutes!!

The Conductor exits.

KIMMI. Okay—something's definitely wrong with you, Doc. Something's totally wrong and it's freaking me out.

PROFESSOR DAVIS. I'm sorry, Kimmi. I can explain. Just—

A beat. Professor Davis turns his head.

PROFESSOR DAVIS. Take my hand.

KIMMI. Uh . . . what?

PROFESSOR DAVIS. *(Speaking louder.)* Take my hand.

Professor Davis squeezes Kimmi's hand forcibly.

KIMMI. Wha—

Kimmi looks down at her hand and realizes her trust has been betrayed.

KIMMI. Omigosh! Doc—what are you d—?

Abigail and Ciera emerge from hiding spots on stage. The flickering light above the ticket window turns into an intense strobe light, violently oscillating between on and off. Kimmi screams as Abigail runs up behind her with a chloroform-soaked cloth and covers Kimmi's nose and mouth with it. Kimmi's scream is cut off as she is knocked out cold. Abigail, Ciera, and Professor Davis carry Kimmi's body out of the train station. The lights return to normal as Diana, Vivian, Scott, and Captain Boggs are left onstage.

DIANA. What on earth just happened?

VIVIAN. Kimmi's gone—they—they took her.

Everyone ad-libs panic for a couple moments, talking over each other—except Scott, who surprisingly processes what needs to happen in a calm way.

DIANA. We must run after them!

VIVIAN. They're going to take her down to the garden—we have to get there first!

CAPTAIN BOGGS. And here t'think Frankie's scum—I fancy I give him two fists a'my mind when we find'im.

Scott shouts with uninhibited confidence.

SCOTT. Guys!

Everyone abruptly stops to listen to Scott.

SCOTT. We have literally no time to panic like this. Yes, Kimmi's been taken, but we know where they're going and we know that this train is the fastest way there. They will not kill her until they get her in front of the rose. So we'll get down to the cave and someone's going to make the rose bloom and uncover the legendary treasure . . . tonight.

DIANA. What are we to do with the witches and the professor?

CONDUCTOR. All aboard!!!

SCOTT. We'll deal with them. C'mon guys—let's go!

Scott, Diana, Vivian, and Captain Boggs hurriedly exit onto the train as the curtain falls.

Platform Peril

Act Two, Scene 4

This scene takes place in two locations—One side is at the entrance to the cave of the Thousand-Year Rose outside the garden and the other side is a train car, taking place at the same time, about thirty minutes later. Train noises are heard in the background periodically to intensify the sense of peril in the scene. Abigail, Ciera, and Professor Davis drag Kimmi into the garden scene.

ABIGAIL. We're right back where we started with a pure heart in tow . . . oh I can see the treasure now! And it's all going to be mine!! Wake up, Kimmi, you're not gonna want to miss this.

Abigail prods Kimmi as she wakes up. Without missing a beat, Kimmi picks up right where she left off, furious with her Professor.

KIMMI. Doc—how could you? I just don't get it—

ABIGAIL. It would be wise for you to not be so trusting next time, my pretty.

CIERA. Next time?

ABIGAIL. Ugh, Ciera—what?

CIERA. I mean, I think it's a little silly that we'd have to kidnap her again.

ABIGAIL. Tread lightly, Ciera. You're the sister I like.

CIERA. Aww, really?

ABIGAIL. Tread lightly.

CIERA. But there's going to be a next time?

ABIGAIL. I misspoke. There will be no next time for Ms. Larkin. A little dark magic is going to make that happen. All in good time.

PROFESSOR DAVIS. You're going to . . . kill her?

ABIGAIL. That's none of your business, "professor."

PROFESSOR DAVIS. Uh, I didn't agree to that—

ABIGAIL. We don't get to agree. There's me—and then there's Ciera—and then there's you. You're as expendable as your student here.

KIMMI. Okay, okay, I get that you wanna kill me. Sure, whatever. You're a wicked witch and the only way you can have a pure heart needed to find Desrosier's treasure is by exploiting a loophole in the prophecy or whatever. I'm fine with that. I mean, I'm not fine with that, but I get it. What I don't understand—Doc? Why? None of this makes sense . . . I had no idea you were a bad guy! Nobody did!!

A beat.

KIMMI. Except maybe that one time when Elizabeth Peaches got her paper back from 103, but she got over that, I think.

Kimmi's bitter feelings creep back in.

KIMMI. Omigosh, Liz totally did not deserve a C on her paper on the Aztecs. That was fifteen pages and countless hours of her freshman spring she's never getting back!!

ABIGAIL. Oh, shut up!

A train whistles offstage. The focus shifts to the train car. Scott sits next to Vivian on the train. Captain Boggs is seated next to Diana. Scott turns to Vivian.

SCOTT. You don't, uh, think Kimmi's actually gonna be—done for—do you?

VIVIAN. Mmm . . . I don't think so. My sisters make a lot of threats, but I think they're bluffing. I don't even think their magic is powerful enough to kill.

SCOTT. Is yours?

VIVIAN. Why would I need to find that out?

SCOTT. I mean, you are a witch . . . Aren't you?

VIVIAN. Sure. I'm a witch. But I'm just . . . me.

Vivian falls quiet as the train abruptly comes to a stop.

SCOTT. Why are we stopping?

CONDUCTOR. *(Offstage.)* Good evening. We hope that you are enjoying your train ride to Olcott. Unfortunately, the train has broken down and we are not presently aware how we may start moving again. Passengers are encouraged to pray to the deity of their choosing until further notice.

Diana and Captain Boggs simultaneously perform the Catholic sign of the cross.

They silently notice each other.

SCOTT. What do we do now? We're not at Haystack Station yet, are we?

DIANA. It's just a little ways down the track; we could certainly hoof it from here. I suppose we just need to find a way to exit.

SCOTT. But how? They won't open the doors for us—

CAPTAIN BOGGS. They made emergency exits for a reason, didn't they?

Captain Boggs crosses to the emergency exit to attempt opening it. Captain Boggs punches the door and grunts in frustration.

SCOTT. What's the problem?

CAPTAIN BOGGS. It's jammed shut. Can't get it.

SCOTT. Hmm. Maybe we could . . . we could bust open a window!

CAPTAIN BOGGS. How ya'gonna do that?

VIVIAN. No, no, Scott. I have a better plan. Step back—

Vivian concentrates on the door and makes a swiping motion with her hand. The door is destroyed in a powerful explosion, as everyone on the train looks at Vivian with gaped open mouths.

SCOTT. That was so cool.

CAPTAIN BOGGS. We might get in a little trouble for that one.

VIVIAN. *(Not agitated per se, just matter-of-factly.)* Do we have time to care about that right now?

CAPTAIN BOGGS. Guess not.

CONDUCTOR. *(Offstage.)* What was that noise?

DIANA. That's our exit, my darlings!!

Scott, Diana, Vivian, and Captain Boggs jump out the hole in the wall. A train whistle is heard, switching the focus of the scene back to the witches and Kimmi.

PROFESSOR DAVIS. Abigail, I'm all right with helping you find the treasure and take over the world.

ABIGAIL. Obviously.

PROFESSOR DAVIS. But if you're going to kill this girl who had nothing to do with you or your plan—she at least deserves to know the truth about me.

ABIGAIL. Fine, make it quick. Don't monologue. It's just weak.

PROFESSOR DAVIS. Kimmi—I'm not the man you think I am.

ABIGAIL. Guess we're monologuing.

KIMMI. You can say that again.

CIERA. He's not the man you think he is.

KIMMI. *(Sarcastically.)* Oh, thanks.

PROFESSOR DAVIS. I'm highly skilled in the field of deception. A bit of a master actor.

KIMMI. Omigosh—you have a PhD in theater? You're not even a real professor then, are you?

PROFESSOR DAVIS. No, not quite.

Professor Davis turns to Abigail and Ciera.

PROFESSOR DAVIS. I think I'll change now . . .

CIERA. Ewwwww . . .

ABIGAIL. Nobody wants to watch you change.

KIMMI. I'm so confused.

ABIGAIL. Just—go behind that rock. I'll finish your monologue. I'm better at it anyway.

PROFESSOR DAVIS. Fine.

Professor Davis steps behind a large rock.

ABIGAIL. You ready?

PROFESSOR DAVIS. *(Unseen.)* Yep!

Abigail begins to use a wavy motion from her hands as powerful magic sound effects are heard and smoke is emitted from behind the rock. Abigail monologues as her hands dance.

ABIGAIL. Our ugly traitor of a sister, Vivian, almost got away with running away and letting you get the treasure and keeping us away from you. We would've just gone back to our nap and waited for her to come back with you in tow—if she'd have been a better liar. But she's just a terrible goody two shoes, isn't she? Can't even craft a good lie. No, I had to take matters into my own hands and get you myself. Vivian was never to be trusted.

KIMMI. I don't care what Vivian did to you—you probably deserved it. Who is Frank Davis?

ABIGAIL. Ugh, you're insufferable. I can see why you and Vivian became friends.

KIMMI. Who is Frank Davis??

ABIGAIL. We tricked you, Kimmi. We got you so good. All this time . . . Wow! He really is good at what he does, isn't he?

KIMMI. I don't get it—

ABIGAIL. The man you thought was Professor Davis when you went to the train station . . .

PAREZCO. *(Unseen.)* I am the master of impressions!

ABIGAIL. . . . was this Bozo!

Parezco enters. Abigail and Ciera cackle.

PAREZCO. I am . . . Parezco!

KIMMI. You have got to be kidding me. That guy?? Gosh, I can't stand that guy.

ABIGAIL. Made us promise a bit more than I was willing to pay, but we knew you just blindly trusted everything that the professor said to you. We had

Bozo over here do his thing and you fell for it.

PAREZCO. My impression work is like magic.

ABIGAIL. Of course, I gave him some actual magic to help with his appearance.

PAREZCO. C'mon Kimmi, how was my portrayal of your dear old professor?

KIMMI. Honestly?

PAREZCO. You're a well-educated critic. Give me a review!

KIMMI. Pretty bad. Like, awful. I knew something was weird the moment I saw you. I mean, you looked and sounded exactly like him, but c'mon—that was only because of magic. You didn't get the mannerisms, the quirks and—OMIGOSH! What did you do with the real Frank Davis??

ABIGAIL. The Professor Frank Davis and his mistress were knocked out cold on the couch with medium-sized bumps on their heads.

CIERA. I got to whack 'em.

ABIGAIL. Rest assured, Kimmi, your dear old professor will be fine. We knocked him out just long enough to wake up in the morning. He'll wake up to know both the treasure—and his intern—are gone forever.

KIMMI. Right. I forgot—you're going to kill me.

PAREZCO. I still think that's a little much. I mean, you're going to get the treasure, right? And give me ten percent? Why does the girl have to die? That seems weak.

KIMMI. He's not wrong.

ABIGAIL. We'll discuss your cut and your understanding of villainy later, bozo.

PAREZCO. Yes ma'am.

A train whistle is heard. Diana, Captain Boggs, Vivian, and Scott fall onto the outside of the train car. Diana dusts herself off.

DIANA. Let's never do that again, now, shall we?

CAPTAIN BOGGS. Jumping outta train at my age's not my idea a'fun anymore.

DIANA. Thank my lucky stars nobody's hurt—

The train is heard chugging, evidently moving again.

SCOTT. Yes—we're going to save Kimmi and get the treasure. And fight the witches. And the professor . . . Here we go.

Vivian leads Scott, Diana, and Captain Boggs offstage. A train whistle is heard, shifting the focus to the witches.

ABIGAIL. Ciera! Bozo! To the garden! Thanks in advance for the transplant, Kimmi.

Abigail draws a dagger, with a murderous glint in her eyes.

ABIGAIL. From the bottom of my cold, icy heart.

KIMMI. Transpl—*(Eyes go wide.)* what? Wh—omigosh—you're actually . . .

going to kill me.

Abigail, Ciera, and Parezco cackle as they drag Kimmi offstage as she screams. A perilous, runaway train is heard in the background amid the cackling, whistling a couple times as the lights dim.

.

Lo, How a Rose E'er Blooming

Act Two, Scene 5

The Cave of the Thousand-Year Rose—an identical setup to the very first scene. At center stage, there is a raised stone pot filled with soil. An elegant rose is carved or painted on the side of the pot.

It's nighttime. Crickets chirp, lights are dim. The Gardener, hooded, meanders the garden, humming a tune in a minor key to himself, as he plants seeds methodically. It appears he has done this for a thousand years . . . because he has. He stops humming after a couple moments, not stopping his work for a second. He continues making his rounds through the garden as he speaks, to nobody in particular.

GARDENER.
On this night, a heart is shattered
For all things good had disappeared.
E'en so, a garden grows in the cave—
While the rose waits a thousand years.

Abigail, Ciera, and Parezco drag Kimmi into the scene. The Gardener appears to pay them no attention, continuing his labor. Abigail corners Kimmi with her dagger.

ABIGAIL. All right, Kimmi, new idea: I have a proposition for you.

KIMMI. Okay.

ABIGAIL. What if I don't kill you?

KIMMI. I like that. I like that a lot.

ABIGAIL. You see, I've had a change of heart.

CIERA. Awww!! I'm so proud of you!

ABIGAIL. It's no longer necessary to kill you.

KIMMI. *(Sarcastically.)* I couldn't agree more . . .

Abigail backs up to the X in front of the Thousand-Year Rose as she lowers the dagger.

ABIGAIL. So I'll just . . .let you go with my . . .change of heart.

KIMMI. Uh . . . what?

Abigail steps on the X. There is a flash of crimson lightning and a violent roar of thunder. The Gardener drops his equipment and looks up from his work, locking his eyes on Abigail. Kimmi clutches her heart in shellshock, like she's seen a jump scare.

KIMMI. Omigosh!!

GARDENER. Someone sets their feet before the Thousand-Year Rose.

The Gardener crooks his bony finger out toward Abigail and comes to a conclusion.

GARDENER. It will not bloom for you.

As if nothing happened at all, the Gardener resumes his work.

CIERA. Huh. It didn't bloom for you, either.

ABIGAIL. We're witches, Ciera. You seem to forget.

GARDENER.
At dawn, the rose shall bloom
When the pure of heart draw near
The wicked may seek its beauty,
But the treasure they'll ne'er find here.

ABIGAIL. Okay . . . Riddle man over here is really annoying—I got the pure of heart down here—isn't that enough?

KIMMI. Well, even if your heart actually did change . . . you still couldn't get the treasure.

ABIGAIL. What are you talking about?

Kimmi is not a great liar.

KIMMI. There's still the . . . uh . . . artifacts.

ABIGAIL. Artifacts?

KIMMI. Yeah. In order to ensure someone with a pure heart who truly cared to seek the treasure would find it, Desrosier . . . Omigosh—that gardener guy has to be Desrosier. Desrosier. Rose. Thousand-Year Rose. Wow, this guy really got the mileage out of his name, didn't he?

ABIGAIL. What do artifacts have to do with any of this??

KIMMI. Desrosier sealed the treasure with two spells—one on the rose that would only bloom for a pure heart a thousand years later—

ABIGAIL. Yeah. Everyone knows that.

KIMMI. And then he also hid five artifacts around the city of Hanenbough that the pure heart must present before the rose when the thousand years pass.

ABIGAIL. You're bluffing. What did he hide, since you know so much?

KIMMI. Uh . . . well . . . obviously, there's the locket that had the treasure map inside. And . . . then he hid a brooch in the old theater and a flask-shaped . . . flask at the church in the forest. There was a . . . skeleton key in Castle Coca Féir., and . . .

Kimmi sees the dagger in Abigail's hand.

KIMMI. A dagger.

ABIGAIL. So even though we have you and you've got this pure heart thing . . .

KIMMI. You can't get the treasure because you don't have the artifacts. And neither do I.

Vivian, Scott, Diana, and Captain Boggs burst into the garden.

CAPTAIN BOGGS. Kimmi!

ABIGAIL. A little late to the garden party now, aren't we? Did the search for magical artifacts hold you all up?

Blank stares all around. Abigail turns to Kimmi.

ABIGAIL. Well, that's certainly suspicious. Your friends seem to know nothing about these artifacts. Ciera—hold her down. Bozo—check her bag!

Ciera holds Kimmi down and Parezco takes Kimmi's bag from her, dumping it out. Some personal artifacts fall out (a candy bar, a cell phone, etc.), but none of Desrosier's items.

PAREZCO. Well, I can see someone's into couponing . . . Hmm . . . No, I got nothing.

DIANA. Ugh—what is Parezco doing here?

PAREZCO. My, my, sweetheart—

DIANA. Please don't call me that. You are not the King yet, and I'll hate to be your Queen.

PAREZCO. After our auditions today, I went and got a quick job as a Frank Davis impersonator! I'm getting a very nice check.

CAPTAIN BOGGS. Frankie—so . . . wait—

ABIGAIL. Long story. I don't have time to go over it with all of you. So Kimmi—why don't you go ahead and "set your feet before the Thousand-Year Rose"? X marks the spot!

Parezco and Ciera hold Kimmi and drag her toward the X. Kimmi attempts to go limp to slow their progress.

ABIGAIL. Now I have to think of what delicious end you will all meet once I'm done with Kimmi—

SCOTT. *(Soberly powerful.)* No.

ABIGAIL. You'll defy me?

SCOTT. Yes. I will. And so will your sister.

ABIGAIL. Vivian! Oh, Vivian—I almost forgot about you. What do you have to say for yourself? Disgracing the family and all?

VIVIAN. I did what was right.

ABIGAIL. But you are a witch. Doing what is right is a little different when you're evil—which is kinda, y'know, the point of being a witch.

VIVIAN. Yes. I'm a witch. I'm a woman who can do magic. That is what it means to be a witch—nothing else. Hate is a choice. Evil is a choice.

ABIGAIL. *(Mockingly.)* Well done, Vivian, there's your degree put to use. Six minus four?

Vivian spitefully holds up two fingers.

VIVIAN. Do your own math.

Abigail is taken aback.

ABIGAIL. Well—you might've done what was right, but you lost. All of you lost. And I'll hold—

Abigail swipes her hand and holds it out, producing a magic sound effect as she puts Scott, Diana, Vivian, and Captain Boggs in a magic chokehold.

ABIGAIL. —all of you here to watch me walk away with the treasure, because now our chosen one is standing before the Thousand-Year Rose—and she will make that thing bloom.

DIANA. *(Painfully eked out.)* Kimmi, do something!

Kimmi looks back and forth.

KIMMI. Quick! Ciera—let me go.

Ciera drops her hold on Kimmi.

CIERA. Okay!

Kimmi pushes Abigail and runs offstage. This causes Abigail to break focus and drop her hold on Scott, Diana, Vivian, and Captain Boggs.

ABIGAIL. Wait—after her!

Abigail, Ciera, and Parezco run after Kimmi. We hear a fight occur offstage. Scott, Diana, Vivian, and Captain Boggs look back and forth at each other in confusion as they get up. Professor Davis—the real Professor Davis—emerges with an ice pack on his head, tantalized by the setting.

PROFESSOR DAVIS. Just as I saw it years ago . . . like not a single day had passed. Mystifying!

Kimmi emerges triumphantly behind Professor Davis.

KIMMI. Wow—that was super lucky you and Maryann were here in time. I definitely needed backup there.

Maryann enters, putting her earrings back in and evidently blowing some sweat, blood, and Ciera's tears off of her arms, having just come from a fight.

SCOTT. Grandma!

MARYANN. Scott!

Scott hugs Maryann.

DIANA. What happened to you?

MARYANN. I saw Kimmi start a fight with the witches and that weird impressionist guy and she needed help. They won't be going anywhere anytime soon.

CAPTAIN BOGGS. Y'laid a beatin' on'em?

DIANA. A woman of your age?

MARYANN. How could I not? After all, I am a Krav Maga instructor.

KIMMI. Omigosh—so earlier when I just kinda said that?

MARYANN. I was shocked!

KIMMI. So . . . what happened to you two?

MARYANN. We were almost out the door when one of those witches came and hit us over the head.

PROFESSOR DAVIS. Kathleen came and found us, so we weren't out long. You didn't answer your phone and we knew you were headed to the garden. We hopped in a cab and came as quickly as we could, but—

Professor Davis removes the ice pack from his head.

PROFESSOR DAVIS. What on earth has happened? It seems we missed something big.

KIMMI. You had an impersonator.

PROFESSOR DAVIS. An . . . impersonator? That sounds exciting!

KIMMI. Exciting . . . is one word to describe it. They kidnapped me, dragged me down here—

SCOTT. While we got on the train and headed for Haystack Station—

DIANA. But then the train broke down—

VIVIAN. So then I blew up a wall on the train with magic and then we jumped out—

CAPTAIN BOGGS. An' then we came down t'the garden an' you found us.

KIMMI. Wow. That's awesome!

PROFESSOR DAVIS. Simply astounding!

VIVIAN. Kimmi—now that we're safe . . . let's get that rose to bloom, yes?

Kimmi nods. In the process of crossing to Kimmi, Vivian inadvertently steps on the X. There is a flash of crimson lightning and roar of thunder. The Gardener abruptly stands up, drops his equipment, and cranes his neck to see Vivian, who has stopped in her tracks.

GARDENER. Someone sets their feet before the Thousand-Year Rose.

The Gardener crooks his finger out toward Vivian and smiles as he waves his hand in the direction of the rose. The rose grows and blooms in one fluid motion as everyone—very much including Vivian—is in awe of what is happening. Abigail and Ciera enter, beaten up. Abigail is livid.

GARDENER. Behold—the Thousand-Year Rose.

ABIGAIL. You have got to be kidding me. All this time the pure heart was Vivian?

KIMMI. Yes. I wasn't "the chosen one." I mean, none of us were. Vivian has a pure heart. But so does Doc. And Scott. And Diana. And Boggs. And Maryann—

ABIGAIL. *(Cutting her off.)* Well so what, Kimmi? None of that even matters! The rose bloomed and now the treasure is mine. Ciera! We dig!

Ciera and Abigail cackle as they dig on the X to discover a small treasure chest. Abigail opens the chest and is disgusted that it's just a meager collection of coins.

ABIGAIL. You expect us to take over the world with this? This is ridiculous. Come on, Ciera. Let's leave these losers in the dust. There is no treasure of Hanenbough.

Abigail and Ciera exit as they leave the treasure chest behind on the cave floor.

Kimmi picks up the treasure chest and opens it, inspecting the little collection of gold coins.

KIMMI. Well, here's our treasure. This is fine, I guess. I was kinda expecting like a more obscene amount of treasure, y'know? This is kinda . . . Well, it's not that. I'm not disappointed, I'm just . . confused. Was any of this worth all the effort you've put into it? That any of us put into it?

PROFESSOR DAVIS. Of course it was, Ms. Larkin. I was trying to say earlier tonight that the treasure is as real as you and me. It's not been about what's inside that chest.

Professor Davis gestures to his heart.

PROFESSOR DAVIS. It's been about what's inside this one. Think about it. All of you: think about the treasure you found on the way to the rose.

As the adventure party ponders what they may have found, Gardener offers his poem.

GARDENER.
  One dark night, a heart was shattered
  For all that was good had disappeared.
  E'en so, a garden grows in the cave
  While the rose waits a thousand years.
  At dawn, the rose has bloomed
  For the pure of heart drew near.
  The wicked have sought the beauty
  But the treasure they ne'er found here.
  For the treasure is the beating heart
  Held fast in grips of fear.

The Gardener crosses to the Thousand-Year Rose and gently plucks it from the pot.

GARDENER.
  When the gales thrash the ocean
  And the rolling thunder leers—

The Gardener places the rose in Kimmi's hands. Kimmi drops the treasure chest at her feet.

GARDENER.
  E'en so, a garden grows in the cave
  While the rose waits a thousand years.

All hang in hushed reverence as they look on each other and realize they have each found the treasure they were meant to discover—Kimmi, Scott, Diana, Vivian, Captain Boggs, Professor Davis, and Maryann.

Kimmi looks at the rose in her hand and takes in the moment.

KIMMI. Wow.

Kimmi and Professor Davis smile back and forth at each other.

The hushed reverence continues for just another moment. Kimmi turns to Professor Davis with a puzzled look on her face.

KIMMI. So what are we doing for the rest of the summer, Doc?

THE END.

SEE AMID THE WINTER SNOW
est. 2018

PETER FENTON

In stillness or in snowstorm, true love is measured by who you will show up for — and who shows up for you. My whole life, you've always made Christmastime special and more importantly, you've taught me everything I know about loving well in friendship and romance. *See Amid the Winter Snow* is dedicated to Mom and Dad.

See Amid is also dedicated to my Midwest mama, IdaLynn, to whom I'm grateful with my life that she bet Jim Fenton an ice cream sundae he couldn't get a date with Beth from the front desk.

Author's Preface to See Amid the Winter Snow

P ractically every artist puts out a Christmas album at some point in their career. Maybe it's a cynical cash grab, maybe it's a letter from the heart born out of love for the season, maybe it's a little both—but here's my Christmas album. Welcome to Santa Claus's North Pole, welcome to *See Amid the Winter Snow*.

Every Christmas Eve when I was a kid, my siblings and I would leave a letter for Santa Claus alongside whatever milk and cookie offerings we had for him that year. We'd ask about things like the reindeer, or Mrs. Claus, or if he had any children of his own—and every year, my father, Jim Fenton, would write a detailed letter back in character as Santa Claus. In these replies, alongside some thinly-veiled pleas for the Fenton children to be kind and share their toys, my father would spin these rich stories of Santa's day-to-day life at the North Pole, with clever references to holiday media worked seamlessly into Santa's speaking voice. It made Santa Claus and the lore surrounding the North Pole all the more real for these three children with wild imaginations. And so, in a way, *See Amid the Winter Snow* is a journey through a yuletide world I've built in my head from my boyhood in the '90s, all thanks to my dad's clever storytelling.

This fantasy world in the Great White North was laid dormant when I stopped believing in Santa Claus (I do have to hand it to my dad, though, his elaborate stories kept me on the hook believing in Santa far longer than the average child), but returned when I was on my journey of self-discovery.

I think in many life stories, there is a familiar, traceable pattern to our relationships with self and shame we follow: first, we know who we really are as kids—we follow our instincts and unbridled passions and let ourselves run wild. As teenagers, then, when we become aware that other people have opinions and we want to measure up to whomever we wish to impress, we internalize a degree of shame toward whoever we were as kids, and then in adulthood, if we do the proper work on ourselves to deconstruct the influence of others—whether it is real or perceived—we can fully re-discover that person we were so proud to be as children.

I very fondly look back on my junior year at Wheaton College as one of the most formative times of my life. When the class film festival left me ready to throw out my writing career before it really began at the end of sophomore year, I had taken junior year as an opportunity to give myself a second chance. While I do not envy going through the experience of all that uncertainty I held about who I was made to be or what I was going to do about him, I so appreciate just how free I was in that window of time to explore my own personality and follow what came naturally.

One of those things that came naturally to me was singing. While I had already been in the world of theatre for quite some time, I really had not invested much in singing—which is odd, for a couple of reasons. For pretty much my entire post-pubescent life, people have commented on my deep speaking voice and asked me if I sing, and prior to junior year, I would kind of shy back and deflect—maybe I would even change the subject—but I did always love to sing, whether I was a kid repeating nursery school rhymes, a member of the drama club in high school, or a member of the worship team at summer camp. I had always admired the Wheaton College Men's Glee Club and when I stopped fearing judgment from others (and most importantly, I stopped fearing judgment from myself), I followed my instincts to audition and joined the club in the fall semester of 2015.

There was such thoughtfully silly energy pulsating through every aspect of my experience with the Men's Glee Club at Wheaton—our warm-ups at rehearsals, our social activities, our lore that was attached to various relics passed between members year in and year out—it was truly an environment that encouraged me to embrace the imagination I've been blessed with and provided no shortage of inspiration for future work—very much including *See Amid the Winter Snow*.

"See Amid the Winter Snow" is the title of a relatively obscure Christmas carol, but it was part of our Glee Club set for the 2015 Wheaton College Christmas Festival. When our conductor introduced the piece to us, she had indicated this song was a classic and an old favorite of hers, but nonetheless, here I was, face-to-face with the song for the very first time. The lyrics to this nineteenth-century English carol by Edward Caswell go,

> *"See amid the winter snow,*
> *Born for us on earth below—*
> *See the tender lamb appear,*
> *Promised from eternal years.*
> *Hail, thou ever-blessed morn!*
> *Hail, redemption's happy dawn!*
> *Sing through all Jerusalem—*
> *Christ is born in Bethlehem!"*

My imagination ran wild as these lyrics washed over me. I fell in love with this hymn, how the very title commands the listener to look in the middle of everything going on around them—in the case of this song, the winter snow—so they may comprehend what is of lasting importance—the birth of Christ. It's a powerful image and a beautiful title that stuck with me through the writing of *The Thousand-Year Rose*, all the way to when I ultimately wrote this script after graduating from Wheaton. *See Amid* premiered as part of the 2019 Fringe Theater Festival in Philadelphia, directed by my dear friend Amanda Pasquini and we co-produced it with Chelsea Cylinder, who originated the role of Daisy Scarlett.

I don't think there is too much more fanfare I need to give to properly introduce you to *See Amid*. I say this not because I think it's a lesser work than *Good Knight and Goodbye* or *The Thousand-Year Rose*, but when I think about where this work fits in the overall canon of Peterfentonland, *Knight* and *Rose* were each earth-shaking for my life direction and personal growth, and I thus have a lot of emotion tied up in those. *Knight* was my first time trying my hand at writing, *Rose* was deciding to take the next step, and now *See Amid*? On a personal development level, it was nothing more than taking the next step after that. It's the first work I wrote as an adult.

What you hold in your hands with *See Amid*, independent of my own lived experience as the author, probably will feel very much in line with what I've written in *Knight* and *Rose*. Perhaps you will see some growth from work to work, but at the end of the day, what really is *See Amid*? It's a silly little Christmas play. Nothing more, nothing less.

I pray this one brings a smile to your face, since life is too short for bad holiday media.

The Sundae Bet

Act One, Scene 1

T he North Pole, The Present. The set is ultimately simple to allow for varied locations to be communicated through a couple set pieces. We see a backdrop of a snowy, Christmassy forest. At upstage center is a magnificent, stationary Christmas tree, seen as a fixture throughout the entire play.

It's a peaceful cold. We are at a snowy woodpile outside a converted shed apartment, just down the hill from Santa's Workshop at the North Pole. A lone tree stump with an axe stuck into the center is surrounded by logs and firewood. A young urban professional-type elf enters the scene and splits logs one-by-one on the stump with the axe. This is MITCHELL.

Into the scene strolls a SNOWMAN, a muppet-like full homage to Burl Ives' character in Rudolph the Red-Nosed Reindeer. His given name is Frosti. He speaks with a warm country twang, like Dolly Parton.

SNOWMAN. I've lived a good, long life for a snowman. Now most of you folk don't ever realize it, but when you're a Snowman—you're lucky if you even live a week. There's a few considerations to keep in mind: If the weather's gonna change—yer gone. If the neighborhood kids decide to get real mean and knock y'down—yeah, yer gone. If, say, the magic ice queen learns how to control her powers learning the power of love and bringin' summer back to her kingdom—

Snowman grins, completely in on the joke.

SNOWMAN. "Let it Go", 'cause yer gone, baby! But I'm a lucky old bag of ice. Now the secret to my very long life is that I live at the North Pole—no matter when in the year you visit, step out on those city sidewalks—in the air, there's a feeling of Christmas. You can go to the meadow and build your own snowman, pretend he's Parson Brown for all I care—

Snowman realizes he's gotten off track.

SNOWMAN. My point is—I've lived a long time and I ain't going nowhere until global warmin' gets me. So I maybe got a week, so listen up: I wanna impart some wisdom to you youngins before I'm . . . neutralized.

Mitchell exits.

SNOWMAN. Now I have a few stories from my day, but even if I lived a hundred years, I'd never forget the story of Mitchell and Daisy.

Act One, Scene 2

North Pole House Party, Two Years Ago. Snowman stands at center stage. The rest of the cast enters, in party attire. Mitchell enters from one side of the stage, DAISY and IDALYNN from the other. Mitchell is holding a cup of punch. Daisy and Mitchell make eye contact.

SNOWMAN. Now yes, at the time there was a nasty fight for city hall—

Daisy and IdaLynn cross to the dance floor area.

SNOWMAN. And yes, the elves went on strike, but that's not the entire story here—

Mitchell notices the two lady elves—Daisy is intuitive, feminine, and creative with a heart warm enough to melt the North Pole. The other, her cousin IdaLynn, is wily and pragmatic with a low tolerance for nonsense. She sports an engagement ring.

DAISY. There's no way this works.

IDALYNN. There's no way this doesn't work! I'd club him in the head and drag him over to meet ya if I could.

IdaLynn waves to Mitchell as he sips his punch. Mitchell spits out his punch a little. IdaLynn nudges Daisy, as if to say, "Here we go!"

SNOWMAN. Because buried in that avalanche of news and politics and what-have-you was the simple story of Mitchell and Daisy.

Mitchell crosses to Daisy and IdaLynn on the dance floor. Daisy and IdaLynn grin.

IDALYNN. Hey-hey! Never thought I'd get ya on the dance floor tonight!!

MITCHELL. I'm just full of surprises.

IDALYNN. Well anyway, Mitch—I've told you about my cousin Daisy, right?

Mitchell and Daisy make eye contact.

MITCHELL. Yes. Yes, you have.

Act One, Scene 3
Mitchell's Office, The Next Day. Mitchell sits at his desk, picking at a little bit of food. IdaLynn sits across from him with her lunch.

MITCHELL. So what's the deal with Daisy?

IDALYNN. She had a great time with you last night!

MITCHELL. Oh yeah?

IDALYNN. And she's been going on and on about wanting to double date with Jerry and me sometime.

MITCHELL. *(Gesturing to IdaLynn's ring.)* Congrats—by the way!

IdaLynn flashes her ring.

IDALYNN. Oh thank you!! Jerry really went all out-

MITCHELL. It's a nice ring. You're a solid couple. I mean, if I ever got engaged . . . I'd definitely hope—

IDALYNN. Hmm?

MITCHELL. Never mind.

IDALYNN. Well funny ya mention that—would ya maybe wanna go out sometime?

MITCHELL. I—really?

IDALYNN. All four of us? Me and Jerry, you and Daisy?

MITCHELL. You're asking me out . . . for her?

IDALYNN. Don't be ridiculous, Mitch. I'm telling you that ya need to ask her out!

MITCHELL. Not really. You're setting up a double date and asking me to be

part of it with a girl I just met and—

IDALYNN. Ah-ha! You see the problem too. See, Jerry and I just bought a house, we're getting married—I'm not in a million years letting Day bring a first date-

MITCHELL. Well. I don't think I can do that. I'm really busy with work and I—

IdaLynn laughs.

IDALYNN. You know what I think? I think you're scared. I bet you think you *can't* get a date with Daisy.

Mitchell laughs.

MITCHELL. You bet?

IDALYNN. Let's make a bet, Mitch. I bet you won't get a date with Daisy.

MITCHELL. You're ridiculous.

IDALYNN. How 'bout for an ice cream sundae? From Lickity Split's?

MITCHELL. How many toppings?

IDALYNN. Five. Seven. All of them. I don't care!

MITCHELL. What's her number?

Act One, Scene 4
Various Locations Around the North Pole (a Boutique Coffee Shop, Mitchell's Apartment, Town Square, and a Painting Studio), montage over the course of a

year. IdaLynn exits. We hear happy couple music play. Daisy is seated at a table in the Coffee Shop.

Mitchell crosses to Daisy, carrying two coffees. He sits down next to her. They kiss.

Mitchell and Daisy cross to Mitchell's Apartment and sit on a couch, each holding a glass of wine. Mitchell and Daisy clink their glasses as Daisy kisses Mitchell on the cheek.

Mitchell and Daisy cross to Town Square, holding hands. Mitchell and Daisy walk upstage, hand-in-hand, pointing out all the interesting things they see.

Mitchell and Daisy cross to the Painting Studio. They pick up finished identical still life paintings and pose with them. Snowman enters and takes their picture.

SNOWMAN. Ahhh! Perfect!

Daisy and Mitchell look at each other. They kiss as the happy couple montage music ends.

In the Name of Christmas Magic

Act One, Scene 5

Granny's Cottage, The Next Day. The cottage set fills one side of the stage. There is a menorah displayed somewhere in the living room. Daisy sits on the couch, doing something mindless.

Daisy hears a knock at the door.

MITCHELL. *(Offstage.)* Daisy!

Daisy grins and opens the door. Mitchell is holding a present.

DAISY. What are you doing, I thought we weren't gonna do gifts this y—?

MITCHELL. I know. I just think you'd like this. Open it!

Daisy opens the gift, pulling out a distinctive red coat—bringing to mind Red Riding Hood.

DAISY. Oh, Mitch! I was just thinking about going out and getting something like this.

MITCHELL. I'm glad I wrote that down.

DAISY. What?

Mitchell pulls out a small notebook and flips to a page.

DAISY. *(Grins.)* You take notes on our dates? And just—carry that notebook around?

Mitchell flashes a shy smile.

MITCHELL. You think it's weird?

DAISY. Of course it's weird! But I love it. You're so . . .thoughtful—

MITCHELL. Thoughtful gift-giving is definitely in my blood. So to speak.

DAISY. Oh, really now?

Daisy and Mitchell kiss. They continue their conversation inaudibly as our attention is drawn to the other side of the stage. Santa's Workshop fills the other side of the stage.

Santa's Workshop, The Previous Night. It's completely still. The room is dark. A workbench of half-finished toys lines the center of the room. Along the wall are several boxes of completed toys for delivery. We linger just a moment too long in the silence, it grows eerie.

Suddenly—a CRASH!! Glass shatters.

A MYSTERIOUS FIGURE enters Santa's Workshop, on a mission. They make a beeline toward the boxes of toys. The dim lights on the break-in at Santa's Workshop go out.

Meanwhile, as we return to the other side of the stage, Daisy has put on the red coat. She's pacing, nervous.

DAISY. I can't believe—all this time together and I'm only meeting your parents now.

MITCHELL. Well, you know they're busy elves.

Mitchell notices Daisy is tense about the whole thing and attempts to console her.

MITCHELL. I'm an only child, so it's going to be tough no matter who I'm dating. It's not like I have a brother out there making worse decisions for them to make comparisons.

DAISY. *(Playful eye roll.)* You, sir, are a shoe-in to win boyfriend of the year. No matter who they are or how much power they have, at the end of the day—your parents are just elves doing their best.

Mitchell's eyes light up. He pulls out his notebook and scribbles down the quip.

MITCHELL. I like that! You came up with it yourself?

DAISY. Yes, but actually believing it is a different thing altogether.

MITCHELL. That it is.

Mitchell and Daisy exit.

Act One, Scene 6

Santa's Workshop, Later That Day. The workshop set fills the entire stage—it's something of a crime scene, having been ransacked the previous night. Snowman enters.

SNOWMAN. Now, Christmas was coming in just a few weeks, so the rush at the workshop was picking—Oh! I plumb forgot to tell you what Mitchell even does for a living. Silly me. Mitchell handles Public Relations at Santa's

Workshop.

SANTA CLAUS enters, cleaning up debris he can find—slowly. Physically, he's exactly who you think Santa Claus would be, very closely resembling the traditional American interpretation from "A Visit from St. Nicholas."

SNOWMAN. And I just want to give some peace of mind to all you kids out there: the rumors you've heard—they're not true. Santa Claus is as real as I am. And he's gettin' old.

SANTA. What's that now?

SNOWMAN. That's not any kinda judgment—it's become a lot to handle for the right jolly old elf, so he put together an elite office staff. There's Lachelle in Elven Resources, Brian handles payroll, and IdaLynn is his right-hand lady.

IdaLynn enters the workshop and crosses to Santa. She carries a tablet.

IDALYNN. Hey-hey!

SANTA. I thought you left hours ago, what're you still doing here?

IDALYNN. Oh I did! Worked on the house for a bit. We're tiling the backsplash! Anyway, I came back to finish organizing the reports from Ireland.

SANTA. Anything interesting?

IDALYNN. Yes, actually! There was a girl—think her name was Vivian—she blew up a train back in May and she still earned a spot on the Nice List. You should check it out, the report was insane!

IdaLynn closes the file and looks around.

IDALYNN. But Santa, what on earth happened here?

SANTA. Small break-in. Just a box of toys missing—

IDALYNN. Small break-in??

SANTA. I'm not worried.

IDALYNN. Uh. Okay. G'night, Santa!

IdaLynn exits. Santa is more distraught than he's leading on. MAUREEN GAINES CLAUS enters, carrying two mugs. While her husband is a traditional interpretation of Santa Claus, Mrs. Claus is anything but. She's a pantsuit politician type in the vein of America's Hillary Rodham Clinton or Kamala Harris; or Germany's Angela Merkel.

MAUREEN. Eggnog, dear?

Santa takes a mug and sips.

SNOWMAN. Sure, folks know Santa has a wife, but that's usually the end of it. But y'all should know—*(Air quotes.)* "Santa's Wife"—is Maureen Gaines Claus, beloved Mayor of the North Pole. She's been mayorin' about as long as Santa's been deliverin'.

MAUREEN. Sorry I couldn't come sooner—busy day in my office. Was anything stolen?

SANTA. A couple tools. A box of toys.

MAUREEN. Who would have any reason to do such a thing?

Santa chugs his eggnog as Snowman steps forward.

SNOWMAN. Yes Virginia, Santa's Workshop felt the pinch of global population growth and his answer was as follows: Sometime in the late 90s, he quietly bought a factory in Shenzhen—*(Clarifying.)* China—to keep up producing enough toys to supply to all the good kids in the world. Santa took a pay cut and the elves were put on pay freeze—still workin' full time with benefits. No one lost their jobs to folks in China. But Santa chose to keep his solution a complete secret. Those of you who have kids out there—and maybe those of you who were kids once—might understand why he thought it was a good idea to not be truthful in the name of "Christmas magic".

Santa sets the mug down as he and Maureen resume picking up debris. Snowman exits.

SANTA. How was work, dear?

MAUREEN. Today's not really been our day, Kris Kringle.

SANTA. I've never understood that name.

MITCHELL. *(Offstage.)* Mom? Dad?

Mitchell and Daisy enter.

MITCHELL. Hello?

Maureen and Santa set the debris down and cross to Mitchell and Daisy. Maureen hugs Mitchell.

MAUREEN. Mitchell! And there she is! Hello, Daisy!

Maureen hugs Daisy. Daisy shakes Santa's hand. Mitchell surveys the surround-

ings.

MITCHELL. Dad, what happened here? Has the press seen this yet?

SANTA. Nothing of value was stolen. Just a box of toys, really—

MAUREEN. Now, Daisy—tell me anything! Everything! How'd you meet?

DAISY. Well, a little over a year ago, my cousin IdaLynn and I were at Lachelle's house party, and she introduced me to Mitch—we had a great time that night, but he was too scared—

MITCHELL. Not "scared"—

DAISY. *(Grinning.)* Mitch was too scared to ask me out, so Ida made him a little bet—

MAUREEN. Oh, yes—the sundae bet! And you're a teacher?

DAISY. Yep! I teach fourth grade at Blazing Yule, mostly science and language arts. We're right across the street from you at City Hall.

MAUREEN. We'll have to get lunch sometime. It's funny you mentioned City Hall, though. Mind if I change the subject?

DAISY. Go right ahead.

MAUREEN. Today I received word that Ebenezer Whitfield has filed official paperwork and will be challenging my seat.

Santa laughs; dismissive.

MITCHELL. The name rings a bell—

DAISY. Who's Ebenezer Whitfield?

MAUREEN. He's . . . Oh, he's harmless. He runs that penguin slash polar bear farm outside the Village. So my decision has been made: I will seek another term as mayor. I love my job and I know I'm good at it.

MITCHELL. *(To Daisy.)* She has a JD, graduated with honors.

DAISY. No kidding!

MAUREEN. I suppose I could retire and just be "Mrs. Claus": staying home, baking cookies, and hosting teas—but I'm deciding to continue fulfilling my profession, which I began long before I settled down with Santa. *(Taps Santa on the shoulder.)* No offense.

SANTA. None taken.

MITCHELL. Fair enough.

MAUREEN. Which brings me to Mitchell. Will you run the campaign?

MITCHELL. I can't walk away from my full-time job, can I?

SANTA. You are head of Public Relations at Santa's Workshop.

MITCHELL. I speak on behalf of our company so we maintain appearances and everything comes out in our favor.

SANTA. And what does an average day amount to, son?

A beat.

MITCHELL. I split a lot of firewood for you.

Maureen scribbles a number down on scrap paper. She hands the paper to Mitchell and Daisy.

MAUREEN. Right. So—here is the stipend I'm offering you:

Mitchell can't believe what he's reading. He babbles. Daisy helps make sense of Mitchell's babbling.

DAISY. He'll do it.

MITCHELL. All right. I suppose I'm running your campaign.

Daisy beams.

MAUREEN. Launch week starts a month from today. I've already booked an exclusive with Channel 7, an interview with the N.P.T., and then on Friday I'll preside over the Reindeer Games.

Maureen, Mitchell, and Daisy exit. IdaLynn enters, carrying a box appearing to be opened and resealed.

IDALYNN. This wouldn't happen to be the box of toys you're missing?

SANTA. Might be.

Santa pulls out a pocket knife and slices the box open. The box is full of toys with an envelope tucked to the side. IdaLynn picks up a toy.

IDALYNN. That's weird. I don't recognize any of these—

IdaLynn inspects the label as Santa grabs and pockets the envelope.

IDALYNN. What language is this label?

Santa hastily grabs the toy and box.

SANTA. That's Elvish.

IDALYNN. Santa. We speak Elvish. That looked like some kind of Asian language—

SANTA. Have you met Dan in R&D? Brilliant guy, just came back the other day, he was consulting for Nintendo. Must've slipped into Japanese.

IdaLynn suspects (correctly) that Santa is lying.

IDALYNN. Uh—okay. Whatever. I think I'll go finish tiling my backsplash—

SANTA. Yes, absolutely go home—but when you get a moment, can you review the security footage from last night? Tell me what they were really after?

IDALYNN. Sure. Why?

SANTA. I can't tell you. Yet.

IDALYNN. Uh. Sure thing, Santa!

IdaLynn exits.

Maureen Gaines Claus

Act One, Scene 7

Town Square, a Month Later. Snowman enters and addresses the audience as the set transitions behind him from Santa's Workshop to Town Square. A podium sits at center stage in front of the Christmas tree.

SNOWMAN. Oh, hold your Wassailin' for just a sec, I'll tell you more about IdaLynn and Santa soon, I promise. Mitchell began his work on the re-election campaign for Maureen Gaines Claus—everything was going swimmingly when launch week arrived.

We hear TV news fanfare as certified hunk TV reporter SCHYLER enters, carrying a microphone. He looks like an airbrushed Ken doll—the kind of pretty boy newscaster who can get away with saying anything he wants on television. Thankfully for the viewing public, he's more vain than he is clever.

RITA. *(Offstage.)* We turn it over to Schyler Hines in Town Square. Schyler?

SCHYLER. *(To Audience.)* Hi! Yes, thank you. Thank you. This is happening in a big way. Thank you.

RITA. *(Offstage.)* Schyler??

Schyler checks his earpiece.

SCHYLER. Thank you, Rita. I'm in Town Square and you're watching Channel 7's exclusive coverage of the 2020 North Pole Mayoral Race—shaping up to be the first true contest for the seat in nearly two centuries. Don't think too hard about that.

Maureen enters, escorted by Mitchell and Daisy. Maureen stands at the podium, waving to her constituents.

SCHYLER. Mayor Claus is formally announcing her bid for re-election tonight, with her own son managing her campaign—and word is she has big plans for a new term.

A spotlight shines on Maureen standing at the podium as she begins her speech.

MAUREEN. Good evening—

The spotlight abruptly switches to the Snowman as Maureen silently continues her speech.

SNOWMAN. Now—I'm just bein' real honest here, campaign speeches are boring as sin. So I'm just gonna say I think it's better for all of us if we just skip ahead a bit.

The spotlight switches back to Maureen as she reaches the conclusion of her announcement.

MAUREEN. It's true; I sweat the details of policy, whether we're talking about the exact level of peppermint in the Candy Cane Forest, the number of maple syrup facilities on Avalanche Street, or the cost of your firewood. Because it's not just a detail—it's a big deal. And it should be a big deal to your mayor.

We hear thunderous applause.

MAUREEN. My name is Maureen Gaines Claus—and I'm here to stay!

The crowd cheers.

MITCHELL. All right, for selfies with the Mayor—form a line right over here, Mayor Claus will be with you shortly!

Mitchell helps Maureen down from the podium. Daisy and Mitchell make eye contact and share a lingering smile. Schyler crosses to Maureen.

SCHYLER. It may be cold outside, but I'm here with a Mayor hot off a campaign announcement. Hello there, Mayor Claus!

Act One, Scene 8

Whitfield's Farmhouse, The Same Time. Maureen, Mitchell, Daisy, and Schyler remain on stage in the Town Square Set, which fills most of the stage, but Whitfield's Farmhouse is tucked into an obscure corner of the stage. Schyler continues his interview with Maureen from the previous scene.

SCHYLER. How's it feel to launch your historic campaign? Running for the first time against an official opponent?

A well-to-do mid-career political strategist watches Maureen's interview, looking a little out of place in the humble farmhouse. This elf's entire presentation reminds us of Mitchell in about 15 years. This is ROMULUS WOLF. Snowman crosses to Wolf.

MAUREEN. You know, Schyler, I'm choosing to welcome the challenge. Elves of the North Pole deserve a real voice at the polls and it's my hope that our campaign will demonstrate why a vote for Maureen is a vote for the North Pole.

SCHYLER. Well, I have to say, Ebenezer Whitfield is in for quite a battle—

Wolf furrows his brow as Schyler and Maureen continue the interview, inaudible.

SNOWMAN. Now the elves down in the village liked Maureen a lot—but just on the outskirts of town—Ebenezer Whitfield did not.

Snowman gestures to Wolf.

SNOWMAN. Well, maybe that's not true. Ebenezer Whitfield was—(Notices Wolf.) Oh! No, that's not Whitfield. *(Laughs.)* That's very funny though, I can see how y'all might think that, but—no. This is Romulus Wolf. Now Romulus—oh Lordy. I don't like your name. Did y'ever have a li'l nickname? Rommy? Romney?

WOLF. Call me "Wolf".

SNOWMAN. Okay. I can live with that. Now see, the Wolf—did they ever call you "The Big Bad Wolf"?

WOLF. Let's stick with "Wolf".

SNOWMAN. Now, okay—The Wolf paid a visit to Ebenezer Whitfield to talk him into running for mayor. Wolf was the brains of the operation, and Whitfield was. Hmm . . . Whitfield was . . .

WOLF. Our voters need to take you completely seriously, Ebenezer. They have no idea who you are and we need to make a great first impression—

A simple elf in a flannel shirt tucked into Wrangler jeans with a trucker cap, carries in a plate of bacon. He's also wearing a stained apron. He looks like he would have a more promising career herding moose in Minnesota or governing Alaska than having a real political career. This is EBENEZER WHITFIELD.

WHITFIELD. You can just leave the "taking me seriously" up to me. Bacon?

Snowman exits. Wolf takes a piece of bacon.

WOLF. Claus is going to be tough to beat. You'll get laughed off the stage if we don't do something about *(Gestures to Whitfield.)* This. *(Repeats the gesture.)* "This" does not bode well for us.

Whitfield puts a piece of bacon in his mouth.

WHITFIELD. *(Talking while chewing.)* You need to relax—Mrs. Claus is just a celebrity. And what's a celebrity except your voice is loud and voters know your face? She'll just make her points and know what she's talking about and they'll listen to her and vote her back into off—Oh.

Wolf hands Whitfield a stack of notecards.

WOLF. Exactly. So I got us an interview with Schyler Hines on the 6 O'Clock tonight.

WHITFIELD. You what?

In the Town Square set, Maureen and Schyler shake hands. Maureen crosses to Mitchell and Daisy to cool off.

WOLF. Stick to these notes and you'll be fine.

Whitfield fumbles through the notecards.

WHITFIELD. Remind me why I gotta say all this highfalutin mumbo-jumbo?

WOLF. Having notes in front of you allows both you and I to have peace of mind and total control.

WHITFIELD. You are better at comin' up with words than me.

Schyler crosses to the Farmhouse set. We hear Schyler's trademark news fanfare play.

RITA. *(Offstage.)* We turn it back to you, Schyler.

Snowman enters.

SCHYLER. Thank you, Rita. We are taking a moment to bring you word from Ebenezer Whitfield. I'm ambushing him right now to ask this very important question: What on earth do you have to tell the North Pole today?

Spotlight appears abruptly on Snowman.

SNOWMAN. Now again—I don't like campaign speeches. As you've gathered, Ebb Whitfield isn't the most eloquent fella—

Snowman exits. Spotlight disappears.

WHITFIELD. But before I go, I have to take a moment and refudiate those claims that some elves out there in our great Village think I'm not a professional like Mrs. Claus. I just wanna say—

Wolf nods along off-camera, Whitfield's speech is going perfectly. Whitfield tosses the notecards away.

WHITFIELD. They're right!

WOLF. *(Whisper-shouted.)* Ebenezer!

WHITFIELD. Yeah, she may have her money and she may have her fancy soaps, but nobody knows the system better than me. And I alone can fix it!

SCHYLER. And what kind of change will you bring to the system?

WHITFIELD. Look, you keep your change. I wanna say to all you out there fixin' problems: don't retreat . . . reload!

Schyler glances aside to the audience.

SCHYLER. Yikes. *(Turning to Whitfield.)* Always a pleasure, Mr. Whitfield.

WHITFIELD. Oh, sure!

SCHYLER. Reporting for Channel 7, this is Schyler Hines and I am very attractive. Back to you, Rita.

Schyler exits.

Act One, Scene 9

Town Square, A Few Minutes Later. Maureen, Mitchell, and Daisy chitchat at center stage. Wolf and Whitfield cross from the Farmhouse set to Town Square.

WOLF. I can't believe you.

WHITFIELD. I said what was on my mind. The elves like it when you tell the truth—

WOLF. They think they do.

Whitfield points at Maureen.

WOLF. Ebenezer—

Whitfield crosses to Maureen, cartoonishly sticking out his hand to meet her. Wolf trails him.

WHITFIELD. Wouldn'tya know—it's the lady of the hour! Ebenezer Whitfield, Candidate for Mayor of the North Pole!

Maureen shakes Whitfield's hand.

MAUREEN. Oh—hello, Ebenezer! Nice to finally meet you face to face, and—who's this?

Maureen extends her hand to Wolf.

WOLF. Call me Wolf, Mrs. Claus.

MAUREEN. Call me Maureen.

Wolf and Maureen shake hands. It's icy. Whitfield unknowingly cuts the tension by speaking up.

WHITFIELD. Look at all this! You have a line of elves and a speech and a big fancy banner—doesn't it all feel special?

MAUREEN. In the broadest sense, sure.

WHITFIELD. I'm just tickled pink about all this—this is gonna be such an adventure for both of us!

MAUREEN. Well, at the end of the day—you and I are just two elves who care deeply about the Village.

Whitfield looks to Wolf. Wolf mimes to Whitfield what he should say.

WHITFIELD. Oh yeah, sure. I, too, care about our village. Ta-ta!

Whitfield and Wolf exit. Maureen leans over to Daisy.

MAUREEN. Get me a drink.

DAISY. Ginger beer?

MAUREEN. Double bourbon. Rocks.

Daisy exits. Maureen caresses the sides of her head.

MAUREEN. Goodness. Really? Him? For mayor? I'll mop the floor with him.

MITCHELL. You and I know that, but we have to play the game pretending he's a serious candidate. You are accessible and you are smart—that's the narrative we're spinning right now. We can't go negative right out of the gate—

Daisy enters with a whisky cocktail. She hands it to Maureen.

MAUREEN. Oh, thank you, Daisy. I took selfies with that whole line of elves and I can talk in complete sentences. We can destroy Whitfield. I want to destroy him. No, I want to destroy his campaign manager!

DAISY. Please do.

MITCHELL. We'll get there, Mom. It's just too early.

A beep goes off on Daisy's phone. Daisy pulls her smartphone out and sees a notification.

DAISY. Oh! Mitch—our table's ready.

MITCHELL. Table?

DAISY. At Jovie's?

MITCHELL. Oh! Right. Mom—are we good to pause for the night?

MAUREEN. Fine by me.

Mitchell and Daisy exit. Maureen chugs her whisky cocktail in a single continuous sip.

MAUREEN. Ay-yai-yai.

Maureen exits.

The Elephant in the Steakhouse

Act One, Scene 10

Santa's Workshop, Same Time. Santa and IdaLynn study security footage on IdaLynn's tablet. IdaLynn points to the screen.

IDALYNN. I couldn't get a clear view of the guy's face—but he knew what he was looking for. He grabbed one box—one box. Why'd he do that? Especially if he just gave it all back the next day?

SANTA. Well . . .

IDALYNN. Santa. What's going on here?

A beat. Santa clears his throat.

SANTA. It's about time you know the truth about Santa Claus.

IdaLynn's eyes widen.

IDALYNN. You didn't kill anyone, did ya?

IdaLynn grabs Santa by the arm.

IDALYNN. I'd bury a body for ya.

Santa pauses. He pulls an envelope out of his suit pocket.

SANTA. Whoever our thief is . . . he didn't just give the toys back. He slipped this letter in the box.

Santa hands IdaLynn the letter. She opens it, not sure what to expect.

IDALYNN. *(Reading aloud.)* "Dear Santa Claus, There are things I want for Christmas, but I won't list them. I have been very, very naughty . . ."

A beat. IdaLynn's tone shifts.

IDALYNN. *(Continued.)* " . . . but not as naughty as you. If you don't send six *thousand dollars* every week to the following address, I will tell everyone what you've done. Signed, Krampus." Santa—what are they talking about? Who's Krampus?

SANTA. Probably an alias. Krampus is this myth of a half-demon half-goat thing that will drag German children to Hell if they're naughty before Christmas.

IDALYNN. Well. That's bleak. Okay—seriously. Did you kill an elf?

SANTA. No, of course not.

IDALYNN. Okay. Uh, I'm gonna get outta here. Maybe work on those reports from China—

SANTA. Don't worry about China yet. Take a break. Work on your house or something.

IDALYNN. If ya say so! We're tearing out cabinets now!!

IdaLynn punches Santa in the arm.

IDALYNN. Everything's gonna be okay. We'll get through this. I believe in you, Santa Claus.

Santa watches IdaLynn exit. He doesn't have the same faith.

Act One, Scene 11

Jovie's Steakhouse, Twenty Minutes Later. We are at the fanciest restaurant in the North Pole. A five-star dining room looking like the classiest Christmas party you've ever been to. Mitchell and Daisy are seated at a table. The table adjacent to them is vacant, but otherwise the restaurant is pretty busy. Snowman enters.

SNOWMAN. Now, I have to say there is no finer dining here at the North Pole than Jovie's —if you ever get a chance to get up here, make a reservation and tell 'em you know Frosti. Well—actually, maybe don't. They did fire me. It was amicable, but they did fire me years later.

Snowman crosses to Mitchell and Daisy.

SNOWMAN. I'll be darned—Mitchell Claus! Never thought I'd get to meet you. Did I hear a hunky birdie on Channel 7 say you're running your Mama's campaign?

MITCHELL. Oh—you got me.

SNOWMAN. You must be smart as a whip, Mitchell Claus. And I don't know many sons who'd do this for their Mama. Oh! Silly me. You're here to do that whole restaurant thing. Name's Frosti, I'll be takin' care of you tonight. Can I start y'all off with something to drink?

DAISY. I'll have a glass of your Chardonnay.

MITCHELL. Make it two.

DAISY. Glass of ice on the side?

Snowman nods, exits.

DAISY. Thanks! *(To Mitchell.)* So today, I taught my kids about "the elephant in the room".

MITCHELL. What?

DAISY. It was our idiom, for the day. I introduced it and said, "There's an elephant in the room that nobody wants to talk about"—and then Jason's little eyes lit up and he asked, "Where??" It was so cute!

Mitchell laughs.

DAISY. So I asked him, "Jason—if an elephant were really here in the room with us, wouldn't it be weird if nobody said a thing about it?" And he sat there, letting it stew—and he said, "I think that would smell very bad."

Mitchell smiles.

DAISY. So then, I said, "when you have a problem that's just so big and you know it's there but nobody says anything about it and it's weird—that's "the elephant in the room," and I turned to Jason and said, "And it would smell very bad."

Mitchell smirks.

MITCHELL. So why that one?

DAISY. I want my students to know that if something's a big deal—you should be able to talk about it. You don't have to pretend like you don't see it—

Mitchell nods.

DAISY. But anyway! Today, the headmaster called me into his office!

MITCHELL. *(Playfully.)* Oh no—was Miss Scarlett in trouble?

Snowman enters, delivering two glasses of white wine and a side glass of ice.

SNOWMAN. You two are just precious!

Snowman exits.

DAISY. The opposite of trouble! He told me Vice Principal Wigglesworth was fired! They thought of me to replace him! I have an interview!

MITCHELL. Outstanding!

DAISY. I mean—this is the perfect next step for my career and—sorry. Enough about me. Your mom sounded great today! You're working so hard for her. I find it very sexy.

Mitchell laughs.

MITCHELL. Thanks. It's tough to get away, but it's important to put work out of my head—

Out of the corner of his eye, Mitchell sees Whitfield and Wolf enter.

DAISY. Mitch?

Whitfield and Wolf cross to the vacant table. Mitchell rises and shakes Whitfield's hand.

WHITFIELD. Hey! I think we met earlier—Ebenezer Whitfield.

MITCHELL. Yes—sort of. Mitchell—Mitchell Claus. And this is my girlfriend, Daisy.

Daisy shakes Whitfield's hand, followed by Wolf's.

DAISY. Hello.

WOLF. What an enchanting little plus one you have, Mitchell.

DAISY. Uh—thanks.

Wolf slips Daisy a business card.

WOLF. Call me Wolf. We're just having a celebratory dinner and then we're off to work on *la résistance*. You understand, Mr. Campaign Manager.

MITCHELL. Indeed I do.

WHITFIELD. We hope you're prepared for every possible disaster.

WOLF. Have a lovely evening, Mitchell Claus. Daisy.

WHITFIELD. We really can't thank your father enough.

Wolf and Whitfield sit down at the table next to Mitchell and Daisy.

MITCHELL. "We can't thank your father enough." What did my dad do for them?

DAISY. I don't know. Mitch, those guys suck. Let's just ignore them, and like you said—put it out of your head—

MITCHELL. *(Spiraling.)* No, this—I really have no idea. What does this mean? Why would—? I just—

DAISY. Can you try? For me?

Mitchell squeezes Daisy's hand.

DAISY. All right.

Mitchell and Daisy sip their wine in silence. It's tense all around. Snowman enters.

SNOWMAN. My lord, talk about an elephant in the room. And well, as their server, I couldn't say nothing—I just shut up and smile and get my twenty percent tip at the end of the meal and move on with my life.

Whitfield and Wolf exit. Mitchell and Daisy exit.

SNOWMAN. Now Mitchell and Daisy weren't so fortunate, since their problems seemed to follow them over the river and through the woods as they went to Granny's house.

Chinese Take-Out

Act One, Scene 12

Granny's Cottage, A Few Hours Later—Nighttime. IdaLynn enters, carrying a bag of Chinese take-out food and her tablet.

IDALYNN. Granny? Day? I'm home! I have food!

IdaLynn plops down on the couch and removes boxes of takeout from the bag, piece by piece, onto the coffee table.

GRANNY. *(Offstage.)* Is that you, Idey?

IDALYNN. Who else would it be, Granny?

GRANNY SCARLETT enters, a perpetually worried New York Jewish grandmother type—wearing a distinctive nightgown. She's carrying a butcher knife.

IDALYNN. Granny!! What's with the murder knife?

GRANNY. Well, Yvonne Horowitz told me at lunch today that right here at the North Pole, her grandson Jonathan—you remember Jonathan. Such a nice boy. Dreadful case of lupus, but he's very nice.

IDALYNN. Granny—

GRANNY. You only ever hear about women getting lupus, but Yvonne Horowitz—she told me that Jonathan's doctor said eleven percent of lupus cases are male. He got prescribed some kind of—

IDALYNN. Granny? The murder knife?

GRANNY. His apartment was broken into and someone stole his clothes. And here I think if that happened to me—

IDALYNN. If you really are worried about the riff-raff breaking in, ya might want to take the spare key out from under the doormat.

GRANNY. Out of the question. What's the occasion for all this?

IDALYNN. Well, I wanted some mood-food in my system because tonight, I'm compiling the naughty/nice reports from China—

Granny brushes sawdust off IdaLynn's shoulder.

GRANNY. No, why are you all covered in sawdust?

IDALYNN. Cabinets!! I tore out all the cabinets in my new kitchen! Now come on, ya want some food?

GRANNY. All I want's a pork egg roll.

IDALYNN. I got 'em, Granny.

Granny picks up an egg roll and turns away.

GRANNY. Okay, good night.

Granny exits. Snowman enters. IdaLynn makes a plate of food and has a seat.

She picks up her tablet and opens it.

IDALYNN. Cen Sennan—verified Nice. *(Moves to next file.)* Zhang Zekai—Nice; good. *(Moves to next file.)* Yin Chenhao, Wu Haolun—what order were these even filed in?

Snowman crosses to IdaLynn.

SNOWMAN. IdaLynn came across a detail that surprised her.

IdaLynn studies the screen closer.

IDALYNN. "Toymaker at Santa's Workshop?"

SNOWMAN. IdaLynn made a quick call to Lachelle in Elven Resources, but Lachelle had no idea who those boys were. So IdaLynn went right to the source.

Snowman exits. IdaLynn makes a quick call on her cell phone, followed by a second.

SANTA. *(Offstage.)* Ho-ho-ho, you've reached Santa Claus!

IDALYNN. Santa!

SANTA. *(Offstage.)* Ha! Gotcha! I'm sorry to say I can't take your call. Please leave your message after the tone and be sure to tell me what you would like for Christmas.

IDALYNN. Santa, I finally found something useful on the workshop break-in and the toy-with-Asian-label thing, but it's in your stuff! We need to talk. Now. Call me back the moment you get this, I'll be up all night.

A beat.

IDALYNN. Also, I want one of those adult coloring books this year.

IdaLynn sighs. She clicks off her phone. The door swings open. IdaLynn sets the tablet down as Mitchell and Daisy enter.

IDALYNN. Hey-hey! You two were out past curfew! I'll give you two some space—

DAISY. No, Mitch isn't staying.

Mitchell sits down. He looks at the tablet.

MITCHELL. I don't think I've ever seen you without that thing.

IDALYNN. Yep. Got a long night ahead of me. You guys want some Chinese food? I've got tons—orange chicken, veggie lo mein, the egg rolls are pork I hope—

GRANNY. *(Offstage.)* Yes, they were!

IDALYNN. The walls are so thin in this house, aren't they?

GRANNY. *(Offstage.)* Yes, they are!

IDALYNN. Anyway—I can't eat all this myself...

MITCHELL. Oh, why not?

Mitchell makes a small plate for himself. He picks at it but doesn't end up eating much.

IDALYNN. How is Jovie's? Jerry and I keep meaning to try it out—

DAISY. Ebenezer Whitfield was there. Right next to us.

IDALYNN. Jeez, really?

MITCHELL. Yeah. He said he can't thank my father enough. I don't understand what that means. What would he do for them? Look, if nothing's going on—my mom could probably phone her whole campaign in and still win. But I've just got a bad feeling about Whitfield. There's gotta be something we don't know. And I'm terrified of finding it out.

IDALYNN. And you could be right.

DAISY. You could be right.

Mitchell rises.

MITCHELL. It's getting late. I should go. Split some firewood.

DAISY. Yeah, I should get to bed soon.

Daisy rises to walk Mitchell to the door.

DAISY. What will you write about in your notebook from tonight?

MITCHELL. Oh—uh. Haven't thought about it.

DAISY. You could say "there was an elephant in the room".

MITCHELL. What?

DAISY. From before. My lesson today.

MITCHELL. Oh. Yeah. Sorry.

A beat.

MITCHELL. That's a nice red coat you've got.

DAISY. Well—a really great guy with really great taste gave it to me.

MITCHELL. Exquisite taste!

Daisy laughs. Mitchell and Daisy kiss.

MITCHELL. Good night.

DAISY. Good night, Mitch.

Mitchell exits. Daisy immediately throws Mitchell's plate into the trash as she plops down next to IdaLynn. Granny enters, carrying a rifle.

DAISY. Granny?

GRANNY. Would you believe Yvonne Horowitz told me at lunch today that—

DAISY. Granny, is that a gun??

GRANNY. Pauline Stein fell down her stairs, so Elaine comes in to work on her, and she said that Elaine's mother-in-law Annetta—oh, what was her name? She's very nice. But she's from Florida. Well, Annetta just gave her neighbors a pair of swans as a housewarming gift. Named them Neal and Barbara—isn't that precious?

DAISY. Granny, the gun??

GRANNY. Oh, this? The nice elf in the Sporting Goods section said it was a Red Ryder, Daisy.

DAISY. You'll shoot your eye out! Granny, you don't need a gun.

GRANNY. Well, Yvonne Horowitz—the big-boned lady—her grandson Jonathan, you remember Jonathan?

Daisy does not remember Jonathan.

DAISY. Yes, I remember Jonathan.

GRANNY. I'm not going down like him. The day someone breaks into my house, I'm gonna need a gun.

Daisy rolls her eyes. Granny grabs another egg roll and exits.

IDALYNN. So . . . when's the big interview?

Daisy lights up.

DAISY. It's next week! They're going to decide around Christmas, too! Everything's going to move so fast.

IDALYNN. And this job would be kinda—everything you want right now?

DAISY. Yes! My contract's up at the end of the year—and if I sign it again, I'm stuck in the classroom for three more years. I love my students, but I really want to help teachers be teachers, you know?

IDALYNN. It's awesome! What does Mitch think?

DAISY. We didn't really get to talk about it. Did you see it's snowing outside?

Daisy picks up a TV remote and turns on the TV.

IDALYNN. Yeah, I heard there's this big storm starting tonight.

On the TV is the News at 11. We hear news fanfare.

SCHYLER. *(Offstage.)* Everything you need to know about the snowstorm after this short break.

MAUREEN. *(Offstage.)* I'm Maureen Gaines Claus and I approve this m—

Daisy reflexively clicks off the TV with the remote. IdaLynn and Daisy are both surprised that Daisy did that.

DAISY. Sorry. I—

Daisy turns the TV back on. We don't hear anything clearly coming out of the TV.

GRANNY. *(Offstage.)* Hey girls? I could use another egg roll. Mind bringing one upstairs?

IDALYNN. You got it, Granny.

IdaLynn picks up an egg roll and exits. Daisy rises. Snowman enters.

SNOWMAN. And there Daisy stood, alone in the living room watching the snowfall as she wondered what lay ahead for Mitchell and for her—and how it was all going to fit together, if it was going to fit together at all.

Yuletide Pandemonium

Act One, Scene 13

Town Square, The Next Morning. The stage is fairly empty, only the Christmas Tree at center stage is present. Snowman enters.

SNOWMAN. Y'all ever been outside when it's snowing? When it's raining my flesh everywhere? Maybe don't think too hard about that. When the weather outside is frightful, it's so easy to get lost. Things get buried as the landscape changes—but nothing actually goes away. So you better try your darndest to find it or it'll be lost until spring. And if you live at the North Pole, you will literally never see it again.

Mitchell and Maureen enter. Newspaper columnist HOLAHAN enters and shakes Maureen's hand. She shakes Mitchell's hand afterward.

SNOWMAN. The storm—both the literal one and the symbolic one—were well underway.

HOLAHAN. Hi, Jodi Holahan from the North Pole Times. Right off the bat, Maureen: why another term?

MAUREEN. Everyday North Pole elves need a champion and I want to continue to be that champion—because when the North Pole is filled with Christmas joy, the world is filled with Christmas joy.

HOLAHAN. Let's take a little stroll—a walk and talk.

MAUREEN. Certainly!

HOLAHAN. Now, the platform you're running on would be the most progressive the North Pole has seen to date. What was the thinking behind—?

Maureen and Holahan exit. Mitchell's phone rings. Daisy enters, phone to ear. Mitchell puts his phone up to his ear.

MITCHELL. Hi Daisy!

DAISY. They cancelled school today! Want to come over and bake some cookies? Maybe help me prep for the interview? I made flash cards—

MITCHELL. Oh! Didn't realize that was so soon. I'd love to, but I'm with my Mom at her—

DAISY. Oh—yeah, right. Okay! Talk to you later, bye!

Daisy exits. Santa enters, forlorn. Mitchell hangs up the phone.

MITCHELL. Dad—Dad? What's wrong?

IdaLynn bursts in, angry. Maureen enters.

IDALYNN. There you are! You've got some explaining to do here, buddy. Ya might as well have killed someone.

MITCHELL. What's she talking about? What's going on?

We hear Schyler's trademark news fanfare. Schyler enters, microphone in hand—and not a hair out of place.

SCHYLER. Here comes Santa Claus, right down Santa Claus Lane. Lean your ear this way: is jolly old Saint Nicholas carrying a dark secret?

Santa turns to leave. Schyler follows him like a trashy tabloid reporter.

SCHYLER. Hours after Mayor Claus launched her re-election campaign, Channel 7 received an anonymous document from Santa's Workshop suggesting toys came in mass shipments from a factory in China owned by—you guessed it—Santa Claus. Santa, can you confirm these documents are authentic?

SANTA. Yes, but—

SCHYLER. And yet, you have claimed from essentially the dawn of time that every single toy on Christmas Eve is made by elves at the North Pole.

SANTA. In the past we claimed that, but you've got to understand—

SCHYLER. Lies. Outsourcing. Deception. What other skeletons is Santa Claus hiding in his Yuletide closet? Reporting for Channel 7, this is Schyler Hines and I am very attractive. Back to you, Rita.

Schyler exits. IdaLynn shakes her head.

MITCHELL. Dad . . . Why?

SANTA. I didn't have a choice. The world had too many people. Couldn't overwork my elves and not pay 'em. So I went to China and bought a factory, uh . . . Under the table.

MITCHELL. Dad . . . You're operating a sweatshop . . . a sweatshop. How—?

IDALYNN. We can fix this. We can spin this—I'll rally anyone I can!

IdaLynn exits. Mitchell turns to Santa, realizing a lot about his own life and his father's in one moment.

SANTA. Mitchell—

MITCHELL. I—I get it.

Mitchell exits.

MAUREEN. Well, I have a campaign to win here, so I hope the North Pole understands what you've done.

Maureen exits in one direction, Santa exits in the other. Snowman enters.

SNOWMAN. And oh Lordy, they did *not*! The piece Channel 7 ran on Santa's alleged sweatshop threw the village into chaos.

A group of PROTEST ELVES enter. The protesters carry signs reading:
   "HO-HO-HORRIBLE"
   "YOU'RE A MEAN ONE, MR. CLAUS"
   "AWAY WITH THE MANAGER"
   "MAUREEN, DID YOU KNOW?"

ELF 1. Can you believe this? I've been making toys my whole life and I haven't had a raise in fifteen years!

ELF 2. And to think he sits there telling the world who's naughty and nice?!

ELF 1. I'm livid!

ELF 2. I'm appalled!

IdaLynn enters.

IDALYNN. I'm convinced!

The protest elves turn to listen to IdaLynn.

IDALYNN. *(Speaking rapidly.)* That the situation at hand could very well be more nuanced than a simple good versus evil and the capitalist world we seem to live in left Santa with one hand tied behind his back and maybe we shouldn't rush to conclusions because Santa Claus has a lot on his plate and could very well have our best interests at heart but circumstances make it difficult to get the whole picture because things are usually more complicated than they appear to be when they're boiled down to a single sound bite that's easy to watch on TV or read on the internet—

The other elves shoot IdaLynn a death glare.

ELF 1. Get out.

IdaLynn exits. Protest Elves exit.

SNOWMAN. This was all anyone was talking about for weeks. A story this juicy gave that Christmas Ham Schyler Hines material that was practically writing itself.

Schyler enters, carrying a poster board.

SCHYLER. A re-election campaign that started as a cakewalk for Maureen Gaines Claus has quickly turned to fruitcake. When asked "Do you trust Mayor Claus?", elves on the street overwhelmingly say:

Schyler holds up the poster board—it reads, in big block letters:
   NO.

SCHYLER. "No".

Act One, Scene 14

Mitchell's Office, a Week Later. Mitchell sits at his desk, working away on some paperwork drudgery. Maureen enters, carrying a trashy magazine. She slaps the magazine onto Mitchell's desk.

MAUREEN. Do you believe what they're saying about me?

MITCHELL. Mom, come on. The Times report came out fine. Why are you even reading the Cosmopolarton?

MAUREEN. Well excuse me for living, Mitchell. I didn't even talk to them!

Maureen picks up the magazine and flips to the story.

MAUREEN. "Chronicles of Mayor Maureen: The Lying, the Snitch in a Warzone" Whose fantasy world are they living in? This is awful—

Mitchell takes the magazine.

MITCHELL. Come on, Mom. We've got bigger issues to deal with than *(Checks article byline.)* Lewis Clive Stapley.

MAUREEN. No, Mitchell. This coverage is demeaning and frankly, really sexist. This would never happen if I were a man with a wife up to shady business. I'll be devastated—devastated if I lose my office over something your father did.

MITCHELL. And so would I. We can beat this. We will beat this. I'm doing a press conference in a couple days about China. That should be a start—

MAUREEN. Crush them.

Maureen exits. Mitchell returns to work at his desk. In an obscure corner of the stage, Daisy enters with the headmaster, DR. WILDER.

WILDER. Miss Scarlett, really and truly—excellent interview. You demonstrate that your career's off to a great start.

DAISY. Thank you so much!

Wilder and Daisy shake hands.

WILDER. I'm confident that you're going places—even if you don't get it this time.

Daisy hadn't considered there was a chance she wouldn't get the job.

DAISY. Oh—thanks. Just curious: How many other interviews do you have?

WILDER. Maybe three, four internal candidates.

DAISY. *(Slightly embarrassed.)* Best of luck.

Wilder exits. Daisy crosses to Mitchell and sees he has the weight of the world on his shoulders. Daisy smiles, softly.

DAISY. Knock-knock.

Mitchell looks up.

MITCHELL. Hey! Hey, I'm still coming over tonight.

DAISY. Yeah, I know. It was just getting late and I just—I don't know. Wanted to see you.

Mitchell returns to his work.

DAISY. My interview went okay.

MITCHELL. Oh—great! Did your flash cards help?

DAISY. Hey, question for you. I thought we were doing our gifts together, on Christmas Eve. What was with the—?

MITCHELL. Oh! No, no, that's not your whole Christmas gift, I just—felt like giving you something.

DAISY. That's very sweet of you. I'm just so curious . . . Why that? You know I really don't care about gifts all that much—I'm a teacher. This time of year, I get so many mugs and picture frames and other junk nobody needs. Jason gave me a peach-scented candle and then told me, "actually, my Mom wanted to get rid of it." I got a re-gifted candle, Mitch.

MITCHELL. Did you not like my gift?

Daisy did not particularly like it.

DAISY. No, no—the bird's great; I just—do we really live in the right climate for a pear tree?

Mitchell takes Daisy's hand.

MITCHELL. Seriously, don't worry—you're getting a better gift tomorrow.

DAISY. Okay. Can I take you home, mister? I've got all the stuff to make sugar cookies—

MITCHELL. I'll be ready, just give me ten.

Mitchell's phone rings. He picks it up.

MITCHELL. Hello? Yes, hi Noelle—I was just about to call you first, Noelle. *(Brief pause.)* Yes, th—Angela did say—

Mitchell exits, phone to ear. Daisy exits.

Act One, Scene 15

Town Square, Two Days Later. The stage is once again fairly empty, with only the Christmas Tree at center stage present. Snowman enters.

SNOWMAN. Things were still going downhill in a handbasket for the Claus campaign. The Union of Workshop Elves threw another hurdle their way—

Union Leaders GOLDSMITH and FRANKEN enter.

GOLDSMITH. And so, due to recent questions surrounding the business practices at Santa's Workshop, it is with great pleasure that on behalf of the U.W.E., we—Goldsmith, Franken, and Murray—

FRANKEN. Three kings of the industry!

Whitfield enters.

GOLDSMITH. Offer our unanimous endorsement to Ebenezer Whitfield!

A crowd applauds. Whitfield shakes Goldsmith's hand.

SNOWMAN. It had turned into a perfect storm for Whitfield to somehow become a serious candidate.

WHITFIELD. Thank you. Thank you. Mr. Chairelf, workshop elves, and fellow citizens—I will be honored to formally accept the U.W.E.'s endorsement for Mayor of the North Pole. Y'know, I was just your average hockey son when I signed up to run for mayor.

The crowd applauds.

WHITFIELD. I love those hockey sons. You know, they say the difference between a hockey son and a pit-bull? Chapstick.

We hear thunderous applause as Whitfield waves. Whitfield, Goldsmith, and Franken exit.

SNOWMAN. Look, I never entertained the thought of voting for Whitfield, but I'll give credit where credit's due: he killed it that day. Y'all know what they say about a broken clock—but anyhow, the days went by and—

A crowd of Protesting Elves enter, angrier than before, crossing the stage to exit. Protest signs this time read:
  "KEEP YOUR SECRETS, LOSE YOUR ELVES"
  "DREAMING OF A WHITFIELD CHRISTMAS"
  "TREASON'S GREETINGS"

PROTESTERS. *(Chanting.)* Ho-ho-ho! He's gotta go! Ho-ho-ho! She's gotta go! Down with Claus! Down with Claus!

SNOWMAN. Oh yeah, all this mess made the elves go on strike, too. Bless their little hearts. Anyhow, IdaLynn and Santa were still playing that game of whodunit—

IdaLynn and Santa enter.

IDALYNN. It's gotta be Whitfield. He had everything to gain by setting this off. Nobody votes for him if he doesn't pull this.

SANTA. But he's been on the Nice List his entire life. I'd be surprised.

IDALYNN. So . . . I happened to make a call this morning to Whitfield's penguin slash polar bear farm and asked if he wanted help . . . remodeling the farmhouse.

SANTA. IdaLynn Marble.

IDALYNN. Hey—this time of year, everyone needs an Elf on the Shelf to figure out what they're really up to.

SANTA. Ho-ho, of course! Keep your ears open. Make a list, check it twice...

IDALYNN. I'm on it!!

IdaLynn and Santa exit. Mitchell enters, along with a small crowd of journalists. Schyler's fanfare plays as he enters and takes center stage.

SCHYLER. And after several silent nights, re-election campaign manager and son of the fallen power couple Mitchell Claus speaks out live in a press conference regarding Santa's Workshop business in China.

Schyler exits.

MITCHELL. We now welcome any questions.

Hands go up all around. Mitchell points to BERG.

BERG. Jeffrey Berg, Snowflake Press: Were you or Mayor Claus complicit in covering up your father's purchase of the factory?

MITCHELL. No. Absolutely not. Maureen Gaines Claus was blindsided with this news, as was I. Mayor Claus's administration will work closely with

Santa's Workshop to find a way to close the factory in China while keeping up with the global—

Another journalist, JONES, butts in. She had not really listened to what Mitchell said.

JONES. Brenda Jones, Elves Magazine: Are there plans to close the workshop here at the North Pole?

MITCHELL. Absolutely not. As I was saying—

JOURNALIST. Can you give an approximate date at which all toys will be imported from overseas?

MITCHELL. It seems there has been a fundamental misunderstanding about my father's motivations. None of this—

WHITFIELD. *(Offstage; Shouted.)* Just quit runnin' yer mouth and tell the truth!

Whitfield and Wolf enter.

WOLF. Good. Command the room.

Mitchell rises.

MITCHELL. Whoa, this is not Okay.

Mitchell and Whitfield stand toe to toe with each other. The journalists encircle them, like they're about to watch a cockfight. Wolf stands at Whitfield's side.

WHITFIELD. Yer mom and dad have been eroding the traditional values this Village was built on.

WOLF. Point the finger.

Whitfield points his index finger at Mitchell.

MITCHELL. Excuse me? My parents have done nothing but sacrifice for the good of this town—and world.

WHITFIELD. And they think they can just rest on that. We know that Santa and Mayor Maureen are nothing more than pirates. They came in with their parrots on the shoulder and their jolly rancher flag and they just went all over buryin' their treasure and swiggin' rum and fightin' sea monsters—

WOLF. *(Flatly.)* What?

WHITFIELD. They didn't think we'd smarten up and ask for an explanation, but durnit, it's time for the Claus family to explanate.

MITCHELL. I'm sorry?

WHITFIELD. I get a kick out of it when other elves say I'm too simple-minded or plainspoken, but I'm the only one with a plan to save this town.

MITCHELL. What plan?

WHITFIELD. The Whitfield Plan is simple, and that's to keep our working elves here. They're hard-workin' toymakers—let's use common-sense and put 'em back to work.

BERG. Can you outline some specific details for this Whitfield plan?

WOLF. I'll take this one. Nobody wants to see our precious way of life here at the North Pole change, and so, rather than running the Claus family out of town, we plan to restore things to the way they've always been. Upon his election, Mayor Whitfield will sponsor the opening of a factory here at the North Pole. We'll sell the toys wholesale to Santa's Workshop, and that income will be repurposed for Public Works. All toy making could return to the North Pole as we all help each other.

MITCHELL. Wow. That's actually kind of great.

WHITFIELD. You sure are good at talking, aren't ya?

WOLF. Yes, thank you.

Whitfield, Wolf, and Journalists exit. Mitchell steps away. Daisy enters. She and Mitchell walk hand in hand around the Town Square.

DAISY. What's with the birds? Three days in a row now, you've sent me birds. The doves, the chickens—

MITCHELL. Yes, I had the chickens shipped from France. *Très bon,* no?

Daisy lets go of Mitchell's hand and turns to him.

DAISY. Mitch, I'm really not in the mood for you to keep a secret from me, can you please just tell me what's—?

MITCHELL. Trust me, Daisy. I know what I'm doing.

DAISY. But . . . why?

Mitchell's phone rings. He picks it up.

MITCHELL. All right, what are we thinking, Mom?

Daisy looks at Mitchell as she shakes her head. Snowman enters.

SNOWMAN. It seemed the Whitfield campaign offered Santa's Workshop something of an olive branch in time for Christmas—but there were still a few things to be resolved. And the heart of the real story was getting lost, buried in the snow.

Mitchell turns around and walks toward City Hall. A new crowd of Protest Elves march toward City Hall. Daisy turns around to see the crowd approaching.

PROTESTERS. *(Chanting.)* Ho-ho-ho! He's gotta go! Ho-ho-ho! She's gotta go! Down with Claus! Down with Claus!

Daisy is enveloped by the crowd, lost in the protest.

END OF ACT ONE.

Dancing in the Eye of the Storm

Act Two, Scene 1

Town Square, Five Days Later. Snowman is alone onstage, speaking directly to a member of the audience.

SNOWMAN. Who even knows how I came to life? Might've been some magic or something, 'cuz I just remember someone put this hat on me and I started dancing—*(Notices the lights are up and the show is back on.)* Oh, wonderful! Y'all are back! Did everything come out Okay? Good, good. So, where were we? Erm—The elves went on strike. They were on strike for exactly five days. Daisy was havin' a cow—more on that in a second. In the meantime, Santa Claus took the first step to end the strike—

Santa and Schyler enter. Schyler holds a microphone up to Santa.

SANTA. You do not have to forgive me. I betrayed your trust and contributed to unfair labor practices in China. Moving forward, the factory in China will close and I will be more direct about my practices. Thank you, and God bless the North Pole.

A crowd applauds. Santa exits. Daisy enters, evidently heading home from a long school day. Wilder enters behind her.

WILDER. Miss Scarlett?

Daisy turns to see her headmaster.

DAISY. Oh! Dr. Wilder. What can I do for you?

WILDER. We've come to a decision. Walk with me.

Daisy and Wilder exit.

Act Two, Scene 2

Santa's Workshop, Four Days Later—The Afternoon of Christmas Eve. The Workshop floor is nearly set up for the Christmas Eve Ball later that night. Maureen and Mitchell enter and place some centerpieces on tables.

MITCHELL. I can't believe you still want to throw this party. You're trailing Whitfield now by sixteen points.

MAUREEN. The elves ended the marches—I'd think it would look worse for the campaign if I didn't throw this shindig. I need to play the part of, "Oh, this isn't about politics—let's have a Christmas Eve Ball!"

Snowman enters. Maureen exits.

SNOWMAN. The Christmas Eve Ball. My lord, would you believe I haven't told you about the Christmas Eve Ball yet? I'm not on my game—pull yourself together, Frosti. Anywho, every year, Maureen threw the Christmas Eve Ball, thanking the North Pole for a year of hard work ending with Santa's annual trip around the world—

Santa enters, carrying a sack of presents. Santa grunts in distress as the weight becomes too much.

MITCHELL. Dad—my God, Dad—you're gonna destroy your back—

Mitchell helps Santa guide the sack to the floor.

MITCHELL. Let me help you with the rest.

SANTA. Well, this is the last bag. I've got to get on the road here in a moment. I've got one of my standbys guiding the sleigh tonight. He's got this bright, sort of shiny nose—

MITCHELL. Like a lightbulb?

SANTA. Yeah, it got him disqualified from the Reindeer Games—

MITCHELL. I do recall hearing about that.

A beat.

SANTA. Mitchell, I'm really sorry about leaving you out of the loop—

MITCHELL. Dad—I'm fine.

SANTA. You're my son. Your mother and I had always wanted to raise—

MITCHELL. Really, Dad. I—

Mitchell and Santa make eye contact. Mitchell and Santa wordlessly have a full moment of reconciliation.

MITCHELL. Thanks.

Santa smiles.

SANTA. How's Daisy?

MITCHELL. What? Oh—we're great. I've just been so busy. But we're great. I, uh, haven't told anyone this yet, but I'm actually going to propose. Tonight.

Mitchell pulls out an engagement ring and hands it to Santa.

MITCHELL. For a week and half, I've been sending her a gift, every day getting more elaborate until tonight when I propose. Tonight is the grand finale, I've hired a big band—twelve drums.

SANTA. Ho-ho, how wonderful!

Mitchell beams.

MITCHELL. Now let's get this to the sleigh.

Mitchell picks up the sack of toys. Daisy enters. Mitchell and Santa exit. Mitchell re-enters.

DAISY. What on earth are you doing, Mitch?

Daisy points offstage. We hear a cow moo.

MITCHELL. Isn't it great? You'll never have to milk the thing yourself!

DAISY. Yeah—I figured that out when eight Mennonite ladies showed up at my door to milk the cow. Every day, these gifts just keep getting weirder: a private show of *Swan Lake*, an *actual* swan lake—and you're not explaining a thing! I just feel like I'm losing my mind over here and to top it all off, the headmaster told me—

Mitchell holds Daisy.

MITCHELL. I wouldn't say you're losing your mind.

DAISY. Well. Thanks. Now—let's have fun tonight, okay? Promise me you won't ditch the party and work or chop wood.

MITCHELL. Not without you.

Mitchell kisses Daisy on the cheek.

DAISY. I'll put on my favorite red coat tonight.

MITCHELL. Which red coat?

DAISY. The one you gave me.

MITCHELL. Oh! Outstanding.

DAISY. I love you.

MITCHELL. I love you, too.

Daisy and Mitchell exit.

Act Two, Scene 3

Santa's Workshop, Later That Night—Early Evening on Christmas Eve. We hear classy swing music playing, the Christmas Eve Ball is underway. Snowman enters and crosses to center stage as party guests mill around him.

SNOWMAN. It was beginning to look a lot like Christmas again. Every elf in the village was thrilled to arrive at the ball.

Snowman gestures toward the entry. Granny and IdaLynn enter. Granny has a sour expression.

GRANNY. I can't believe you dragged me out of bed for this.

IDALYNN. Granny!

GRANNY. I probably could've stayed in my nightgown—

Wolf and Whitfield enter. Whitfield is wearing his normal outfit, but with a tie added that he thinks looks good. Granny looks up and down at Whitfield.

GRANNY. I definitely could've stayed in my nightgown.

Granny exits in a huff. Wolf crosses to IdaLynn.

IDALYNN. Granny!!

WOLF. Good evening, IdaLynn.

IDALYNN. Nice to see ya, Wolf.

WOLF. Care to join me for an hors d'oeuvre?

Wolf and IdaLynn cross to an hors d'oeuvres table. Maureen enters with Schyler and Snowman, who are carrying several identical baskets.

MAUREEN. Just set them on the table right over there—

Schyler and Snowman set baskets on a table. Daisy and Mitchell enter and mingle with others nearby. Maureen crosses to Mitchell and Daisy.

MAUREEN. Daisy! You look wonderful! So good to see you.

Maureen hugs Daisy.

MAUREEN. How are you doing? How's your class?

DAISY. I'm okay. I have a great class this year, but life just keeps happening and you work so hard sometimes only to—

MAUREEN. Good to hear. Now, Mitchell, come with me a moment—

Mitchell and Maureen walk away. Daisy spots IdaLynn at the hors d'oeuvres table with Wolf.

WOLF. Fascinating. I'd love to trade some notes on Santa Claus. Perhaps you know a few things I don't.

IDALYNN. Well, I'm at Whitfield's house all the time these days if ya wanna swing by and talk.

WOLF. Oh yes. And how is that going?

IDALYNN. It's a real fixer-upper, and well—so is Whitfield. *(Laughs.)* Just making a little extra cash to work on my own house before I marry this one—

IdaLynn goes to punch Jerry on the arm, but Jerry isn't there. Daisy crosses to hors d'oeuvres table.

IDALYNN. Where'd Jerry go?

WOLF. Daisy Scarlett. You look beautiful tonight.

DAISY. Thank you, Mr. Wolf.

Wolf picks up a mini quiche and leaves the hors d'oeuvres table.

IDALYNN. Day, you've gotta try these mini quiches! I've had like six already!

Daisy tries a mini quiche.

DAISY. Florentine?

IDALYNN. Yeah, I think so. I wish we'd gotten little cards telling ya what's what. Nothing hurts more than biting into something and being surprised.

DAISY. Really? Nothing hurts more than that?

IDALYNN. Try biting a raisin cookie thinking it's chocolate chip.

Mitchell crosses to center stage.

MITCHELL. If I could have your attention, please.

Music fades down. A spotlight shines on Mitchell.

MITCHELL. Before my mother started her re-election campaign and before we learned the truth about Santa Claus, my girlfriend, Daisy, said to me, "No matter who they are, at the end of the day, your parents are elves doing their best". So now, I invite you to give it up for my Mom—an elf doing her best—Maureen Gaines Claus.

The crowd applauds. Maureen hugs Mitchell as Mitchell joins Daisy in the crowd. Maureen steps into the spotlight.

MAUREEN. Thank you, Mitchell. And thank you all for being here tonight. It brings me such joy to see all of you here, even with unanswered questions or bitter feelings. And those questions and feelings may be justified—but it means the world that we have come together for one night as the North Pole. It is truly wonderful to see you choose to be here for each other and show up for the town we love so dearly, with so much going on in our town, our world—it's like a blizzard. And yet you're here—*(Pause.)* I'm moved.

You chose to see amid the winter snow and be here, for each other, and the greater good in which we believe.

Crowd applauds. The lights return to normal and the classy swing music resumes.

MAUREEN. And so, all that I ask tonight is that we put politics aside and just have a ball! Before you go, please take a basket. Merry Christmas to you all!

The crowd cheers and resumes dancing. Mitchell and Daisy cross to the table with baskets.

DAISY. Well done, sir!

Daisy picks up a basket.

MITCHELL. I have you to thank for that.

Mitchell kisses Daisy on the cheek. Daisy grins.

DAISY. Mitch—I'd love if you asked me to dance right now.

MITCHELL. Hmm. Miss Scarlett, do you wish to dance?

Daisy removes her coat and sets the coat and basket on a coat rack. Mitchell and Daisy cross to the dance floor. They dance.

Meanwhile, Wolf is scrawling something in a notebook. Whitfield crosses to him, carrying a basket identical to Daisy's.

WHITFIELD. Woul'ja just put that thing away? We're at a party.

WOLF. We agreed you would make an appearance at the Christmas Eve Ball in a show of diplomacy and I'm here so you don't put your foot in your mouth. So, enjoy yourself—but watch your tongue.

WHITFIELD. No.

WOLF. What?

Whitfield yanks the notebook out of Wolf's hands.

WHITFIELD. I'm not gonna have fun unless you do.

Wolf reaches for the notebook.

WOLF. Come on. Give that back—

WHITFIELD. You'll get this back after you've had a little fun. Go ask someone to dance or something, I dunno.

WOLF. Fine.

Wolf scans around the room and sees Daisy on the dance floor, swing dancing with Mitchell.

WOLF. May I cut in?

MITCHELL. Uh—no.

DAISY. Mitch. It's fine.

Wolf and Daisy dance. Mitchell is pushed to the sidelines, watching. Snowman crosses to Mitchell.

SNOWMAN. Now Daisy was determined to have fun that night, so she thought nothing of dancing with someone else, but Mitchell on the other hand was more than a bit jealous. Seeing his fiancée-to-be with an elf who was decidedly a better dancer was very much not part of his perfect plan.

Mitchell crosses to IdaLynn.

MITCHELL. You wanna dance?

IDALYNN. Sure!

Mitchell and IdaLynn cross to the dance floor. They dance somewhat near Daisy and Wolf. Whitfield crosses to Maureen, removes his hat, and bows.

WHITFIELD. Mayor Maureen—

MAUREEN. Oh, no need to bow, Ebenezer. Are you heading out?

WHITFIELD. Not yet. Listen, I'm sorry for the attacks and my one-line quips and my gizmos and my hoo-hahs. It's all politics. It's inexcusable.

In the background, we see Schyler and Snowman flirting with each other.

MAUREEN. That's very big of you. No offense taken, I know you're running a campaign, same as me.

WHITFIELD. Well you said it best, Maureen. Tonight's not a night for politics. So, you wanna dance? Whaddiya say?

Whitfield extends his hand.

MAUREEN. Oh—why not?

Maureen and Whitfield cross to the dance floor. They dance. Now we have three mismatched pairs dancing at the front of the stage, each holding individual conversations: Daisy and Wolf, IdaLynn and Mitchell, Maureen and Whitfield. Music transitions from upbeat swing into an ominous tango.

MAUREEN. So I'm very curious Ebenezer—penguins? I had no idea there were penguins at the North Pole.

WHITFIELD. Yeah, I've been tryin'a teach 'em how to fly. Hasn't gone so well.

MAUREEN. I admire your perseverance.

Whitfield spins Maureen as she laughs, uninhibited. She's enjoying herself more than she expected.

WOLF. I can tell you're a dreamer, Daisy Scarlett.

DAISY. Excuse me?

Wolf pulls Daisy closer.

WOLF. I see it in your eyes: I know you're more than a mere plus one for Mitchell Claus. Tell me your story.

DAISY. That's hardly any of your business, Mr. Wolf.

Wolf spins Daisy.

WOLF. Have you told Mitchell Claus your story?

DAISY. Mitchell is great.

WOLF. But does he know your dreams? Has he ever asked?

Wolf lifts and turns Daisy. Mitchell sees Wolf's lift and haphazardly lifts and turns IdaLynn, nearly dropping her. IdaLynn laughs. Daisy looks over to Mitchell.

MITCHELL. So how's the farmhouse?

IDALYNN. It's not bad! It's nice having a little more money coming in—would you believe my homeowner's insurance specifically doesn't cover a busted ejector pump??

MITCHELL. Do you still think Whitfield is Krampus?

IDALYNN. No, not anymore. He's a sweetheart and he's too dumb. But ya know what? That Wolf guy gives me the creeps.

Mitchell and IdaLynn continue dancing. Daisy makes eye contact with Wolf.

DAISY. I want to open my own school someday.

WOLF. Is that so?

DAISY. Thought I had a chance to start making it happen, but I—it'll be awhile before I can.

WOLF. I'm sorry to hear that.

DAISY. I—I love Mitchell. I love him, but I'm lost.

Wolf spins Daisy. They continue to dance.

Mitchell smiles as he spins IdaLynn.

DAISY. Gosh, there's so much going on in my life. It's like this party. And I should be happy—I really should, it's a party! But just like tonight, I'm wandering through this crowded room, looking for the elf I love. And sometimes I find him—for a moment. So then I take that moment to breathe for just one second—but then I see he's gone. Off to another room, another conversation, another hors d'oeuvres tray—and he hates parties like this! But I can't dwell on it. No. I have to pull myself together and go looking. He's everything to me. And I know he doesn't feel the same way about me. I feel horrible to even think—but it's true. He doesn't care about my dreams. He never has.

Wolf smiles.

WOLF. You are quite the dancer.

Whitfield spins Maureen.

WHITFIELD. To be honest, it blows my freakin' mind to think ye'r married to the no-profits toy giant and of all the things you could do, you want to do some local government thing.

MAUREEN. I'm sure that's how all this may look to the outside world.

WHITFIELD. Every so often, someone like me can see somethin' from that outside world.

Maureen smiles—she's made a friend.

MAUREEN. I suppose you can.

WHITFIELD. You know, I once saw Russia from my house!

Maureen laughs—she's made a dumb friend.

MAUREEN. I'm sure you did.

Mitchell turns to IdaLynn.

MITCHELL. And you've not learned anything about Whitfield's workshop?

IDALYNN. That's the other thing. Wolf's the guy with those answers!

Daisy laughs.

DAISY. And there I go, bearing my soul to a total stranger.

WOLF. Not a stranger—I'm a friend.

Mitchell and IdaLynn leave the dance floor and head to the bar.

DAISY. Well—I would guess you have dreams then, too?

WOLF. Oh yes. I dream that Whitfield will win the election so we can open the factory. Really, this will save Christmas.

Wolf spins Daisy.

WOLF. The village is well-funded by Santa's Workshop and of course—all the children of the world will receive elf quality, North Pole toys on Christmas morning.

DAISY. Wait—how will you staff this factory? There's not enough toymakers to even begin—

WOLF. I'm confident that will not be an issue. We just need time and votes.

Mitchell, with his cocktail, sees IdaLynn sipping out of a mug.

MITCHELL. Open bar and you get hot chocolate? Really?

IDALYNN. With schnapps.

MITCHELL. Ah. Good choice.

Mitchell and IdaLynn clink their glasses. They watch Wolf and Daisy dance on the floor.

IDALYNN. I just have a gut feel he's Krampus.

MITCHELL. But you don't have any proof.

IDALYNN. Exactly!! Hey I was just thinking about this today: I never got you that ice cream sundae. You remember?

MITCHELL. How could I forget? Funny you mention that, though.

Mitchell pulls out the engagement ring and shows it to IdaLynn.

MITCHELL. I'm gonna propose tonight.

IDALYNN. Mitch! That's huge!! Do it now!!

MITCHELL. Now? Like now-now?

IDALYNN. Yes, now-now! Come on!! Get her away from that Wolf!

IdaLynn bounds toward the dance floor. Mitchell follows. She pushes Daisy out of the way and grabs Wolf.

IDALYNN. I'll cut in!

IdaLynn and Wolf dance. Daisy laughs.

DAISY. Thanks!

Daisy turns around to see an eager Mitchell.

DAISY. Hey stranger.

MITCHELL. Do you—wanna get out of here? Go back to my place and, uh—bake some cookies?

DAISY. I'd love to!

Daisy and Mitchell leave the dance floor as IdaLynn leads Wolf in some not-great dancing.

MITCHELL. You ready to go?

Daisy and Mitchell cross to Daisy's coat, which is on top of her basket. Whitfield's basket is hanging next to Daisy's coat on the coat rack.

Daisy grabs her coat and Whitfield's basket. We hear Schyler's trademark news fanfare as Schyler crosses to center stage.

SCHYLER. It was truly heartwarming to see our candidates dance together and connect elf to elf rather than rival to rival, as Mayor Claus called us to do:

Maureen and Whitfield laugh as they continue dancing.

SCHYLER. To look beyond circumstance and be there for our fellow elf. Reporting for Channel 7, this is Schyler Hines and I am very attractive.

Schyler exits. A spotlight follows Snowman as he crosses to center stage while the rest of the cast exits.

It's Cold Outside

Act Two, Scene 4

Mitchell's Apartment, Twenty Minutes Later—Night of Christmas Eve. The apartment fills half the stage, while the Christmas Eve Ball set fills the other half. Snowman stands at center stage.

SNOWMAN. And you know something? That probably would be an all right place to end the story. So everything turned out all right.. There was nothing else remotely of interest going on that night. The end.

Snowman walks offstage and all is quiet for a moment. A beat.

Snowman returns to center stage. He smirks.

SNOWMAN. Oh, come on! I can't believe y'all almost fell for that! Of course our story's not over! Now, Mitchell and Daisy had left the Ball under codeword "baking cookies"—

Mitchell and Daisy enter. Daisy sets the basket down and takes off her coat.

DAISY. We are actually going to bake cookies though, right?

MITCHELL. That was my plan.

Mitchell and Daisy sit down on a couch.

DAISY. I really appreciate that you wanted to leave the ball early. I just feel like lately we've been—frozen. But for the first time in forever, I feel like we can—

Mitchell looks straight ahead. Daisy looks at Mitchell.

MITCHELL. We have to be thinking about our next move.

DAISY. I'm so happy you bring that up.

MITCHELL. Tonight was a good sign—

DAISY. Yeah, I think it was!

MITCHELL. We just have to capitalize on it.

DAISY. Yes, of course! So—

Mitchell looks at Daisy.

MITCHELL. So the media's going to be all over my mom tomorrow—

Daisy's heart sinks. We hear an oven ding.

MITCHELL. I'll get it.

Mitchell exits. Daisy looks at the basket as our attention is drawn to the other side of the stage.

On the other side of the stage, we see the coat rack from the Christmas Eve Ball with an identical basket to the basket Daisy left with hanging on it. Whitfield and Wolf enter.

WOLF. I'll admit. That was fun!

Wolf picks up the basket off the coat rack. He opens it.

WHITFIELD. I'll say! Mayor Maureen is a great dancer! Is she single?

Wolf finds the basket empty. He spirals.

WOLF. No—no.

WHITFIELD. Don'chaknow, I walked right up to her and said, "I think we oughta dance" and she just thought it was the kindest jester—

WOLF. My notebook—where's my notebook? Do you still have my notebook?

On the other side of the stage, Daisy opens the basket to see a notebook.

DAISY. Oh—is this Mitch's . . . ?

Daisy picks up the notebook.

WHITFIELD. No, I put it in the basket and didn't touch it!

WOLF. This—this—I need my notebook!

Whitfield pats Wolf on the shoulder.

WHITFIELD. My mama always used to say, if you bring work to a party, ya can't get mad if someone walks off with it. We're all decent elves here. When someone finds out it's not theirs, they'll just bring it back—

Wolf bolts offstage. We return our full attention to Mitchell's apartment on the other side of the stage. Snowman enters as Daisy opens the notebook.

SNOWMAN. Well—anyway, so Daisy was having a rough go of things. Because, obviously, the most pressing thing on her mind—she never got a chance to re-gift that scented candle . . .

Daisy glares at Snowman.

SNOWMAN. Oh, are we not making jokes about this yet? All righty, then. So a little like a kid sneaking a peek at their presents a night early, Daisy thought she was taking a sentimental flip through the private thoughts of her boyfriend, but this story took a darker turn when she realized this was the notebook of one Romulus Wolf—his name was Romulus, right?

DAISY. *(To herself.)* Profit margins . . . private bank account . . . Who is "Krampus"?

SNOWMAN. So now miraculously, all the questions everyone had been asking about the campaign, the Krampus—Daisy had stumbled backward right into those answers. I swear, you can't make this stuff up! But she wanted to talk to Mitchell about something—anything—else. She didn't dare bring up that elephant she saw in the room.

Mitchell enters with a plate of cookies. Daisy tosses the notebook on the floor.

MITCHELL. Our second batch of snickerdoodles!

Mitchell and Daisy each take a cookie and chew in silence. Mitchell picks up a second cookie.

MITCHELL. We've done worse.

DAISY. Always the optimist, aren't we?

MITCHELL. I'm feeling optimistic, yeah. The Ball could be great for our momentum. Because remember, everybody hated Mom not even a week ago, but I think we can really spin this into our favor—

DAISY. Mitch.

MITCHELL. I don't know, what would you do? You always have an idea. I mean, in this situation, you have so many moving parts—

DAISY. Mitch.

MITCHELL. I'm getting ahead of myself. We don't know what any of this means yet, they won't update the polls until—

DAISY. I didn't get the job.

MITCHELL. Oh. I'm sorry.

A beat. Daisy rises, turning away from Mitchell. A tear rolls down her cheek.

DAISY. It's fine. I just—I really wanted it. For me.

Mitchell crosses to face Daisy and hug her.

MITCHELL. Hey. Hey—I don't think any less of you for failing this one t—

DAISY. It's more than that. You have the weight of the world on your shoulders with your mom's campaign and the China mess, and those are so important and of course I support you, but it's like all I am to you is that girl who teaches little kids and shows up when you need a plus one. I'm your girlfriend, Mitch, but it just feels like all I am to you is—

MITCHELL. I'm sorry you feel that way. I know just the thing to cheer you up.

DAISY. Oh?

Daisy sits down. Mitchell joins her.

MITCHELL. You've noticed my gifts for the past eleven days.

DAISY. The ones with no rhyme or reason, yes.

MITCHELL. What did you think of the trampoline the other day?

DAISY. It's neat—but you really hired all those property owners jumping around on it? That's ten broken arms waiting to happen—

MITCHELL. I had to make sure it was broken in! But I—I have one final gift for you. It's at the woodpile—want to see it?

DAISY. Mitch, you're not listening to me. I didn't care about the stuff you've gotten me the past eleven days.

MITCHELL. What?

DAISY. I don't want a lot for Christmas.

Daisy dumps all the cookies from the plate into her basket.

DAISY. There is just one thing I need—

Daisy rises from the couch and heads for the door. Mitchell rises.

MITCHELL. Help me understand—

DAISY. I'm not in a place to have this conversation with you right now, Mitchell.

Daisy crosses to exit.

DAISY. I really can't stay.

Mitchell picks up Daisy's coat from the couch. Daisy sets the basket down.

MITCHELL. Babe, it's cold outside.

Daisy snatches her coat and buttons it up.

DAISY. I've got to go away.

MITCHELL. Babe, it's cold outside.

Daisy throws the red hood over her head. She picks up the basket.

DAISY. I'm going to my Granny's. Merry Christmas.

Daisy exits. We hear a wolf howl. Mitchell watches in utter bemusement.

The Hood, the Wolf, the Granny, and the Axe

Act Two, Scene 5

The Snowy Woodpile Outside Mitchell's Apartment, Moments Later—Night of Christmas Eve. A tree stump surrounded by firewood sits in the center. Mitchell has adorned the area with soft white lights and framed photos of him and Daisy, with a banner reading, "DAISY SCARLETT, WILL YOU MARRY ME?" in the background. Snowman enters.

SNOWMAN. Ah, you just hate to see it. Now, most of you folk don't ever realize it, but when you're a snowman, you're lucky if you even have one friend. After all, what are you even supposed to do with a snowman when you've rolled him together and stuck a carrot in his face? Unless you can laugh and play just like you and me, there's not much to do. So I love a good story where the characters up and do something about the ones they love.

It's getting hot. Snowman fans himself.

SNOWMAN. Oh, Lordy. Well, global warmin's a real thing threatening some of us more directly than others, so I say let's run and we'll have some fun, now, before I melt away.

Snowman exits. Daisy enters, tears rolling down her face. She's carrying the basket. Daisy notices the engagement decorations. It washes over her that

Mitchell was planning to propose—which makes her feel worse. She hears footsteps.

DAISY. Hello? Is someone there?

WOLF. *(Offstage.)* Someone.

Wolf enters.

WOLF. Bit of a cold night to be walking by yourself, Daisy Scarlett.

DAISY. Oh—hello, Mr. Wolf. T—to what do I owe the pleasure?

WOLF. I came to personally reclaim an important item of mine that I couldn't help but wonder if you walked off with.

DAISY. I—don't know what you're talking about.

Wolf surveys the surroundings. He picks up a framed photo of Mitchell and Daisy.

WOLF. Isn't it funny? This little shrine to you. Looks like someone was planning to ask a big question—and yet here you are. All alone. Talking to the one elf who swept you off your feet tonight.

Wolf sets the photo face-down on the stump.

DAISY. Please leave me alone. I'm just trying to get to my Granny's.

WOLF. Why don't we walk together?

DAISY. No.

A beat.

DAISY. I can't believe that you—you're a monster.

WOLF. So the notebook was in your basket.

Daisy stammers in a sad attempt to change the subject.

DAISY. Just—how—how could you—Mitch's mom is a fine mayor. Why—Whitfield?

WOLF. Oh Daisy, you naïve little girl. Nobody's saying Maureen is a poor mayor. Ebenezer Whitfield is just a dream come true.

DAISY. He's a fool.

WOLF. You're right. Ebenezer Whitfield is a fool.

Daisy is shocked to hear Wolf speak so bluntly.

WOLF. For a full year, I've been working on that fool. He really does love this town and thinks he's got an idea how to run it—and he's just that dumb. Defeating Mrs. Claus was certainly going to be a challenge, she runs circles around him in policy and poise. But then last Christmas, I saw a present from Santa Claus given to Whitfield—he's gotten sloppy, you know. A big label reading "Made in China". So I broke into the workshop and stole a box of toys to see for myself. I had quite a lot of fun writing those letters, calling myself Krampus and making Santa Claus squirm. Seeing things ripple out to crumble Maureen's campaign was just the star on top of the tree. But what a pity, here we are and you know so much. We can work out a little deal, you know, to leave things quietly.

Wolf caresses Daisy's hand. Daisy yanks it away.

WOLF. So hand me the goodies in the basket, little girl. Things will end badly if you don't.

DAISY. I really don't know what you're talking about, Mr. Wolf—nothing but cookies in here. Would you like one?

Daisy pulls out a cookie from the basket.

WOLF. No thanks. I had liver with some fava beans and a nice figgy pudding. Couldn't go until I got some.

DAISY. Well—Okay then. I'm just going to my Granny's house with some cookies. Over the river and through the woods—

Daisy laughs, nervous.

WOLF. Over the river and through the woods, you say?

Daisy rapid-fire looks in both directions. She stomps on Wolf's foot, with a precision strike from the heel of her stiletto into his toe. Wolf shrieks, caught completely off-guard. Daisy exits, basket in hand, hood on head.

Act Two, Scene 6

Mitchell's Apartment, About a Half Hour Later—Night of Christmas Eve. Mitchell sits on the couch, staring at nothing. Silently screaming. Upset and confused, but stoic.

We hear the door creak open. Mitchell turns his head in hope—it's IdaLynn. IdaLynn enters, carrying a giant ice cream sundae.

IDALYNN. *(Singsongy.)* Congratulations!!

MITCHELL. What?

IDALYNN. You're engaged, stupid! You've earned the sundae!! Lickity Split's wasn't open, so I had to improvise. Hope ya like whatever I could find in Jerry's pantry.

IdaLynn plunks down on the couch.

IDALYNN. Mitch? Everything Okay? Where's Day?

Mitchell shakes his head.

In the audience, Daisy enters, hurrying along the forest path. Wolf enters, trailing her.

WOLF. Daisy . . . I just wanna talk, Daisy . . .

Daisy stops. She removes a stiletto and turns back, ready to attack. Daisy exits. Wolf exits. Our attention returns to Mitchell's Apartment.

IDALYNN. So—you leave the ball, you're baking cookies—what happened? When'd it get weird?

MITCHELL. When I took the cookies out of the oven, she was reading something—from a little notebook.

IdaLynn sees the notebook on the floor. She laughs.

IDALYNN. This wouldn't happen to be that notebook, would it?

IdaLynn flips through the notebook.

IDALYNN. Wait—Mitch, this is Wolf's. And I've read this exact letter before. Wolf is Krampus!

Mitchell takes the notebook from IdaLynn.

MITCHELL. Whoa, this is straight-up evil. So . . . Daisy knows all this—

IDALYNN. You don't think Wolf's out there? Day could be in danger.

MITCHELL. How do we know for sure?

IDALYNN. We don't. But what do ya know?

MITCHELL. I love her.

IDALYNN. So quit chopping wood and run after her! *(Claps twice.)* Up and at'em!

Mitchell gets up.

MITCHELL. I'm bringing my axe.

Mitchell and IdaLynn exit.

Over the River and Through the Woods

Act Two, Scene 7

T*he Snowy Forest, Moments Later—Night of Christmas Eve. It's a bleak mid-winter scene. Daisy enters. Her cell phone rings. She sets down the basket to pick it up.*

DAISY. Mitch—thank God. I'm so, so sorry. Listen—

On the other side of the stage, Mitchell enters, phone up to ear. IdaLynn enters, carrying Mitchell's axe.

MITCHELL. It's fine. We'll talk later. Has Wolf found you? IdaLynn and I are on the way.

DAISY. Yes—I—How?

MITCHELL. The notebook. It was at my place.

DAISY. Wolf's following me. I think I lost him for now.

MITCHELL. I highly doubt that.

DAISY. Excuse me?

MITCHELL. You're running through snow in high heels.

Daisy nods.

DAISY. Fair.

MITCHELL. Well—Okay. You'll be safe when you get to Granny's. Don't dawdle along the way and don't talk to anyone else. These woods are dangerous.

DAISY. Mitch. I need you to trust me.

Daisy checks her battery percentage.

DAISY. Crap, my phone's about to die.

MITCHELL. Okay—uh—how do we know you're safe?

DAISY. I'll break up some cookies and leave crumbs on the ground. Follow my trail to Granny's and you'll know I got there.

MITCHELL. I don't know—

DAISY. We have to think fast here. You have a better idea?

MITCHELL. It's just such a waste of good cookies.

Daisy's phone dies. Mitchell stops to look at his phone.

MITCHELL. Dangit.

IDALYNN. We need elves on this. Call your mom!

MITCHELL. What? Why? The mayor shouldn't be involved in any of this—

IDALYNN. I don't care who she is—Day's in danger. If you don't call her, I will!

Mitchell and IdaLynn exit. Daisy takes a cookie from the basket and breaks it. Wolf enters and crosses to Daisy. Wolf stops to look at the moon.

WOLF. I admire the moon this evening, how it glistens on the snow.

DAISY. Get away from me, Wolf.

Daisy turns to see Wolf.

WOLF. I grow bored with you playing dumb, Miss Scarlett. What is it you want, Daisy? You want the moon? Say the word and I'll throw a lasso—

Wolf mimics throwing a lasso.

DAISY. I don't want the moon, I want a restraining order.

WOLF. Your wit carves me like a Christmas ham.

DAISY. Don't flatter me.

Wolf monologues to the audience as he approaches Daisy. Daisy takes this opportunity to exit.

WOLF. You have the goodies in the basket. If all I need to do is throw some money to make you shut up and forget, I'm prepared to do that. Hand me the notebook and I open my checkbook. A little money could go a long way toward opening a school, you know—

Wolf looks at where Daisy had been.

WOLF. And—she's gone.

Wolf sighs. He picks up his cell phone. On the other side of the stage, Whitfield enters, phone up to ear.

WHITFIELD. Oh hey! How ya doin'? Did ya get your notebook back?

WOLF. Listen, Whitfield. I think I need your help.

WHITFIELD. Well isn't this incredulous! I've been dreaming of the day you'd call me to say, "Ebenezer—"

Wolf picks up a piece of cookie.

WOLF. Yeah. So I'm going to need you to meet me in the woods at the river. We'll get my notebook out of that basket.

Wolf eats the cookie piece.

WOLF. And I might want some of those cookies, too.

Wolf exits. Whitfield exits.

Act Two, Scene 8

The Snowy Forest, About a Half Hour Later—Night of Christmas Eve. Snowman enters, wracking his brain trying to remember something important.

SNOWMAN. Now I hate to interrupt, but there's somethin' real important I'm forgetting and it's gonna eat me like a snow cone if I can't figure it out—

Schyler enters. He brushes Snowman's back.

SCHYLER. What's up, babe? I've been sitting at the bar for a while and

Schyler Hines does not get stood up.

SNOWMAN. My sincerest apologies. Y'all, this is my boyfriend: Schyler Hines! I've been tellin' them all about you.

SCHYLER. All good things, I'm sure.

SNOWMAN. Oh! Here's a thought—I'm tellin' that story of when Daisy ran off to Granny's House when Mitchell was going to propose to her and that Wolf was bein' real creepy.

SCHYLER. Ah yes, that old chestnut.

SNOWMAN. Can you maybe give us a headline? About the story? When I give you a cue.

Schyler pulls out microphone and speaks into it.

SCHYLER. Well I sure could, Frosti!

SNOWMAN. Okay, Okay, hang tight and wait for my signal.

Schyler exits. Snowman takes center stage.

SNOWMAN. So now, poor Whitfield had no idea what Wolf was really up to, but he sure was happy to be wanted.

Whitfield and Wolf enter. Whitfield picks up a cookie crumb.

WHITFIELD. *(While chewing.)* Why all this trouble for a little notebook? Y'know, I saw some at Target for a dollar!

WOLF. There are some things I'd rather the elves not know.

WHITFIELD. Like what I'm gonna say in my next speech? I never know what I'm going to say most days so that makes two of us, me and everyone else.

Whitfield picks up another cookie crumb and eats it.

WOLF. Follow the crumbs.

WHITFIELD. You know, once we build that toy factory—I really hope we can help Santa—

Wolf points his index finger with force.

WOLF. Follow the crumbs.

Whitfield and Wolf exit. Mitchell and IdaLynn enter, on the run. Mitchell holds the axe.

SNOWMAN. And they all headed deeper into the woods:

Mitchell and IdaLynn exit. Daisy enters, basket in hand, nervously whistling a Christmas tune as she drops cookie crumbs.

SNOWMAN. With Daisy, leaving her trail of cookies—

Whitfield enters, eating the cookie crumbs as he goes. Daisy exits. Whitfield exits.

SNOWMAN. And Whitfield not far behind.

Wolf enters. He gets a thought—a thought he is very pleased with.

SNOWMAN. But the Wolf—well, he got an idea. An awful idea. A wonderful, awful idea.

WOLF. I could just run.

Wolf breaks into a sprint, speeding off the path.

SNOWMAN. Schyler—headline!

Schyler's typical news fanfare plays. Schyler enters, microphone in hand.

SCHYLER. And coming up: An elf running through the forest in high heels on Christmas Eve outpaced by someone wearing literally any other footwear—the story will not surprise you. Reporting for my boyfriend, this is Schyler Hines and I am very attractive. Back to you, Frosti.

Snowman swoons.

SNOWMAN. Thanks, babe.

To Grandmother's House We Go

Act Two, Scene 9

Granny's Cottage, Twenty Minutes Later—Midnight on Christmas Eve. It's an eerie quiet. Nobody is anywhere to be found. The only light on comes from the Christmas Tree. Granny's nightgown and nightcap are laid on the floor, her butcher knife sits on the coffee table, and her rifle is mounted on the wall.

SNOWMAN. 'Twas the night before Christmas and all through the house . . . not a creature was stirring, not even a mouse.

A knock at the door.

WOLF. *(Offstage.)* Granny . . . It's Daisy. I've brought some goodies with me. Hmm—ah-ha!

Wolf finds the spare key and opens the door.

SNOWMAN. The Wolf had arrived on a wing and a prayer—

Wolf enters. He locks the door behind him.

SNOWMAN. —in hopes that his victim soon would be there.

Wolf turns on a lamp. He picks up the butcher knife from the coffee table and flashes a psychotic smile. A knock at the door.

DAISY. *(Offstage.)* Granny! Are you home?

Wolf sees Granny's nightgown on the floor and thinks, "Oh dear God, am I really going to do this?"—he does. He strips and puts on the nightgown.

DAISY. *(Offstage.)* Granny!! I see a light on, are you home?

WOLF. *(Poor falsetto.)* It's just me, Granny, dear.

Wolf sets Granny's nightcap on his head, races to the couch, and lays down, covering himself with a blanket. He clutches the butcher knife.

SNOWMAN. The Wolf here got nestled all snug on the couch, while visions of greed and murder danced in his h—head. I'm sorry, y'all, I thought he went up to the bed for this one. You can't win 'em all.

Snowman exits. Daisy continues to knock at the door.

DAISY. *(Offstage.)* Can you come open the door? I left my key at Mitch's and it looks like the spare isn't here.

Wolf continues to speak in a poor falsetto that wouldn't fool a child.

WOLF. Just pull the bobbin dear, and the latch will go up.

Daisy enters and sets the basket down. She removes her coat.

DAISY. I had no idea you knew how to pick a lock, Granny.

WOLF. I've fallen horribly ill, Daisy. Please have a seat next to me—

Daisy turns to see Wolf in her Granny's nightgown and stifles a shriek, both a little horrified and a little amused.

WOLF. —your dear old Granny.

Daisy crosses to Wolf; incredulous. Snowman enters.

SNOWMAN. Okay, stop—I think it's real important to mention that at no point here did Daisy think she was talking to her Granny. I mean—come on. She knew it was the Wolf but she played along to buy a little time to figure out what in God's green earth she was gonna do about it.

Snowman exits.

DAISY. You know, I think I'll keep my distance. I wouldn't want to get your—germs, "Granny."

Wolf drops the butcher knife onto the floor. He reaches down.

WOLF. Dearest me, I dropped my bedtime knife.

DAISY. My, Granny—what big . . . arms you have?

Daisy smiles nervously; incredulously. Wolf shoots Daisy an equally incredulous look.

WOLF. All the better to hug you with, my dear.

Daisy inches toward the rifle. Wolf rises from couch, knife in hand.

DAISY. And Granny, what big eyes you have.

WOLF. All the better to see you with, my child.

Daisy reaches for the gun. Wolf inches closer.

DAISY. And Granny, what big ears you have.

Wolf throws off Granny's nightcap and snaps back into his normal voice.

WOLF. Now that's just mean.

Daisy grabs the rifle. She clicks the safety mode off.

DAISY. One step closer and I shoot!

Daisy's finger quivers on the trigger. Her whole body is shaking. Wolf smirks.

WOLF. You wouldn't hurt a fly, Daisy Scarlett.

Wolf steps. Daisy fires a warning shot and readjusts her aim.

DAISY. Wanna bet an ice cream sundae?

Whitfield enters.

WHITFIELD. Well wouldn'tya know, that cute little trail of cookies led me here!

Whitfield assesses the bizarre sight of Wolf being held at gunpoint in Granny's nightgown.

WHITFIELD. Now what do we got here? Last time I saw something like this, my family reunion hadn't even busted out the drinks—

WOLF. Ebenezer, go outside.

DAISY. No. Stay.

WHITFIELD. Well goshdarnit! I don't know what I'm s'posed to do since twoa'ya said something.

In the audience, Mitchell and IdaLynn enter, hurrying along the forest path. Mitchell carries the axe. IdaLynn carries the notebook.

MITCHELL. Almost there! Almost there!

They're both sweating. While neither are particularly out of shape, neither Mitchell nor IdaLynn woke up this morning ready for a multi-mile run in evening wear. Mitchell and IdaLynn exit.

Meanwhile, back in Granny's Cottage—Daisy holds Wolf at gunpoint.

DAISY. You disgust me, Wolf.

WOLF. I'm well aware.

WHITFIELD. I don't understand.

DAISY. Wolf realized he could get a better deal once you got elected, selling just enough toys to Santa to avoid suspicion—but then sell the majority to distributors in the US. From your government workshop.

WOLF. What can I say? The world loves North Pole toys and I love money.

DAISY. You were going to make millions—and no one was ever going to find out while you raked in all that cash for yourself.

Whitfield is uncharacteristically sobered.

WHITFIELD. You . . . you never told me that.

WOLF. What a shame. I suppose I have to kill you both now.

Wolf knocks the gun out of Daisy's hand. Mitchell and IdaLynn enter. Mitchell charges toward Wolf with the axe. Mitchell pins Wolf against the wall. Daisy grabs the gun from the floor.

MITCHELL. Game's up, Wolf. We read your notebook. You're cornered.

IdaLynn holds up the notebook. Wolf puts the butcher knife on the floor and places his hands on his head.

WOLF. Okay, Okay—hold up. *(Poor falsetto.)* I'm just a little old lady here.

IDALYNN. Why is he wearing Granny's nightgown?

DAISY. Unclear.

WOLF. It was a silly notebook, I can buy a new one—Nobody's in any real danger. It was all hypothetical, really—

MITCHELL. Hypothetical, huh? Stalking my girlfriend? Attempted murder? Involving Whitfield in whatever this is?

Mitchell gestures to Whitfield in the background.

WHITFIELD. Hey! Merry Christmas, Mitchell!

Wolf hesitates.

WOLF. I don't suppose you all would like some hush money? Let me carry on and we can forget any of this happened? We can go into it together, you know, between the five of us—

MITCHELL, DAISY, IDALYNN. *(In unison.)* No.

DAISY. So what do we do now?

MITCHELL. We've got to call the cops.

IDALYNN. Why didn't we call the cops??

MITCHELL. That is something we should've done.

Wolf snickers.

WOLF. You can call the cops. But I'll be long gone by then. I'll be taking this.

Wolf grabs the notebook from IdaLynn and moves to exit.

WOLF. Merry Christmas to all—and to all, a good night.

Maureen, Snowman, and the grizzled police chief YUKON enter. Wolf is shoved to the side. Mitchell and Daisy set weapons down.

IDALYNN. Hold that Wolf down!

Snowman and Yukon hold Wolf.

MAUREEN. Oh goodness, I was so worried for you, Daisy! Come here, come here.

Maureen envelops Daisy in a hug.

MAUREEN. Now, all right: what happened here?

Yukon scribbles down everything.

MITCHELL. Wolf's a cheat and a fraud. He broke into Dad's workshop and blackmailed him to ensure Whitfield could win the election.

IDALYNN. Once Whitfield built his toy factory, Wolf was gonna cook the books, sell toys all over the world, pocket the money. Looked like he was gonna get away with it.

DAISY. But then I found out—and he tried to kill me to keep his plan in motion.

MITCHELL. That he did.

MAUREEN. Well—I'm glad you called, Mitchell, because I brought Chief Yukon of the NPPD with me. Did you hear all of that, Cornelius?

YUKON. Got everything. We'll have some questions for you at the station.

Yukon slaps handcuffs on Wolf. He leads Wolf offstage.

YUKON. You have the right to remain silent. Anything you say—

WHITFIELD. Hey! Where ya goin' with him?

Whitfield exits.

MAUREEN. Oh dear—Ebenezer! Get back here!

Maureen exits.

DAISY. Should we—?

MITCHELL. Nah.

IDALYNN. It's a lost cause.

Sleigh bells ring.

SANTA. *(Offstage.)* Ho-ho-ho!

MITCHELL. Dad!

Santa enters with Granny. Santa is carrying a sack of presents. Granny has hoof prints on her forehead and incriminating claw marks on her back. IdaLynn and Daisy's eyes widen.

IDALYNN. Granny—what on earth happened to you??

DAISY. Are those hoof prints?

Santa hesitates.

SANTA. Yes, well, one of my reindeer had a little accident. But! I made sure your Granny here got home and what do you know, my whole family is here, too!

GRANNY. Get me in bed, I'm done with this.

DAISY. Is she going to have to sleep naked?

IDALYNN. Yikes.

SANTA. And as luck would have it...

Santa pulls a present out of his sack.

SANTA. Here's a brand-new nightgown, Doris! Merry Christmas and Happy Hanukkah!

Granny grabs the present and exits. Santa hands an adult coloring book to IdaLynn.

SANTA. And IdaLynn—

IDALYNN. You remembered! It's one of those adult coloring books!!

Act Two, Scene 10

The Snowy Woodpile Outside Mitchell's Apartment, A Little Later That Night—Christmas Eve. Mitchell's "engagement shrine" is still set up, one framed photo is face-down. Mitchell and Daisy approach the woodpile hand-in-hand.

DAISY. I didn't get to really admire this earlier—this is all very impressive.

Daisy crosses to the stump. She picks up the framed photo and places it face-up.

DAISY. Mitch—I'm really sorry I didn't say anything sooner. What I saw as this huge problem—

MITCHELL. An elephant in the room?

DAISY. Yes, exactly! I kept thinking you would magically know to ask about my problem, but we'd just gotten into a pattern of not talking about me and I freaked out when you weren't reading my mind.

MITCHELL. You've been there for me through all of this. Even when you didn't feel like it. If that's not love, I don't know what it is. I got lost in—like a blizzard—and you were my light. I didn't realize sticking to my plan meant I wasn't trusting or listening to you. I want you to know I'm here and I support you.

DAISY. Mitch.

MITCHELL. So—with all of that said—and the nightmare we've lived through tonight... Daisy Scarlett,

Mitchell gets on one knee, holding the engagement ring.

MITCHELL. Will you be the next Mrs. Claus?

DAISY. Yes, of course!!

Mitchell slips the engagement ring on Daisy's finger as they kiss. IdaLynn, Maureen, Santa, and Snowman enter, celebrating.

SANTA. Well, Mayor Claus. We're not perfect.

MAUREEN. But I think we did all right.

Maureen kisses Santa. Santa exits.

SNOWMAN. So Mitchell saw his Mama kissing Santa Claus and everything had finally come together. I'll wrap up some of the hangin' bits up for ya with a nice little bow: Wolf was charged with breaking and entering and the attempted murder of Daisy Scarlett—so he went to prison for a long time. With him out of the picture, the election became a fair fight. So Maureen of course won re-election in a landslide. Whitfield actually got his own reality show—something like Ebenezer Whitfield's North Pole. Good for him. Santa closed the factory in China and he brought the entire operation back to the North Pole. IdaLynn got married about a month after all this and left Santa's Workshop to start her own business. She's remodeling homes all over the North Pole.

Mitchell and Daisy step forward.

SNOWMAN. But this was Mitchell and Daisy's story. They decided to leave the North Pole for a while. Mitchell and Daisy both needed some time to be together and heal from the last few months. When they got back, Daisy left Blazing Yule and soon began to make her own dreams come true. Vice Principal Scarlett is now working on a PhD in education theory. Mitchell runs a daily press briefing for the entire North Pole to share how they're all workin' together to keep Christmas magic alive.

Mitchell smiles.

SNOWMAN. But most importantly, Daisy is no longer ashamed to talk about her own feelings and Mitchell is no longer blind to what's going on outside his own life. They were ready to face their next challenges in life and love together.

Mitchell and Daisy kiss. Whitfield enters with a bottle of champagne.

WHITFIELD. A toast to my good friend Mitchell Claus, the richest man in town!

All cheer as Whitfield uncorks the bottle with a POP!

WHITFIELD. And don'chaknow, every time there's a bell, an angel gets his rings?

Blank stares all around.

THE END.

Acknowledgments

With this book being a compilation of three separate, distinct works, it can be hard to really pinpoint who made this book happen specifically. Basically, what I'm trying to communicate here is if I were to list every single person worth acknowledging in the lives of *Good Knight and Goodbye*, *The Thousand-Year Rose*, AND *See Amid the Winter Snow*, we would be here all day. Thank you from the bottom of my heart to each person who worked with me on these projects as part of the casts, crews, beta readers, audiences—it truly took a village to make each individual project come to life. Thank you for being part of my village.

As far as specific individuals for *Shakespeare in the Parking Lot*, there are a few names springing to mind:

Thank you first to Sue Fisher—or Mrs. Fisher, as I knew her for so long—thank you for taking me seriously when I said I could write a better play than this and for your support every step of my way.

Thank you always to my dad, Jim Fenton, for being my first-ever content editor as I went through writing *Good Knight and Goodbye* the first time, helping me to create the best possible script a fourteen-year-old could write, and for believing in me as we navigate the publishing world together.

Thank you to my creative non-fiction editor for this project, Ciera McElroy—it feels so fitting to have a Wheaton classmate be the one to edit my reflections on my work from college. Feels like a full-circle moment. Thank you for catching my mistakes and for asking me the right questions to deepen

ACKNOWLEDGMENTS

my reflections and create a stronger piece.

Thank you to Amanda Pasquini and Chelsea Cylinder for taking on *See Amid* and going along with my outlandish idea to mount a Christmas play in September. Amanda, thank you for how you were able to bring these characters to life and get me thinking about how to improve the script; and thank you, Chelsea, for bringing Daisy to life to the point where I'm still not sure where Daisy ends and Chelsea begins.

Thank you to the Jukebox Theater cast of *The Thousand-Year Rose*: Piper Curda, Maggie Auffarth, Sophia Smith, Taylor Schaible, Caleb Conner, Katy Humnick, Michael Melter, Calvin Graham, Maddie Johnson, Iain Robins, Yari Medina, Rachel Hand, Aaron Hanes, Suzanna Hersey, Phoebe Silva, Mary Neeley, Grace Brazell. It was a truly special moment as an artist to bring that show to life together. Thank you all for how much initiative you took as an ensemble cast to really make my job directing our show a walk in the park(ing lot).

ABOUT THE AUTHOR

Peter Fenton's work has appeared in or is forthcoming from Dadley Productions, Heuer Publishing, OurBible App, and Q Christian Fellowship among others. Peter is an adventurous multi-genre author and screenwriter drawn to creating clever and self-aware works stimulating critical thought and laughter. He wrote and produced the profitable world premiere of his holiday satire *See Amid the Winter Snow* (2019), as well as his dark spiritual comedy, *Abandon All Hope* (2020), a co-production with BraveMaker Media. Peter served as the President and Director of Jukebox Theatre at Wheaton College and is an alumnus of the postgraduate apprenticeship program at Walnut Street Theatre in Philadelphia. As an up-and-coming screenwriter and playwright, Peter is a member of the Dramatists Guild of America.

You can connect with Peter on his website at www.byPeterFenton.com or follow him on Twitter and Instagram @peterfent!

YOUR NEXT READ

ABANDON ALL HOPE
by Peter Fenton

Three college freshmen—a scrappy feminist, a naïve evangelical, and a cocky logistician—arrive in Hell, which appears as an infernal dorm room, challenged to a diabolical game by a fun-loving demon: the winner will gain admission to Heaven at the cost of torturing the others.

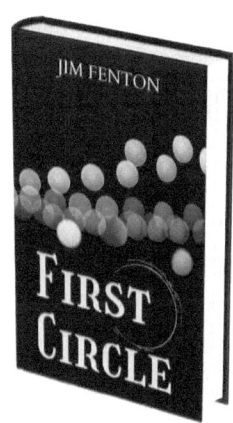

FIRST CIRCLE
by Jim Fenton

Follow the faith and character journeys of six individuals connected to a pugnacious, retired professor battling cancer who are receiving messages crafted by a hand from afar. This magical realism novel from debut author Jim Fenton is a thrilling tale with charming prose!

www.ingramcontent.com/pod-product-compliance
Lightning Source LLC
Chambersburg PA
CBHW020900080526
44589CB00011B/377